Economy, Culture, and Civil War in Sri Lanka

EDITED BY DEBORAH WINSLOW
AND MICHAEL D. WOOST

Economy, Culture, and Civil War in Sri Lanka

INDIANA UNIVERSITY PRESS

Bloomington and Indianapolis

This book is a publication of

Indiana University Press
601 North Morton Street
Bloomington, IN 47404-3797 USA

http://iupress.indiana.edu

Telephone orders   800-842-6796
Fax orders   812-855-7931
Orders by e-mail   iuporder@indiana.edu

© 2004 by Indiana University Press

Library of Congress Cataloging-in-Publication Data

Economy, culture, and civil war in Sri Lanka / edited by Deborah Winslow and Michael D. Woost.
   p. cm.
Based on a workshop held Aug. 25–27, 2000, at the New England Center, University of New Hampshire, sponsored by the American Institute for Sri Lankan Studies.
   Includes bibliographical references and index.
   ISBN 0-253-34420-4 (cloth : alk. paper) — ISBN 0-253-21691-5 (pbk. : alk. paper)
   1. War—Economic aspects—Sri Lanka. 2. War and society—Sri Lanka. 3. Ethnic conflict—Sri Lanka. 4. Sri Lanka—Ethnic relations. 5. Tamils—Sri Lanka. 6. Sri Lanka—History—Civil War, 1983– I. Winslow, Deborah, date II. Woost, Michael D., date
   HC424.Z9D44 2004
   954.9303′2—dc22
                                                      2004000692

1 2 3 4 5   09 08 07 06 05 04

That man I remember well, and at least two centuries
have passed since I last saw him;
he traveled neither on horseback nor in a carriage,
always on foot
he undid distances,
carrying neither sword nor weapon
but nets on his shoulder,
ax or hammer or spade;
he never fought with another of his kind—
his struggle was with water or with earth,
with the wheat, for it to become bread,
with the towering tree, for it to yield wood,
with walls, to open doors in them,
with sand, to form it into walls,
and with the sea, to make it bear fruit.

—Pablo Neruda

Excerpted from the poem "The People," by Pablo Neruda, in
Fully Empowered, translated, with a new introduction, by
Alastair Reid (New York: New Directions Books, 1995).

Contents

Preface

The real lesson from Sri Lanka may be that liberalization is not just a turning point in economic policy. It also involves a profound alteration of social and political life.

David Dunham and Sisira Jayasuriya

This book was born of curiosity. Like many people, we wanted to understand how tens of thousands of people have come to die in Sri Lanka's civil war and what, if anything, the economy has had to do with it. Impassioned curiosity led to a question that soon became a debate, then a workshop, and now this volume. In 1977, the leaders of the Democratic Socialist Republic of Sri Lanka, after decades of battening down national hatches against global economic currents, did an abrupt about-turn and invited capitalism in. Did they inadvertently also set a course that led to heightened ethnic conflict and the tragic civil war that has held the country in its grip since 1983? Yes, some said, liberalizing the economy reduced the role of government, which changed the relative privileges accorded one ethnic group over another and perilously exacerbated social tensions. No, others replied, the Sri Lankan economy was too small to flourish in isolation and opening it up to more foreign investment and trade produced opportunities for people of all classes and ethnicities.

We convened a workshop specifically to address these issues. We invited scholars with a variety of disciplinary perspectives, who had recently been doing research in Sri Lanka, to join us. Together, we quickly learned that the causes of Sri Lanka's civil war are vastly more complex than the simple before-and-after scenario of our original query. National economic policy has contributed to the conflict, but so have many other intertwining developments that have interacted and accumulated over time to produce contemporary Sri Lanka. In fact, the picture that emerged from the workshop discussions was of a war that has not just happened *to* Sri Lanka but in many ways has *become* Sri Lanka, fully as embedded in ordinary lives as in extraordinary emergencies. To better understand its causes, we came to believe that we had to consider how ordinary people live and how they understand that living, as well as the national economy that structures some of the parameters within which they carry on. This book brings together our efforts to do exactly that.

The workshop on the Economy and Ethnic Conflict was held August 25–27, 2000, at the New England Center on the campus of the University of New Hampshire. It was made possible by the early sponsorship of the American Institute for Sri Lankan Studies (www.aisls.org). We are very grateful to Dr. Chandra R. de Silva, now dean of arts and letters at Virginia Commonwealth University, who was then president of AISLS. His interest in our project and his willingness to commit some of the Institute's resources were invaluable. We also thank several anonymous private donors, who helped pay the travel expenses of some participants; the workshop was improved by their generosity. Of course, we owe our biggest debt to the scholars who responded to our open invitation to participate. The hard work, generous debate, and sustained enthusiasm of Francesca Bremner, John Conant, Swarna Kanthi Dharmawardena, Geraldine Gamburd, Michele Gamburd, Arjun Guneratne, Darlene Hantzis, Siri Hettige, Alan Keenan, Caitrin Lynch, Pat Peebles, Sonali Perera, John Richardson, Nisala Rodrigo, John Rogers, Amita Shastri, Kevin Trainor, and Robin Willits made those two summer days both illuminating and enjoyable. In addition, we single out the exemplary work of Alan Keenan and John Rogers as workshop discussants.

Transforming a workshop into a book has only widened the scope of our indebtedness. First, we are profoundly grateful to Kumari Jayawardena, Jayadeva Uyangoda, and the Social Scientists' Association, Colombo, for permission to reproduce Newton Gunasinghe's article, "The Open Economy and Its Impact on Ethnic Relations in Sri Lanka" (chapter 4). It was one of the first, and remains one of the most important, pieces on the topic; both the workshop and this book would have been the poorer without it. Second, we owe a great deal to Rebecca Tolen, our editor at Indiana University Press. Her faith in us and her relaxed professionalism have been crucial to our work.

In addition, we thank Burt Feintuch, director of the University of New Hampshire Center for the Humanities, for a Discretionary Grant; and Tom Trout, associate dean of the University of New Hampshire College of Liberal Arts, for an award from the Alumni Annual Gifts Fund. Their support helped to defray our costs in producing the manuscript and made it possible for us to finish it sooner rather than later. In addition, we acknowledge with gratitude the wonderful work of Kelsey A. Dennis, an amazing undergraduate student, who assisted us in everything from checking bibliographies to cartography, and did it all with impressive competence and amazing good humor.

Of course, none of this would have been possible without our coauthors: Francesca Bremner, Michele Gamburd, Siri Hettige, Caitrin Lynch, John Richardson, and Amita Shastri. We thank them for their wonderful scholarship and their commitment to this project. Over and over, despite the many other demands on their time, they came through for us, and we appreciate it. Finally, we acknowledge our debts to our families. Diane Woost, Gabriel Winslow-Yost, and Israel Yost helped us immeasurably with their support and their patience.

Deborah Winslow
Mike Woost

A Note on Pronunciation
of Sinhala Words

This information on pronunciation is only meant as a rough
guide. The main focus is on the pronunciation of a few key
vowels and consonants. These notes are adapted from Fairbanks, Gair, and de Silva, *Colloquial Sinhalese* (1968) and W. S.
Karunatillake, *An Introduction to Spoken Sinhala* (1992). Readers will find more complete guides to pronunciation in these
works.

Key Vowels

i   High front unrounded short vowel with a sound similar to the short *i*
          in the English words *pit* and *bit*.

ii   Vowel sound in *pit* or *bit* lengthened or sustained, as in *bitter*, al-
          though even longer.

e   Mid front vowel with a sound between the short *e* in the English
          words *yet* and *pet* and the long *a* in the word *bait*.

ee   Vowel sound between *e* in *pet* and *a* in *bait*, lengthened.

ae   Low front vowel, like the short *a* in the English words *bat* or *cat*.

aeae   Vowel sound in *bat* or *cat*, lengthened or sustained, similar to the *a* in
          actor.

a   Low central short vowel similar to the vowel sound in the English
          word *bar* but shorter.

aa   Vowel sound in *bar*, lengthened or sustained, similar to the *a* in *bard*.

u   High back rounded vowel similar to the sound in the English words
          moot or *rude* but shorter.

uu   Vowel sound in *moot* or *rude*, lengthened or sustained, similar to the
          vowel sound in *food*.

o   Mid back rounded vowel similar to the vowel sound in the English
          words *shone* or *clone* but shorter.

oo   Vowel sound in *shone* or *clone*, lengthened or sustained, similar to the
          o in *over*.

Others

y   Similar to the corresponding sound in the English word *yes;* however,
          when used before another consonant or at the end of a word, it is pro-
          nounced like the *y* in *valley*.

t	Voiceless dental stop, similar to the *th* in the English word *thin*.
T	Voiceless retroflex stop similar to the English *t* but pronounced with the tongue further back in the mouth.
d	Voiced counterpart to *t* similar to the *th* in the English word *then*.
D	Voiced counterpart of *t* similar to the *d* in the English word *dough* yet further back.

Acronyms

200 GFP	200 Garment Factories Program
ADEP	Association of Disabled Ex-Servicemen
AGA	Assistant Government Agent
AISLS	American Institute for Sri Lankan Studies
A-level	GCE, Advanced Level
BBC	British Broadcasting Corporation
BOI	Board of Investment
CAS	Country Assistance Strategy
CCPI	Colombo Consumers Price Index
CGR	Ceylon General Railway
CP	Communist Party
CWE	Co-operative Wholesale Establishment
EPDP	Eelam People's Democratic Party
ESAF	Enhanced Structural Adjustment Facility
FIAC	Foreign Investments Advisory Committee
FTZ	Free Trade Zone
GCE	General Certificate of Education
GCEC	Greater Colombo Economic Commission
GDP	Gross Domestic Product
GNP	Gross National Product
GST	General Sales Tax
ICRC	International Committee of the Red Cross
IMF	International Monetary Fund
IPKF	Indian Peace Keeping Force
IPS	Institute of Policy Studies (Colombo)
JC	Jathika Chintanaya (national ideology)
JVP	Janatha Vimukthi Peramuna (People's Liberation Front)
LIAC	Local Investments Advisory Committee
LIC	Low Income Country
LSSP	Lanka Sama Samaja Party
LTTE	Liberation Tigers of Tamil Eelam
MEP	Mahajana Eksath Peramuna (People's United Front, a coalition led by the SLFP)
MIC	Middle Income Country
NGO	Nongovernmental Organization
O-level	GCE, Ordinary Level
PA	People's Alliance
PLOTE	People's Liberation Organization of Temil Eelam

RSL	Regaining Sri Lanka
SL Rs.	Sri Lankan Rupees
TELO	Tamil Eelam Liberation Organization
TULF	Tamil United Liberation Front
UNF	United National Front (coalition led by UNP)
UNP	United National Party
UF	United Front
SLFP	Sri Lanka Freedom Party

Economy, Culture, and Civil War in Sri Lanka

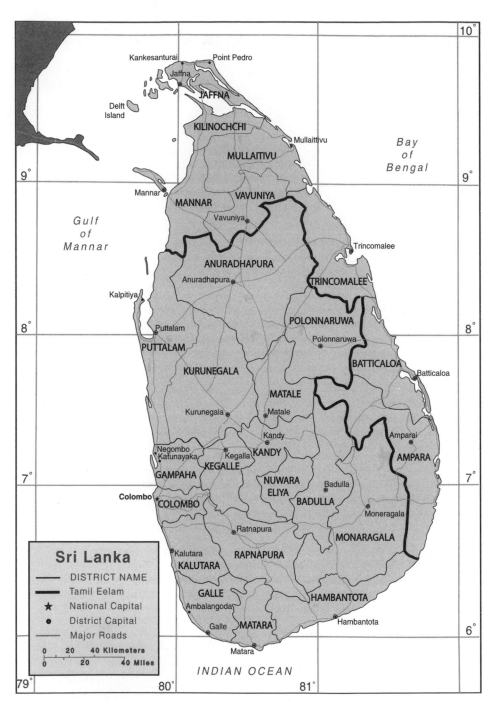

Map of Sri Lanka showing district boundaries and places mentioned in the text.

1 Articulations of Economy and Ethnic Conflict in Sri Lanka

Deborah Winslow and Michael D. Woost

On July 24, 2001, a small but well armed group of guerillas—members of the Liberation Tigers of Tamil Eelam (LTTE)—mounted a daring assault on Sri Lanka's only international airport and the adjoining military air base. The attack was intended to mark the anniversary of the infamous anti-Tamil violence of 1983 and also to retaliate against the Sri Lankan government for more recent events, including what the LTTE termed indiscriminate bombing of civilians in the north. Anniversary hostilities had been anticipated, so airport security was tight; hundreds of air force troops were present at the base. Nevertheless, despite these precautions, a mere 14 LTTE insurgents managed to wreak serious havoc. They first raided the base, where they demolished eight military planes and damaged another ten. They then moved on to the civilian airport and destroyed six commercial airliners, while airline employees and travelers cowered behind suitcases, furniture, and check-in counters. When the shooting stopped, 21 people were dead: 7 airport security workers and all 14 Tigers (123India.com 2001).

In the aftermath of this attack, the government closed Katunayake International Airport for 36 hours. Lloyd's of London imposed war zone insurance rates on both the airport and the ports,[1] and for months afterwards, international carriers curtailed their Sri Lanka schedules and demanded ticket surcharges to pay the rising insurance costs of doing business there. Not surprisingly, both tourism and foreign investment plummeted. Thus the events of July 24, 2001, were not only a tragedy for those on both sides who lost their lives; they also were a blow to government economic plans for Sri Lanka's Sinhalese-dominated south. Perhaps this was not yet the straw that broke the back of Sri Lanka's southern economy—tourism resumed, the surcharges gradually were lifted, and travel to and from the country was approaching normal within a year. But the July 24 raid undeniably was a particularly difficult twist in the already tortuous economic path traveled by the Sri Lankan government since 1983, when the war with the Tamil separatists began in earnest.

In July 1983, the worst communal riots in Sri Lanka's history—full-scale anti-Tamil attacks—took place in the capital, Colombo. The violence was so widespread and so destructive that it closed Colombo down for almost two weeks, even as it spread to other cities and towns throughout the country (Tambiah 1996: 94–95). Estimates of the total number of people killed during those awful days range wildly, from 350 to 4,000, but all agree that hundreds, even thousands, died and tens of thousands more were injured (Eller 1999: 95; Tiruchelvam 1999: 192). In addition, as many as 100,000 Tamils in Colombo alone, and another 175,000 elsewhere, were rendered homeless (Rotberg 1999: 7).[2] Property damage totaled hundreds of millions of dollars; an estimated 18,000 homes and 5,000 shops were destroyed (Herring 2001: 40).

The generally cited catalyst for the 1983 riots was a series of events in the northern Tamil city of Jaffna. First, there had been what was reported as a rampage by government, primarily Sinhalese, troops. In reprisal, Tamil separatists ambushed an army truck and killed 13 Sinhalese soldiers. The army then chose to bring the dead soldiers' bodies south and put them on public display in a Colombo cemetery, a display that in the end was cancelled despite the agitated crowds gathered to greet them (Tambiah 1996: 95). The violence that followed seemed almost predetermined, an anti-Tamil pogrom, especially because the dead included 53 Tamil prisoners in a maximum security Colombo jail. There also were many reports of official involvement, the use of voter registration lists to locate Tamil households, apparent police acquiescence, and even provision of transport for the so-called mobs (Ross and Savada 1990: 205–206; Snodgrass 1999: 100–101; Somasundram 1999: xviii; see also Bremner, this volume). Since then, in both scholarly and popular analyses, it has become axiomatic that the events of the summer of 1983 "turned a conflict between the state and radical Tamil youth into an ethnic war" (Herring 2001: 163). That tragic summer is seen as the watershed for an increasingly polarized society and the escalating losses of two decades of foregone income and investment as the government deployed its limited economic resources[3] to fight the war and to repair the destruction it wrought.

We do not disagree about the significance of "'83," but we believe that to understand such transformative processes, we need to open them up to a different kind of analysis. In this book, we and our contributors try to bring into the discussion, in as substantive a way as possible, not only the larger contexts of violence but also people's everyday orientations: the shifting articulations of understanding, practice, and experience that have been central in the expansion of violence in Sri Lanka generally and in the war's production and reproduction particularly. Together, we document at various levels, from national to neighborhood, how both ordinary and extraordinary practices and policies have articulated into events of violence, both mundane (surveillance and expanding cultures of fear) and spectacular (war and riot).

The "economy" is our opening into these linkages—not macroeconomic analysis alone, as has been increasingly common in recent analyses of civil war in Sri Lanka and elsewhere (e.g., Arunatilake et al. 2000; Berdal and Malone 2000; Esman and Herring 2001; World Bank 2000) but the economy understood as part of an always changing Sri Lankan social formation.[4] Thus, while the first essays in this volume do the important work of laying out changes in national economic policy over time, held up against larger patterns of violence, the essays that follow map the complex and various ways in which Sri Lankan people directly engage the economic and social reproduction of the society in which they live—"the view from below" (Mwanasali 2000). Here, we suggest, is the real ground zero, the site where, as people struggle to make their livings and their lives, they both comprise and constitute the contexts of violence and war. In this sense, context is, as the culture theorist Jennifer Slack put it, "not something *out there, within which practices occur or which influence the development of practices.* Rather, *identities, practices, and effects generally constitute the very context within which they are practices, identities, or effects*" (Slack 1996: 125).

Of course, the very idea of a "national economy" is necessarily an abstraction from what people do, a useful abstraction that, as our opening essays show us, can reveal how different parts of the whole are linked in relation to the war. But national-level data do not usually capture the informal economy, a sector that expands in the less controlled conditions of civil war (Mwanasali 2000: 149; Rajasingham-Senanayake 1999). Ultimately this whole is grounded not in the "nation" but in the contingent concatenation of practices of people of all strata making their lives in relation to the lives of others. Cost/benefit analysis alone cannot fully account for the particular ways in which the violence has expanded, because the economy is not a subject with a singular logic that overrides all aspects of this complex network of practices. Therefore, we must bring into our purview both the economic situations and predicaments that people encounter and the historically shifting understandings that people have of those situations, to which, ironically but also inevitably, their own participation contributes. The view from below helps us to see how various socioeconomic contexts become linked with each other and resonate with other sorts of hierarchies and contradictions that permeate social life.

We do not argue for the superiority of one methodology over another. Instead, we take a resolutely interdisciplinary tack with essays that connect the Sri Lankan economy with the ethnic conflict at different levels of scale and with different methodologies. Chapters 2 and 3, by political scientists John Richardson and Amita Shastri, provide rich and detailed longitudinal and structural overviews of economic and political change at the national level. In chapters 4 and 5, sociologists Newton Gunasinghe[5] and Siri Hettige use their vast personal and research knowledge of Sri Lanka to link these macroeconomic shifts with changes in opportunities for people of different ethnic groups and classes, seen in categorical terms (such as "Tamils," "elites," "Sinhalese," and "lower class"). Finally, the ethnographic chapters, by sociologist Francesca Bremner and anthropologists Michele Gamburd and Caitrin Lynch, allow us to glimpse through their intensive sited fieldwork the complex and partial ways that people in three Sri Lankan locales are agents within the social and economic arrangements, local and larger, in which they live. We hope that collectively the essays in this volume initiate a renewed discussion of the relation between the economy and conflict, one that brings the economy back to the spaces where people live their lives and attempt to grasp the meaning of how their lives are produced.

Our interdisciplinary array also reminds us that while it is feasible, even useful, to construct a vision of the economy as a structure abstracted from social life, we must not allow that technology of vision (Haraway 1986: 188–196) to lead us into forgetting that the sources of those abstract structures lie with people engaged in socially and culturally meaningful material practices. In this way we hope to avoid at least some of the conceptual distance expressed in such phrases as "political economy" and "cultural economy" (cf. Du Gay et al. 1997; Hall 1997), which may perpetuate conceptual barriers of little salience in the boom and buzz of everyday life. On the one hand, we appreciate that not all practices are meaningful on the same scale. On the other hand, we emphasize that all levels of scale, from local, regional, and national, to international and "global," are produced by human activity (Tsing 2000); indeed, this is what makes possible the interconnections between levels that in the end produce the ethnic conflict in Sri Lanka as an ongoing and tragic actuality.

Sri Lankan Ethnicities

Sri Lanka's population has always been heterogeneous, as one would expect of an island possessed of excellent harbors and a location that was important in regional and interregional trading networks even before Europeans sailed into southern Asia in the early sixteenth century. Archaeological sites, monument inscriptions, and the oldest texts attest to a perpetual ebb and flow of people to and from other countries (Bandaranayake et al. 1990; Ray 1994). But how these various peoples identify themselves and are identified by others has varied significantly over time, with religion, language, and caste frequently given more importance than ethnicity (Rogers 1994; see also Gunawardana 1985, 1990). The contemporary focus on ethnicity apparently derives, at least in part, from the nineteenth-century sociology of knowledge employed by the British, who ruled Sri Lanka as a Crown Colony from 1796 until 1948.[6]

The British believed Sri Lanka's population was made up of three primary ethnic groups or, as they termed them, "races": the Sinhalese, the Malabars or Tamils, and the Moors, as Sri Lanka's Muslims are called (Rogers 1993: 108).[7] The British considered the three basic racial groups to be "fixed entities," with inherent, natural, quasi-biological differences that could be discerned in appearance, aptitudes, and character as well as culture (Rogers 1993: 101). British racial theory de-emphasized religion and caste, which had been more important in pre-British times. Language, however, was seen as an indicator of racial distinctiveness, particularly after it was recognized that Sinhala and Tamil came from different language families (Rogers 1994: 16).[8]

The British also distinguished less essential differences within the three "races." Thousands of Tamil speakers came from southern India to work in plantation agriculture in the late nineteenth and early twentieth centuries; subsequently, an official census and policy distinction was maintained between Tamils who had always lived in Sri Lanka and more recent arrivals, primarily the estate workers but also small groups of Indian traders found in major cities. Likewise, the British divided the Moors into Ceylon Moors and Indian Moors based on how long they had been on the island. The Sinhalese category, too, was divided into Low-country Sinhalese, who lived in the coastal areas and therefore had had contact with European colonial powers since the mid-1500s, and Kandyan Sinhalese, who lived in the internal highland areas and had been ruled directly by Europeans only since 1815. But these internal divisions were seen as elaborations on the basic racial categories, not contradictions to them.

Underlying the British scheme was the assumption that such fixed, bounded categories existed and that the entire population could be brought into a single "all-encompassing framework" (Rogers 1994: 17). This idea persists in contemporary Sri Lanka. The Department of Census and Statistics divides the country's 19 million people as follows: Sinhalese, 74 percent; Sri Lankan Tamils, 12.7 percent; Moors, 7 percent; and Indian Tamils, 5.5 percent, with the balance of about 1 percent made up of Malays, Burghers and Eurasians, Veddahs, and others.[9] Nevertheless, the Sinhalese, Sri Lanka Tamils, and Moors all recognize internal variability not flagged in official categories: the Low-country/Kandyan split remains culturally important for Sinhalese, even though it was dropped as a census division in 1981; Moors on the east coast are socially, economically, and culturally distinctive from those who live elsewhere in the country (McGilvray 1998: 446); and northern and eastern Tamils are in many ways as different from each other as the Indian Tamils are from them (Daniel 1996: 161–162). News accounts frequently combine the Sri Lankan and Indian Tamils and report that 18 percent of Sri Lanka's population is Tamil, but few Indian Tamils have a role in or identify with the LTTE (Daniel 1996: 18–24). Nevertheless, the basic notion that there are three ethnic groups and that they have always been clearly separate from each other is rarely challenged, despite historical evidence to the contrary. That this is so should not surprise any student of conflicts of this sort. Yet, given the way in which the construction of ethnic markers has been used for a variety of purposes to make internal differentiation invisible (or at least less visible), it *is* surprising that so few social theorists have come to question the use of ethnicity as a valid analytical concept.[10]

Over the twentieth century, religion has gained in importance as a marker of ethnicity. Almost all Sinhalese are Buddhists, and most of the Tamils are Hindu, but some of each are Christian. Thus religious divisions have never exactly mirrored ethnic ones: 69.3 percent of the population identify themselves as Buddhist, 15.4 percent as Hindu, 7.6 percent as Christian, and 7.6 percent as Muslim (S. de Silva 1997: 51). However, Sinhalese who are not Buddhist increasingly have found it politically and socially expedient to downplay their religious identity and give more emphasis to their Sinhalese ethnicity (Bartholomeusz and de Silva 1998). At the same time, the more "organic past" (Tambiah 1986: 63), when practitioners of all religions shared some deities, temples, and specialists, is now being ignored. Increasingly since independence in 1948, a single, discrete Sinhalese Buddhist category has been rhetorically opposed to all the rest, who then are by reduction not Buddhists, not Sinhala speakers, and, in some eyes, not true Sri Lankans.

Overview of the Conflict

The civil war that has existed in Sri Lanka since 1983 is primarily between the Sinhalese-dominated government and the Liberation Tigers of Tamil Eelam (LTTE), an armed group formed in 1976 that claims to represent all Tamils of Sri

Lanka.[11] The LTTE seeks the right to Tamil self-determination in their own Tamil Eelam, or Tamil homeland, to be located in the northern and eastern regions where Sri Lankan Tamils have predominated for centuries (see map, p. xvi). In contrast, the large Sinhalese majority lives primarily in the central, western, and southern parts of the island. However, this apparently straightforward geographic partitioning is more complicated than it appears. Many Tamils have long lived outside the "homeland" areas. Furthermore, the Moors, who also speak Tamil but identify themselves on the basis of religion rather than language, are found in the urban areas of the west and southwest, as well as on the east coast where they live alongside the Tamils, although not necessarily on friendly terms, particularly in recent years (McGilvray 1999). Finally, the Indian or Estate Tamils live on or near the central highland tea estates, within the Sinhalese regions.[12]

The war can be seen as an escalation of communal violence that has broken out intermittently since independence in 1948 (see Richardson, Figure 1, this volume), in tandem with official rhetoric and government policies that favor Sinhalese interests and culture. The first major jump in both violence and rhetoric is usually attributed to the 1956 elections. The winning candidate, S. W. R. de A. Bandaranaike, outraged Tamils by running on a pro-Buddhism and Sinhalese-language platform and then, immediately upon election, introducing a bill to make Sinhalese the country's only official language. Tamils also objected to government economic development programs that were resettling Sinhalese farmers into traditionally Tamil areas (Peebles 1990). Bandaranaike himself appeared open to compromise because, after the election, he suggested that Tamil speakers be allowed to use Tamil in schools, exams, and government and, in 1957, he signed an agreement with S. J. V. Chelvanayakam, a senior Tamil leader, to that effect (Eller 1999: 129). The agreement also called for a reconsideration of plans to repatriate the majority of Estate Tamils to India. However, after protests by Sinhalese and Buddhist nationalists, the pact was canceled. Rioting against Tamils broke out repeatedly during these years, but in 1959, after Bandaranaike was assassinated by a Buddhist monk, essentially for not being anti-Tamil enough, violence subsided and a period of relative calm prevailed for over a decade.

The second major period of pre-1983 violence was instigated by the policies of Mrs. Sirimavo Bandaranaike, Bandaranaike's widow and herself prime minister (1960–65 and 1970–77). In 1972, she continued the resettlement programs, carried out repatriation of some Estate Tamils, and led a rewriting of the country's constitution to give official and unique primacy to Buddhism and the Sinhalese language. Simultaneously, university admissions policies were restructured to effect affirmative action for students who took their exams in Sinhala, drastically reducing educational opportunities for Tamil students who up to that time, in large part because of their superior English language skills, had been admitted to the most competitive university programs and professions in numbers far exceeding their proportion of the population (C. R. de Silva 1974). Tensions between Tamils and Sinhalese rose. In 1974, after police killed 11 people at an international Tamil conference, the northern Tamil city of Jaffna was the scene of days of rioting. Finally, in 1976, the major Tamil opposition party, the Tamil United Liberation Front (TULF), called for a constitutional change to create a Tamil homeland.

During the national elections the following year, which replaced Mrs. Bandaranaike with J. R. Jayawardene and "liberalized" economic policies (Richardson, this volume), anti-Tamil rhetoric reached new heights. The summer of 1977 was marred by weeks of Sinhala/Tamil violence. By 1978, Tamil youth had broken away from the TULF to act independently as the Liberation Tigers of Tamil Eelam and pursue the goal of Eelam through force (Rotberg 1999: 7). In 1979, the government passed a Prevention of Terrorism Act, which gave the government broad powers to arrest and hold suspects. Jayawardene declared a state of emergency and sent the Sri Lankan army to the Jaffna peninsula, where army violence soon became commonplace; the events of July 1983 ensued (Eller 2001: 137).

Since 1983, the LTTE, which now has approximately 5,000 soldiers supported by international financial dealings and fund-raising among Tamils resident abroad, has pursued its cause militarily (Lewer and William 2002: 485–486; Rotberg 1999: 8). With the groundswell of support that followed the 1983 riots, the LTTE gradually gained control of the Jaffna peninsula and much of the east coast where it maintained not only military dominance but a parallel civilian government. In 1987, an agreement between India and Sri Lanka brought the spectacularly unsuccessful Indian Peace Keeping Force (IPKF) into the Jaffna peninsula, to facilitate the disarming of the insurgents. In 1990, after military and political defeat, the IPKF withdrew, leaving the Sinhalese population deeply suspicious of India's intentions.[13] The IPKF's departure left the LTTE solidly in control, with their headquarters in the city of Jaffna (Rotberg 1999: 9).

In 1995 and 1996, after the breakdown of peace talks between the LTTE and the government, which was now led by the Bandaranaikes' daughter, Chandrika Bandaranaike Kumaratunga, the Sri Lanka army undertook a new military offensive and regained control of the Jaffna peninsula. In 1999 and 2000, the LTTE took much of it back, although the Sri Lanka army remained in tenuous and constantly threatened control of Jaffna town itself. In 2001, after the LTTE declared a unilateral cease-fire, the Norwegian government attempted unsuccessfully to broker a peace agreement. When those talks collapsed, the war resumed in earnest, particularly after the July attack on the airport. But elections were held at the end of 2001, and there was again a change of government: Kumaratunga's party lost to the UNP (the United National Party, which under J. R. Jayawardene had introduced economic liberalization in 1977), although, as president, she remained part of the government. When the LTTE declared a unilateral cease-fire for December 24, 2001, Prime Minister Ranil Wickramasinghe quickly followed suit, and a formal cease-fire agreement was signed by both parties on February 23, 2002. Peace negotiations, again brokered by Norway, have been under way since September 2002 (see epilogue; also Lewer and William 2002: 490–499). But the obstacles to peace are enormous. Not only is a political solution acceptable to all parties going to be difficult to come by, but after 20 years—a full generation—of hostilities, the war and the ways people cope with it constitute what has become normal life.

Post-Ethnicity and the New Normal in Sri Lanka

Today, modernist and post-Orientalist scholars generally agree that it is not accurate to describe the Sri Lankan civil war, or any so-called ethnic conflict, as simply the most recent outbreak of ancient animosities between essentialized and preexistent groups, such as "the Sinhalese" and "the Tamils" (Rogers 1994). Instead, scholars contend that contemporary political groups, responding to forces and so-ciologies of knowledge set in motion during colonial times, make appeals framed in terms of race, caste, ethnicity, or language to garner political support. Once elected, these same politicians hand out political and economic rewards along community lines. It is in this process that the "economy" and "ethnicity" are expe-rienced together as part of ordinary people's lived experience (e.g., Mwanasali 2000).[14]

However, as the violence in Sri Lanka and elsewhere has expanded and civil wars have become entrenched, an interesting new form of explanation has developed that we call the *post-ethnicity argument*. The post-ethnicity argument is the posi-tion that whatever the impetus for a war's development, whether rooted in the past or the consequence of twentieth-century political and ideological positionings in the language of ethnicity, an explanation of origins no longer serves as an expla-nation of persistence. This is because, over time, war produces a new social forma-tion, one that is grounded in an economy that includes war and violence as a part of the reality in relation to which people are fashioning their lives. We note that this argument can reduce conflict to simplistic "economic agendas" (e.g., Collier 2000a, 2000b) or "social capital" (Goodhand et al. 2000), which we discuss below. But post-ethnicity approaches also allow us to see "how ordinary people adjust their lives to cope with the constraints and opportunities brought about by civil war" (Mwanasali 2000: 152), how those adjustments then become part of what the war is, and therefore contribute to the war's reproduction.

At its simplest, this turn in scholarly positioning for Sri Lanka notes that the war's development has set in train wide-ranging changes that, in interaction with earlier forces, have altered profoundly the economic terrain of Sri Lankan life. The numbers alone insinuate the transformations of the past two decades. At the start of the civil war, the Sri Lanka military numbered 12,000; today, it is over ten times that. In 1985, military spending consumed a mere 1.61 percent of the nation's GDP; by 1996 it was 6.02 percent (Arunatilake, Jayasuriya, and Kelegama 2000: 22; see also World Bank 2000a: 263); and it has continued to grow into the twenty-first century (Shastri, this volume). When the government increases the war budget and hires more troops at better salaries, it may not guarantee military victory, but it does ensure that some men and women find paid employment who otherwise would not (Goodhand et al. 2000: 394–395; Gamburd, this volume). When soldiers in the national forces die, their families receive not only the thanks of a grateful government and an armed escort for the coffin (M. R. Gamburd 1999) but also death benefits that dwarf the incomes that most families would otherwise have: the soldier's salary until the year he would have turned 55,[15] a pension after that, an additional and quite substantial one-time payment, and, by some reports, a new house (Gamburd, this volume; Edirisinghe 2000). Of course, those same soldiers must be clothed, fed, transported, doctored, armed, entertained, and buried, all of which creates other jobs and other markets. Thus directly and indirectly, government military spending, around $1 billion a year (Edirisinghe 2000), can be said to produce economic opportunities for thousands of ordinary people. This is one of the profound ironies of war, only recently studied at the local level.

Instead, when the relationship between the economy and ethnic conflict is described, it is primarily the national whole that is considered. For example, economists at the Central Bank of Sri Lanka have calculated that the conflict had reduced the country's rate of growth by about "2 to 3 percentage points a year" (World Bank 2000b: 12), a figure that is cited widely, usually without discussion of the underlying assumptions of uniformity. Similarly, researchers at the Institute of Policy Studies (IPS) in Colombo estimate that "[t]he war may have cost the equivalent of twice Sri Lanka's 1996 GDP" (Arunatilake, Jayasuriya, and Kelegama 2000: 29). We would ask what these figures might not tell us about the war's economic effects. What does it mean that Sri Lanka's growth rate is "reduced"? Who makes a living, and who cannot? Does everyone suffer the same, no matter where they are? Is it possible that simply as they go about the task of making a living, people's lives become articulated with violence as victims and as perpetrators? We have to remind ourselves that, although useful, structural statistics leave out the lived dimensions that motivate action, construct interests, articulate the local with the national, and move people in and out of the history of the war.

Nevertheless, the IPS study in particular is a painstakingly thorough examination of available macroeconomic data. Their analysis reveals that national resources that could have been available to expand health, education, and other social and economic programs have been used instead to buy weapons and pay soldiers, provide relief services for thousands of repeatedly displaced people, and replace damaged infrastructure. Tourist arrivals have stayed below potential; foreign direct investment has declined; and the country has lost the income and civic participation of hundreds of thousands of its people—Tamil and Sinhala—who have been uprooted, injured, or killed or who have chosen to emigrate and seek better lives for themselves and their families in Europe, Australia, Canada, or the United States (Arunatilake, Jayasuriya, and Kelegama 2000). But such macro analyses need to be complemented with micro ones that consider how people in Sri Lanka have adapted to living under conditions of civil war, how effects measured at the national level are felt differently in different social locations, and, most important, how wartime in practice becomes not just a detour on the road to prosperity for the nation taken as a whole but also a new normalcy written into everyday lives.

Income was not only "lost" during this period; for many, it also was gained. After all, the World Bank report *Sri Lanka: Recapturing Missed Opportunities* also notes that unemployment in Sri Lanka fell to a "historical low" (8.8 percent) in 1999 (World Bank 2000b: 2), and Shastri (this volume) notes an even lower rate of 7.6 percent in 2000.[16] Sri Lanka's overall economy has grown at rates exceeding 4 percent for most years since the war began (O'Sullivan 1997: 97), and it was

6 percent in 2000 (Shastri, this volume). Furthermore, unlike the situation in many countries at war, indicators of social well-being, such as life expectancy, infant mortality rates, and school enrollment, have continued to improve, at least in areas outside the major conflict zones (O'Sullivan 1997: 98–99). But opportunities vary enormously in areas controlled by the LTTE, held by the government, or contested by both; and within areas, they vary by class, caste, gender, and ethnicity (Goodhand et al. 2000). To understand the effects of the war on the economy, the national view must be complemented by a more local one.

One study that does this is Meghan O'Sullivan's comparative research on how Tamil households have coped with the war in the northern areas controlled by the LTTE and the eastern areas actively contested by the LTTE and the government. She found that in some ways they have done better than might be expected because, as she put it, while "some opportunities are destroyed, others are created" (O'Sullivan 1997: 95). However, the situations in the two regions were quite different. In the north, both the government and the LTTE were propping up the war-torn economy, at least until the government reclaimed the Jaffna peninsula in 1996. In the east, daily battles made it impossible for the LTTE to do social support work effectively, trade was disrupted by severe travel restrictions on Muslim traders, and people were more dependent on emergency assistance from the government and from nongovernmental organizations (NGOs). Jonathan Goodhand, David Hulme, and Nick Lewer, in their own comparative study of the quality of life in different regions of Sri Lanka, also found that in uncontested villages—places that were clearly held by either the LTTE or the government—conditions were more conducive to relatively stable lives than they were in contested areas (Goodhand et al. 2000).

Both O'Sullivan and Goodhand, Hulme, and Lewer found that everywhere residents were heavily dependent on government remittances (which continued to flow into LTTE-controlled areas),[17] and many had to abandon former occupations (such as deep-sea fishing and farming) because of security restrictions or because they did not have access to the necessary inputs (Goodhand et al. 2000: 398; O'Sullivan 1997: 113). Nevertheless, life went on as people cobbled together remittances (from the government or family members abroad), LTTE salaries or welfare payments, and new jobs in trade and services (O'Sullivan 1997: 108). Children attended school, took government-run exams, and went on to university at rates approaching those before 1983 (O'Sullivan 1997: 106). Hospitals functioned, although staffs were much reduced, and the situation would have been far worse without the support of foreign NGOs. Life was difficult, but, at least in those war zone areas where the authority situation was clear, many people found ways to move from day to day and to plan for their own futures and those of their children.

Other researchers, too, have found people adapting to economic opportunities produced in the constancy of violence. In the mid-1990s, Darini Rajasingham-Senanayake conducted ethnographic fieldwork in the unsettled edges of the war zones in Sri Lanka. She discovered that in these unsettled areas, the war has produced a "hidden economy" of "illegitimate profit, power, and protection" (1999:

57–58; see also Goodhand et al. 2000). In 2001, while doing fieldwork in an area of rural Moneragala District that he has followed for nearly two decades, Mike Woost found that military employment has become the most recent addition to the already eclectic mix—*chena* (slash-and-burn) gardening, gem mining, and development project aid—that makes up the economy in this particularly marginal region of Sri Lanka. When the *chena* season began, some young men in the forces took leave of their positions and returned home to farm. When the season was over, they found a way to return to the military. Others would take part-time employment in security units ancillary to the army and police, such as "home guards."

Some we talked with—primarily people self-identified as Sinhalese—claimed that the war has become its own reality, its reproduction less and less tied up with the politics of ethnicity and more and more dependent on the politics of profits and the daily struggle to make a living. In 1997, 1999, and 2001, we each met people, in urban Colombo and Kandy and in rural Moneragala and Kurunegala Districts, who worried that the war might never end because a few are getting rich from it and many others have come to depend on it to make a living. In 2001, a spokesperson for the National Peace Council, a private Sri Lankan organization that promotes a negotiated settlement, told a *New York Times* reporter, "It [the economic benefits of military service] diminishes the potential to mobilize rural communities against the war, because they are deriving substantial economic benefits, though at tremendous human cost" (Dugger 2001).

Thus wartime Sri Lanka is not just a stop-gap but a new social formation, one that may provide people relatively predictable ways to survive and, as such, may actually contribute to the war's perpetuation. At the same time, we underline that it is *not* possible to reduce social complexity or even just the war's reproduction to a balance sheet with *costs* in one column and *opportunities* in the other. Costs and opportunities clearly are not the same for everyone. Costs are not the same for Tamil refugees in the north as they are for struggling farmers in the southeast. The thousands who run from air force helicopters presumably do not derive the same meaning from the burning carcasses of aircraft on the airport tarmac as do other thousands who depend on jobs at tourist hotels. Economic analysis must be linked to a broader cultural and ideological analysis of Sri Lanka as a society divided by location, age, gender, class, and ethnicity—social categories that are reformulated by the expansion of violence, both mundane and spectacular.

We underline this point with a more personal example of how the war produced not only a new ordinariness but also one that has differential economic effects and meanings, depending on how one is identified by others. While doing research in Sri Lanka in 1999, we found, as Colombo residents then knew only too well, that it had become difficult to negotiate the city by any vehicle larger than a bicycle. Partly, this was because the post-1977 "liberalized" economy has brought more vehicles to the roads of Sri Lanka, but it also was the result of the increased presence of security forces. In 1999, roads and byways were closed or narrowed by cement barriers and manned checkpoints throughout Colombo (and on major roads throughout the island), creating delays so predictable that like everyone else, we learned to calculate them as part of travel time.[18] But we particularly were impressed by how institutionalized these security measures had become. Barriers and checkpoints, which might appear to the casual observer as makeshift or temporary, were so established that they were indicated on ordinary road maps published by the national Survey Department. Even the expense of maintaining them was underwritten in an orderly fashion by business establishments. Alongside the soldiers, weapons, and barbed wire, neat signs announced that Maliban Biscuits or Bata Shoes or the National Assurance Corporation sponsored a particular checkpoint. A new normality indeed.

However, while for most Sinhalese residents and foreign visitors these barriers were a trivial inconvenience, for Tamil Sri Lankans, such as those on their way to work each morning, the implications were more ominous. They feared and worried over checkpoints, where they were far more likely than either foreigners or Sinhalese residents to be pulled over, taken from a bus, taxi, or bicycle to be interrogated, and even taken away and detained. Perhaps it resulted only in being late for work or some appointment, but even that could be a significant cost. Both Sinhala and Tamil residents suggested to us that employers increasingly were reluctant to hire Tamils because they too often were delayed at checkpoints. It was not that Tamils were unreliable; it was simply that they experienced the "normalization" of security in a particularly costly fashion.

Overall, then, what a post-ethnicity analysis helps us to see is that the war in Sri Lanka today is not a detour; it has become the path taken, a fully embedded part of the social formation, consequence as well as cause. Now the war is not just what is happening *in* Sri Lanka; it has become an important part of what Sri Lanka *is,* a social formation of war that is reproduced in daily life. Nevertheless, we introduce a caveat: Because the post-ethnicity discussions often highlight how people are "managing" (or not) under trying circumstances, they can degenerate into a simplistic economism that pays insufficient attention to the ideological and social contexts with which the economy is imbricated.

Social Capital, Greed, and Other Economisms

The potential dangers that we see in the post-ethnicity approach are evidenced in two bodies of related work: that on war and "social capital," for which our example is the Goodhand, Hulme, and Lewer study, cited earlier; and that which looks at war and "greed," epitomized by recent publications of Paul Collier (2000a, 2000b). We worry that both perpetuate artificial separations between people's many sorts of socially constructed connections to each other and the political and economic contexts that both create and are created by those links in the first place.

The overall goal of the Goodhand, Hulme, and Lewer study was not just to show how the war's effects varied from one part of the island to another, but explicitly to examine "the interaction between violent conflict, political economy, and social capital" (2000: 393). Since Robert Putnam popularized the idea in the early 1990s (Putnam et al. 1993), the notion that "trusts, norms, and networks"—social capital—"can improve the efficiency of society by facilitating coordinated actions" (Harriss 2002: 2) has become something close to development dogma.[19] Supporters argue that social networks—for example, kin ties, clubs, and political groups—increase social capital, which is touted as *the* essential ingredient for organizational efficiency and successful development. Conversely, inadequate social capital is deemed to be a root cause of economic and political failure. That is, the lack of network-building organizations in civil society is seen as a cause, not, as one might expect, a consequence of poverty and inadequate government (Harriss 2002: 29).

Goodhand, Hulme, and Lewer set out to test the accepted wisdom among social capital theorists that "violent conflict has a negative effect on social capital and war zones are considered to be 'zones of social capital deficiency'" (2000: 390). They carried out a series of brief community studies in seven villages in different parts—government-controlled, LTTE-controlled, and contested—of Sri Lanka. Not surprisingly, they found economic problems everywhere, largely because of the disruption of markets and interregional trade, repeated displacement of people, and the economic blockade imposed on Tamil-controlled areas by the Sri Lankan government. But, as we noted above, they also found that life in controlled areas was relatively predictable and that it sustained a new normalcy, which included economic planning (planting crops, for example), dynamic organizations (temple societies, credit schemes, co-ops), and trust in neighbors and the ruling authorities. In contested-area villages, however, it was another story. In these "gray" areas, where neither the government nor the LTTE had full sway, they found a growing "culture of fear," unwillingness to plan for the future (such as a reluctance to plant crops), and rising alcoholism, theft, suicide, and domestic violence.

Goodhand, Hulme, and Lewer conclude, and we agree, that their research findings undermine the "simplistic assumption that conflict undermines social capital" (2000: 402). Instead, they suggest, people have mobilized different sorts of social capital to deal with the conflict. In Tamil-controlled and contested areas, kin, caste, and religious ties—what they term "traditional sources of social capital"—have become increasingly important. In government-controlled villages, new "civil society organizations have mobilized." This is consistent with O'Sullivan's simpler notion that people have found ways to cope, even to progress. But Goodland, Hulme, and Lewer go further. They propose that not all social capital is positive: The "conflict entrepreneurs" can manipulate social capital to create "anti-social capital" (2000: 401); and strengthening social capital within groups ("bonding social capital") can result in weakening social capital between groups ("bridging social capital"), exacerbating divides, such as those between ethnic groups. It is here that we see cause for concern, because in the end what they seem to be arguing for is a liberalized economy and open market competition, which they imagine will give rise to both productivity and social trust.

Yet we know that in Sri Lanka, the open economy has been associated with a decline in trust, a rise in ethnic conflict, and an increase in opportunism (see Gunasinghe, this volume; Hettige, this volume). The social science literature is replete with examples of how party politics and increasing social and economic differentiation have undermined cooperative associations among the Sinhalese (e.g.,

Brow 1996; Winslow 2002) and polarized identities (e.g., Woost 1993; Bartholomeusz and de Silva 1998). Goodhand, Hulme, and Lewer too easily blame the conflict itself for the "erosion of trust" at the local level instead of looking at how local relations always connect with national quests for leadership and hegemony, before as well as during the war.[20]

Equally disturbing is their use of the term "perverse" in contrast to "good" social capital. In a summary table, "bonding social capital"—which we know from their earlier discussion refers to "traditional" forms such as kin, caste, and religious ties—joins "perverse social capital" as part of the "unstable" environment. This appears to replicate a spurious dichotomy between the modern and the traditional, while suggesting that these cultural practices are inherently unchanging and inevitably incompatible with a market economy. This is particularly troublesome because they move on to suggest that "the key question then is how can one invest in and construct 'pro-social' capital" (2000: 404). We are left to ask, by whose standards are certain kinds of social relations positive and others negative?

In the end, Goodhand, Hulme, and Lewer seem unable to transcend the neoclassical economic formulation that is part and parcel of the idea of social capital. They persist in seeing political economy and social capital as distinct, as if there is any capital that is not social and as if political economy and social capital can have different relations to the production of violence. They have re-created a world where one kind of entrepreneur ("conflict entrepreneurs" who "do well out of war") undermines the accumulation of capital of another sort of entrepreneur (the capitalists of the open economy), where modernity is equated with markets and contrasted with an essentialized tradition of caste and kinship, where social ties can be the objects of selective investment, and where policies can be adopted to "construct 'pro-social' capital" by promoting an "enabling environment" (2000: 404). Despite their assertions that "the critical factor is the interaction between social, economic, and political processes rather than notions of social capital divorced from the wider context" (2000: 405), in the end, their analysis props up that conceptual separation, which seems to be inherent in the social capital approach.

Goodhand, Hulme, and Lewer's analysis touches on but does not really explore the "greed or grievance" debate about the causes of war. As noted by Mats Berdal and David M. Malone in *Greed and Grievance: Economic Agendas in Civil Wars,* "The presence of economic motives and commercial agendas in wars is not so much a new phenomenon as a familiar theme in the history of warfare" (2000: 1). But for contemporary civil wars, the issue has taken analysts into new territory, beyond simple profiteering or political manipulation for gain. The articles in the Berdal and Malone volume consider a wide range of topics, from transborder trade and the world arms market, to targeted economic sanctions and international aid.

Perhaps the most controversial research, however, is that by Paul Collier, director of the Development Research Group at the World Bank and professor of economics at Oxford University. In an effort to understand why some civil wars go on for decades, while others fizzle out fairly quickly, Collier put together what he describes as a "large new data base on civil wars during the period 1965–99" (Collier

2000a: 5). He concludes, "Greed matters more than grievance" (2000b: 110). The only exception he allows is in some situations of lopsided ethnic dominance, where oppressed minorities may "take to the gun" (2000a: 9); otherwise, "the modern rebel appears truly to have been a 'rebel without a cause'" (2000a: 9).

Collier's data base consists of information on 73 civil wars in 161 countries, only 47 of which had enough information to make it to the final study sample. The factors he (and his colleague, Anke Hoeffler) included in the study were (1) percentage of GDP coming from the export of primary commodities, (2) geographical spread of population, (3) having recently had a civil war, (4) a diaspora resident in the United States, (5) population growth rate, (6) education levels, (7) ethnic and religious diversity, (8) economic inequality, and (9) lack of democratic rights, which he equates with "lack of political rights" (2000a: 7) and "repression" (2000a: 9). Collier finds that the first five variables are positively correlated with civil wars, the next two are negatively correlated, and the last two—economic inequality and "democratic rights," which are his "obvious proxies for objective grievances" (2000a: 7)—do not predict civil wars at all.

Collier suggests that social scientists who would take grievance seriously are "badly misled" (Collier 2000a: 2), taken in by the public relations discourse generated by rebels who really are no more than self-interested "predators"—a highly pejorative and distancing term, we point out—who "use force to extort goods or money from their legitimate owners" (2000a: 3). They want power, they want wealth, or possibly—but to an economist, Collier claims, it does not really matter—they want justice and need to steal to fight for it. Just as businesses need good images, so do rebel leaders; therefore, they "develop a discourse of grievance in order to function" (2000a: 3). Collier claims that if rebellions really arose out of objective grievances, his measures of a lack of democratic rights and economic inequality would have been better predictors of civil war (2000a: 7).

We see many problems with Collier's analysis. He does not explore case examples to see if the articulated grievances would have been reflected in his proxy variables, which seem the weakest aspect of the analysis even though in many ways they are also the most crucial. He does not engage with or even cite the many social science analyses of civil wars that do explore the construction of grievance (e.g., Danforth 1995, on Macedonia; Daniel 1996, on Sri Lanka; Malkki 1995, on Tanzania; van der Veer 1994, on India). He does not consider the enormous literature on how people may form agency around all sorts of possible identities rather than act on their "objective" class position (e.g., Hall 1996a; 1970). He appears to assume that governments are always legitimate and rebels always illegitimate, and that it is easily possible to tell one from the other. Similarly, he does not seem to imagine that the simple survival strategies of people caught up in civil wars might also sustain conflict.

The overall problem is that Collier proposes a simple, static model for what is after all a tremendously complicated and dynamic situation: an entrenched attempt to transform a society by force, around which the social and material landscape is constantly being remade (Mwanasali 2000: 14–15). Collier implicitly dis-

allows the possibility that the conflict could be the result of the practices and identities—nurtured over time by all kinds of experiences in the society at large—of a
multiplicity of groups engaged in the struggle for power or even, as grassroots studies show, just survival. Culture, ideology, and power struggles disappear to be replaced by simple financial feasibility. Rebel leaders are reduced to a perverse form
of that old staple of neoclassical economics, the rationally calculating generic man
who, given enough funding and the right advertising, can manipulate almost anyone to follow any cause.

Certainly, Collier is not the only analyst to suggest that opportunism and greed,
poverty, and wealthy diasporas play a role in civil wars. But what social science
research makes clear is that these factors cannot be isolated from contemporary
politics, history, colonialism, religious nationalism, and other social processes (e.g.,
van der Veer 1994). Collier's policy recommendations to the World Bank for reducing the risk of conflict do not take account of such complexities. For example,
he promotes economic diversification, long a feature of World Bank and IMF structural adjustment programs, to expand growth and reduce poverty while at the
same time limiting dependence on easily raidable natural resource exports (Collier
2000a: 16). Thinking inside the box constructed by his simple correlations, Collier
seems not to remember that high growth economies can themselves be raided for
private gain, although perhaps more easily by government elites than poor rebels.[21]
He also neglects to mention the growing evidence that both economic liberalization
and development aid are not experienced by everyone equally (for Sri Lanka, see
Abeyratne 1999; Herring 2001; Woost 1993) and are strongly associated with civil
unrest (e.g., Esman and Herring 2001; Walton and Seddon 1994).

In Sri Lanka, it is precisely the transition since 1977, from a relatively "closed"
economy to one encouraging diversification through foreign investment and international trade, that not only helped to bring the civil war about (see in particular
the Gunasinghe and Hettige articles in this volume) but has also helped to sustain
it. Freer trade made it easier for both the government and the LTTE to manipulate
the international webs of humanitarian and development aid to consolidate power,
to receive funds from Sri Lankans resident abroad (Portenous 2000), and to procure
weapons and other necessities for waging war. For those who experienced the
austere and tightly controlled Sri Lankan economy before 1977, it is almost impossible to imagine that such a context could have produced the civil war we know
today, even though widespread shortages of basic necessities (like bread, rice, gas,
and pharmaceuticals), as well as absolute privation, were far more prevalent then
than now. Thus economic liberalization seems to have provided both some of the
motivation and some of the means for the civil war, although we do not want to
downplay the role of a growing culture of violence (Daniel 1996). In this perspective, Collier's recommendations seem dangerous, possibly leading to more conflict
rather than less. Equally important, Collier's work can too easily be used to seek to
delegitimize any kind of grievance, from wherever it is voiced, and, like the post
9/11 discourse of terrorism, to legitimize any means to blot it out.

Collier's treatment of conflict is like the social capital theorists' treatment of social networks in civil society. Each becomes a subject all its own, cause instead of consequence. Collier suggests, "It is natural for observers to interpret . . . [ethnic] conflicts as being caused by ethnic hatred. Instead the conflicts have caused the inter-group hatred and may even . . . have created the groups" (2000b: 13). Structured in this way, conflicts become fetishes in and of themselves, the outcome of financially feasible predation on productive activities, with no other origin or goal, simply another form of accumulation. Haraway suggests that such explanations perform a "god-trick"—they appear to explain everything from nowhere, i.e., their perspective is supposedly that of the neutral, universal observer, with a vision beyond politics (Haraway 1986: 193).

For all these reasons, then, we argue that the insights gleaned from post-ethnicity arguments should be handled with care. We agree that it is important to recognize that the war is not a temporary break in a real Sri Lanka to which life will return once the war is over; there is now a new social formation in which war and violence have been normalized. But even though people have indeed found various ways to build lives and make livings, we should not reduce their lives to those livings. Nor should we forget that the past *does* matter, not in the sense of unchanging animosities between essentialized groups that are acted out in the present but because past social positioning and cultural constructions set up contemporary potentials. Our contribution here is not to unearth new factors but to look at the same factors in a different way, to move from correlation analysis and structural determinants to those ordinary people maintaining their lives, in conditions that always, for everyone, "anticipate" violence (cf. Jeganathan 2000).

But to do this, we return to the question of *how* changes in national policy really do articulate with the economy from below. If we agree that different sectors, groups, and individuals perceive and experience costs and opportunities differently, sometimes even in opposed directions, then what does it mean to call this a "new social formation" and how is its reproduction carried forward? What is needed is a way to understand both the variety of subjectivities and interests at play in this social formation and the way in which subjectivities and agencies emerge in the give and take of making everyday lives. To embark on this effort we need a theoretical framework that will allow us to more adequately grasp such complex articulations of agency.

Articulations

As a first step on this alternative path, we draw on the notion of articulation as it emerged in the work of culture theorists like Stuart Hall. As Hall explains it, articulation is about social linkages that are possible, that may occur if the conditions are right, but that are not inevitable and that always may be changed or broken. In his words:

> [Articulation] has a nice double meaning because "articulate" means to utter, to speak forth, to be articulate. It carries that sense of language-ing, of expressing, etc., but we

also speak of an "articulated" lorry [truck]: a lorry where the front [cab] and back [trailer] can, but need not necessarily, be connected to one another. The two parts are connected to each other, but through a specific linkage that can be broken. An articulation is thus the form of the connection that *can* make a unity of two different elements, under certain conditions. It is a linkage which is not necessary, determined, absolute, and essential for all time. You have to ask, under what circumstances *can* a connection be forged or made? (1996b: 142)

The idea that social linkages are never necessary or obligatory is especially important if we are to see the social order of war as contingent in its construction, rather than as emerging inevitably from transhistorical, intrinsic, and absolute interests such as greed or essentialized and eternal ethnic identities. Hall reminds us that while any particular new arrangement of social linkages is not inevitable, it also is not wholly free of determinations. Each linkage becomes meaningful by bringing elements of historically specific social formations into relation with each other, and when new articulations come about, those previous meanings may be engaged and transformed as well. Hall uses religion as an example:

[Religion] exists historically in a particular formation, anchored very directly in relation to a number of different forces. Nevertheless, it has no necessary, intrinsic, transhistorical belonging-ness. Its meaning—political and ideological—comes precisely from its position within a formation. It comes with what else it is articulated to. (1996b: 142–143)

So when a rearticulation of social forces occurs, "It is not something which has a straight, unbroken line of continuity from the past" (Hall 1996b: 143).

We find articulation a valuable starting point, but we also suggest going beyond Hall's ideas, as stated here, to open up the notion of articulation to more of the rich complexities of social life. The metaphor of cab and trailer might give the impression of linkages between already fixed elements, which is probably not what he intended because the "elements" being articulated are themselves emergent from other sorts of articulations. Building on Hall's own metaphors, we note that both cab and trailer are articulated in separate factories, under different conditions; they are reproduced or maintained in different ways, operating on different resources and principles.

For example, in Michele Gamburd's article (this volume), we learn of Sinhalese men who enlist in the army less because of patriotism than because the overtly masculine identity of soldier is a more comfortable fit for them than being "househusbands" while their wives are working in the Middle East as housemaids. These rural families live within a realm of articulations of practice and identity involving family, caste, class, gender, and more, which they bring with them as they try to connect with the larger economy and society. What emerges is not some imposition of identity and practice from above. To use Hall's metaphor, they are not simply an inert "trailer" now linked to and dragged along with the "cab," which alone has the power of motion, of acting as a subject (the metaphor does, after all, imply an unequal relationship within the linkage). Instead, the linkage changes the range of motion of the cab, even makes requirements and demands on its ability to lead the way. From this angle, subjectivities and agency emerge in the articulation of identities, practices, and social forces already in motion.

At the same time, this is not a simple linear process whose outcome is known in advance. As Hall notes in a critique of economism, people do not enter into these articulations as fixed identities; they become self-conscious of possible identities because of the social forces with which they now are engaging (Hall 1996b: 144). Perhaps if their wives had not been working in the Middle East, even more men would have become soldiers anyway, but with different results. The relationship is, as Hall tells us, dialectical.

It is not the case that the social forces, classes, groups, political movements, etc., are first constituted in their unity by objective economic conditions and then unified as an ideology. The process is quite the reverse. One has to see the way in which a variety of social groups enter into and constitute for a time a kind of political and social force, in part by seeing themselves reflected as a unified force in the ideology that constitutes them. The relationship between social forces and ideology is absolutely dialectical. As the ideological vision emerges, so does the group (Hall 1996b: 144).

While the idea of the dialectic does frame the emergence of identity within a more complex play of forces, in everyday life the dialectic is rarely experienced as a merging of discourse and subjectivity. Rather, the experience is more one of becoming, of recognizing the self in practice, in often new but always unfinished ways. In this volume, Bremner's article provides an example of such processes at work among the 1983 rioters. As Hall cautions, we should not only "see subjectivity as discursively constructed in practice." We also must see that "the 'self' as constituted out of and by difference . . . remains contradictory, and that cultural forms are, similarly in that way, never whole, never fully closed or 'sutured'" (1996b: 145).

In sum, and as the essays in this volume demonstrate, we need to think of articulation as multiple, layered, engaging, transforming, and never final. As we tried to use these ideas to understand the relation between economy and ethnic conflict in Sri Lanka, the late Newton Gunasinghe's 1984 article "The Open Economy and Its Impact on Ethnic Relations in Sri Lanka," reproduced here as chapter 4, became a key starting point. In his analysis, which originally appeared in three installments in the *Lanka Guardian*, a now lapsed progressive news weekly, Gunasinghe took on the task of explaining the 1983 explosion of anti-Tamil violence.

As Hall suggests, Gunasinghe eschewed a simple "straight line" approach. Instead, he argued for looking at how, in a multiethnic society, changes in the structure of the national economy produced effects that built on historically specific social formations but always in ways that were differentiated by class, ethnicity, and other factors. Gunasinghe noted that in the controlled economy years before 1977, Tamil and Muslim businessmen were relatively disadvantaged by not having access to political patronage from the Sinhalese-dominated government, the major player in the economy. After 1977, however, when the role of the government decreased, the Sinhalese lost that advantage; furthermore, because Tamils and Muslims were already well established in the private sector, they now had the advantage of being ready to work in the new open conditions. Not surprisingly, Sinhalese businessmen resented the fact they were losing economic ground in relation to Tamils and Muslims (see also Herring 2001: 156–158). At the same time, many of the urban poor were hit hard by the combination of decreased welfare support and soaring inflation that characterized the early years of the new economy. The poor could see around them, for the first time in decades, highly desirable consumer goods available for sale, and their increased sense of relative deprivation also led to resentment against Tamil businessmen. These resentments were fanned by the government-controlled media and some government ministers into the flames of 1983.

What Gunasinghe does in his analysis is reveal how "elements" articulate around the conflict, even while showing us that they were indeed emergent from other sorts of previous articulations. However, in many ways his argument was more provocative than demonstrated; and as we tried to work with it in 2000, we also felt it needed to be held up to more current developments. Therefore, in August 2000, we held a workshop at the New England Center on the campus of the University of New Hampshire. We brought together scholars from a variety of disciplines— political scientists, economists, historians, sociologists, and anthropologists—who had been doing research in Sri Lanka and who could address Gunasinghe's ideas with different information and experiences.[22] In the end, of course, because of this variety of disciplines, we also found ourselves dealing with formulations attuned to quite different notions of scale, ranging from nation to neighborhood. Putting them together, as we have in this volume, has forced us to deal with the way in which different sorts of articulations may become what Anna Tsing has called scale-making projects. That is, scale is more than just an artifact of research method; it is also part of what is being studied: "Scale is not just a neutral frame for viewing the world; scale must be brought into being: proposed, practiced, and evaded, as well as taken for granted. Scales are claimed in cultural and political projects" (2000: 161). Thus as groups compete and collaborate in their efforts to construct, or affect the construction of, a social order, global, local, and other forms of scale, overlapping and contradictory, are proposed and claimed. If the claims are successful, the benefits of such contingent arrangements of order are generally distributed unequally, though many might derive some temporary access to resources that would otherwise be out of reach.

For example, Woost, in recent research, has found that the international gem trade links a variety of scale-making projects that go deep into and well beyond the boundaries of Sri Lanka. When gem merchants in California search for cheap and reliable sources of gemstones, they create links between buyers in the United States and traders in Sri Lanka. This project links with an already existing gem trading network within Sri Lanka, a network that connects urban traders with rural villages in various parts of the island. In rural areas, the network of gem trading connects the various and sundry scale-making projects of rural people: those who seek new opportunities to provide for themselves; those who dream of being rich and independent (the result of other sorts of scale-making projects attempting to create desires for various commodities produced elsewhere), and those who just seek the pleasure and freedom of being in the jungle with friends. For all these reasons, they scour the countryside mining for gems. A few people will strike it rich, others will acquire some minor input to their household budget, while still others will profit nothing except a break from normal routines.

Thus while not all scale-making projects are successful, when they are, they connect with and reinforce other sorts of projects. Yet such projects are always contingent articulations, which are sometimes planned and at other times stumbled into inadvertently. Many rural miners, for instance, may ultimately have little idea how or why their mining activities are linked to gem merchants in Los Angeles. The merchants, on the other hand, are unlikely to have considered how their own activities would link with domestic consumption and the appropriation of forest lands in rural Sri Lanka. Their only conscious link may be with gem traders they visit or contact in Sri Lankan cities.

From this perspective, the war in Sri Lanka can be seen as a scale-making project that articulates complementary and contradictory—even opposing—projects of lesser scale. For example, the LTTE is trying to create a separate state while the government of Sri Lanka is trying to maintain a unitary state. Yet in the confrontation entailed by these two differently guided scale-making projects, a larger social formation is brought into being: an ethnic civil war. And in *that* formation many groups and projects of scale may be reinforced or strengthened, including the efforts of foreign, national, regional, and local entrepreneurs to expand their range of accumulation by supplying the war effort on either side; of politicians who seek votes and others, such as the Sri Lankan Muslim community, who are compelled to form linkages with the war effort, in one way or another, just to survive; and still others, such as refugees torn asunder from kin and community, whose articulations to extra-local scales of war and nation are not only involuntary but also terribly costly.

Not all Sri Lankans articulate with the notion of national identity in the same fashion. People situated differently—rural, urban, male, female, richer, poorer, Sinhala, Tamil, one caste or another, and so on—will become subjects of the nation (or not) differently, just as they also will vary in how they articulate with the open economy and the war economy. These varied articulations and resulting identities may or may not resonate perfectly with one another. Young men who join the Sri Lankan army or the LTTE because they have no other work connect to others who join because the masculine identity associated with soldiering appeals to them. Both of these articulations are very different from the patriotic stance, which might bring still others to support one side or the other. Thus different subjects may connect for a "moment" in such a way that does not undermine the reproduction of war, or they may connect in a way that helps to expand consensus about the pursuit of war and the legitimacy of violence of one identity against another. But most assuredly the manner of linkage cannot simply be read off the abstract structure of the "economy." People do not just exist in general, as objects outside their day-to-day existence. They act, interpret, understand, and negotiate life based on their own "situated knowledges" (Haraway 1986).

While these knowledges are, as Haraway contends, always partial and contradictory,[23] they provide significant elements that become part of new processes of identity formation, new formations of production, new formations of suffering, and the like. Furthermore, in the process of becoming new subjects, people never quite become the subjects that others may intend them to be. As Althusser said about the process of identity construction (1971), articulations of social ordering often occur behind the backs, and in spite of the intentions, of those involved. Thus, even as the government recruits women to work abroad or in newly constructed export-oriented garment factories, politicians may condemn these same women for abandoning their families or failing traditional standards of being "good girls" (see Lynch, this volume). The outcome of even such conscious attempts at constructing new linkages, bringing people into new positions needed by those in power, is never linear but always shaped by the other sorts of articulations already in motion.

The essays in this volume map this complex context of the ethnic conflict in Sri Lanka at various levels of scale. In Part I, "Articulations of National Economic Policy and Ethnic Conflict," Shastri and Richardson provide a vision of the conflict from above. They each look at the effects of changes in economic policy over time, how these changes have linked with the rise in violence, and what the consequences are for Sri Lankans generally. These macro-view mappings suggest a relationship between policy and conflict, implicitly pointing to patterns of activities and events that can be further explored in more local contexts.

In Part II, "Articulations of Class and Ethnic Conflict," the late Newton Gunasinghe and Siri Hettige, both sociologists, use survey research to map out the ways in which economic policies and the war have changed the structure of opportunities for Sri Lankans in all walks of life. As we have noted, Gunasinghe's essay, written shortly after the riots of 1983, suggests that the riots emerged out of the variety of ways in which Sri Lankans experienced the new "open economy" policies. While class was the basis of his analysis, he tried to show how class interests came to be articulated around ethnicity in the moment of the riots. Hettige's analysis is more current, based on data from a recently completed National Youth Survey. Drawing on this large data base, he is able to show the contingent character of the articulation of the conflict as an "ethnic" one. While not downplaying the polarizations of ethnicity at the center of hegemonic struggles, he points out that not all of the contradictions and difficulties experienced by the youth of Sri Lanka as they struggle to carve out a living can be easily subsumed under banners of ethnicity.

Finally, in Part III, "Material Lives Articulating Violence and War," sociologist Francesca Bremner and anthropologists Michele Gamburd and Caitrin Lynch describe how three local groups—an urban lower-class community in Colombo, rural lower-class villagers in the southeast, and *juki* girls, women who work in garment factories in the Free Trade Zone—have become articulated with the history of violence and war through the material predicaments of their lived experiences. Francesca Bremner's essay is based on 2001 fieldwork with participants in the 1983 riots that precipitated the civil war. Drawing on their narratives of those events, she is able to illustrate how many forms of identity were drawn into the event, only to emerge transformed and even disciplined at the other end. Michele Gamburd draws on several years of recent fieldwork to investigate the linkages between home contexts of violence, concepts of gender roles, and the reasons that poor rural Sinhalese men enlist in the armed forces. Caitrin Lynch looks at public ambivalence about the other growth area of women's work, employment in export zone garment factories. She explores the way moral panic about "good girls" exposed to western immorality (by sewing underwear for Victoria's Secret) resonates with concerns about the vulnerability of the Sinhalese Buddhist nation. This has provided fodder for Sinhala-chauvinist political grandstanding, which may in turn have contributed to men's desire to control women and to the ideological exacerbation of Sinhala-Tamil rhetoric. Her analysis also illustrates just how contingent attempts to articulate subjectivity really are. As politicians scurried to prove their own patriotic nationalism, the outcome was uncertain given all the different motivations and interests that were at play in the controversy.

Conclusion

The way we articulate these theoretical strands is also a contingent linkage, not necessarily the best, but a place from which to think about how economic practices and policies are connected to ethnic conflict in Sri Lanka and how we should choose to analyze those connections. All analysis involves some kind of struggle "over what will count as rational accounts of the world," and these in turn "are struggles over *how* to see" (Haraway 1986: 194, her emphasis). Our particular theoretical connections shape and limit what comes into our visual field, telling us what to see, as well as how, from where, with whom, what is clear, what is not, what is important, and what can be ignored (Haraway 1986: 194). Theory operates as a prosthetic enabling certain ways of seeing that are all partial in the sense of being incomplete and because they arise from a specific position. Consequently, what each technology of vision produces is a situated knowledge that must always be questioned in regard to the position from which it comes and the position to which it leads, since "politics and ethics ground struggles for the contests over what may count as rational knowledge" (Haraway 1986: 193). Thus our goal has been to articulate a technology of vision that takes the material into account but resists economic reductionism. For example, if Collier is right that greed plays a role in the reproduction of the conflict, we contend it is our responsibility to treat that assessment not as a conclusion but rather as an opening to further questions. How and for whom does greed emerge within a specific and contingent context of articulation? If we argue that the economy structurally adjusts identity, we need then to ask how, what identities, why those and not others? Lastly we need to question the very notion that the economy exists as a subject distributing its effects on generic or even multidimensional subjects; rather, we need to see the economy as itself multiple and emergent in the very context of articulation of material practices in motion and in conjuncture.

Individually and collectively, the articles in this volume provide new understandings of how Sri Lanka's tragic civil war has become embedded in the social formation of wartime Sri Lanka. At all levels of scale, we insist on the importance of that embeddedness, of seeing how different aspects of people's lives inter-connect for them, with others, with the society and world at large.

Notes

Woost acknowledges support received from the National Science Foundation, the American Institute for Sri Lanka Studies, and the Trustees of Hartwick College for research in Sri Lanka in 1999, 2001, and 2003. Winslow acknowledges support received from the University of New Hampshire Vice President for Research and Public Service Discretionary Fund for research in Sri Lanka in 1999 and the University of New Hampshire Faculty Development Committee for travel support in 2001. We also thank Francesca Bremner, Chandra R. de Silva, Michele R. Gamburd, Arjun Guneratne, Amita Shastri, and Rebecca Tolen for very useful comments on earlier drafts of this introduction.

1. These rates continued until March 2002, at which time Lloyd's withdrew the surcharges and also returned the $50 million deposit that the Sri Lankan gov-ernment had paid to keep the rate increases from being even higher.
2. For fuller accounts of the events of 1983, see Spencer, ed., 1990 and Tambiah 1986.
3. In 1998, Sri Lanka, with a population of 19 million and an annual GNP per capita of $810, ranked 144th out of the 210 economies reported on by the World Bank (World Bank 2000a: 231, Table 1).
4. Here we will use the term *social formation* when we want to emphasize that "society" is not a fixed entity that persists unchanging through time but is only a tendency marked by a history of diverse practices that at any given moment may or may not resonate with each other and may or may not be linked.
5. Dr. Newton Gunasinghe died in 1988 at age 42. We reproduce his essay here because we consider it a work of seminal importance for the kind of analysis we are trying to put forward with this volume. It was the taking-off point for many of our contributors, and as far as we know, it has not been published out-side of South Asia.
6. The British were the third European power to rule in Sri Lanka. In 1505, Portuguese ships visited the Sinhalese kingdom at Kotte (near what is now Colombo), one of three Sinhalese kingdoms that then existed in the island. The Portuguese returned in 1517 to build a fort, which they initially were unable to hold; but by enmeshing themselves in Kotte politics, the Portuguese managed to gain a foothold in the cinnamon trade and eventually, by the end of the sixteenth century, to take over the Kotte kingdom, the neighboring Sinhalese kingdom at Sitavaka, the northern Tamil kingdom of Jaffna, and most of the western coast. The Portuguese also tried, but for the most part failed, to defeat the interior Sinhalese kingdom at Kandy (K. M. de Silva 1977: 48–60).
   Between 1656 and 1658, the Portuguese were driven out of Sri Lanka by the Dutch, who then took over the coastal areas and ports, holding them until they themselves were defeated by the British in 1796. Throughout the Dutch period, the Kandyan kingdom continued to hold the interior. Only after the British had

ousted the Dutch did the Kandyan kingdom finally fall. The coastal areas taken from the Dutch were initially made part of the East India Company's Madras government, then subject to joint East India Company and Crown rule; only in 1802 did it become a separate Crown Colony. After the British defeated the Kandyans in 1815, the island was unified politically and remained a British Crown Colony until it attained independence in 1948 (K. M. de Silva 1977: 60–61).

7. The British also recognized Europeans, mixed race Burghers and Eurasians, Malays (thought originally to be from Java), and Veddas (allegedly descendents of the island's original inhabitants) as distinct races; but together, these tiny minorities made up just over 1 percent (Denham 1912: 195).

8. See, e.g., the discussions of "races" in the British censuses (e.g., Denham 1912: 194–244; Ranasinha 1950: 150–171).

9. Veddas are said to be descendents of indigenous, nonfarming peoples. "Burgher" is the Sri Lankan term for people of mixed Dutch or Portuguese and Tamil or Sinhalese ancestry. Malays are a separate group of Muslims, said to be originally from Java. These figures come from Soma de Silva (1997: 51), who based them on 1996 estimates by the Sri Lanka Department of Census and Statistics, which are extrapolated from the 1981 census (see also Sri Lanka 2002b). The 2001 census omitted most of the Tamil areas, due to the unsettled conditions (Sri Lanka 2000a). Given the significant outmigration of Tamils since 1983, it is very likely that their proportion of the overall population has declined and that extrapolations from the 1981 census are inaccurate. For this reason, some scholars have suggested using the more up-to-date electoral rolls instead. But because of extensive election-related violence, those rolls may have their own problems. Furthermore, as we write this in 2003, a cease-fire is in effect and some Tamil refugees are returning to Sri Lanka. Given the overall fluidity of the situation, we have chosen to use the 1996 extrapolations, even while recognizing their limitations.

10. It remains a difficult concept to define in any general sort of manner because of the highly varied ways it is defined and experienced in practice. First, language may be the definitive marker, then religion, then dress and religion, and so on. As markers change, so do the sources from which ethnicity as lived gets its emotive power and resonance. Hence to still go in search of a general definition of ethnicity, as if it were truly a thing in itself, with its own universal source of passion and emotion seems ill advised. And yet the attempt to nail down such a universal concept remains a preoccupation with many contemporary theorists of ethnic conflict (see, for example, Horowitz 1985, 2001). Why this is the case deserves much more attention than we can possibly afford it here. Suffice it to say that the position taken here is that the sources of ethnic passion and power are highly varied. Many forms of loyalty and difference (gender, class, patronage, etc.) can be drawn upon in the process of perpetrating what is seen as ethnic violence or conflict. Identities of ethnicity, gender, class, place, and so on, do not exist separate from one another. From this perspective, ethnicity can be seen to operate as an ideological principle articulating many strands of identity, passion, and interest in the production of conflict and/or cooperation. As such, ethnicity is *not* a thing in itself and should not be treated as though it were a singular subject of history; rather, it is only one among many possible ideologi-

cal principles around which many forms of emotion and identity can be made to coalesce as collective agency. Within that agency, other principles of identity, difference, and emotion are made to resonate and coexist, for a moment. Seen from this angle, the passions and experience of ethnicity are also contingent, just as the elements said to represent it are contingent amalgamations of symbols, memories, and histories. Its power and passion emerge both in and through conflict and/or cooperation. It is not a subject that comes preformed to the jagged space of conflict.

11. According to most accounts, although the LTTE has eliminated competing Tamil militant groups, it does not have the unambiguous support of all Tamils. Some Tamils, although sympathetic to the idea of at least much increased Tamil autonomy, deplore the violent methods used by both parties to the conflict (as do many Sinhalese). The LTTE has an international presence, with offices in Paris, London, and Toronto, and extensive support from Tamils living outside Sri Lanka. The LTTE is on the United States' list of banned terrorist organizations, and it is also banned in Sri Lanka.

12. Sri Lanka's Tamil population is usually divided between the "Sri Lankan Tamils" who have lived in the island for millennia and "Indian" or "Estate" Tamils who descend from plantation workers who migrated from India in the nineteenth and twentieth centuries to work on tea plantations. The two groups are distinguishable in dialect and social practices as well as history. See also note 9.

13. India's presence provoked a campaign of violence against the government and its associates by a Sinhalese nationalist youth group called the Janatha Vimukth Peramuna. The JVP had earlier staged an attempted coup in 1971. The 1987–89 JVP uprising was quelled by ruthless and violent suppression by the government and unofficial death squads.

14. Not everyone agrees with all aspects of this basic scenario, of course. Some have argued convincingly that ethnic distinctions and antagonisms between Sinhalese and Tamils did have precolonial political significance, that they were not simply, as has been suggested, colonial creations or the results of colonial policies (e.g., Holt 1996; Roberts 2001). Still, few scholars today would contend that the present conflict is simply a continuation of past ethnic distinctions and animosities, which clearly have waxed, waned, and been hybridized with other concerns in Sri Lanka over the centuries (Rogers 1994).

15. With the extra supplement for being on the front, ordinary soldiers stationed in Jaffna in 2001 earned about $140/month (Dugger 2001), about twice what a factory job would pay.

16. Unemployment stood at about 24 percent in 1973, the highest level recorded since the 1946 census, which was the first to collect unemployment data. Unemployment decreased more or less steadily between 1973 and 1981, to just under 12 percent. After 1983, the conflict initially was associated with a *rise* in unemployment, which hovered around 16 percent until 1990, but it has fallen steadily since then (Central Bank of Sri Lanka 1998: 37, 274; data based on Quarterly Labor Force Surveys from the Department of Census and Statistics). Employment has expanded for many reasons, including increased opportunities generated by the war, but also other factors such as opportunities for work abroad, particularly for women.

17. For the mid-1990s, O'Sullivan found that the government was still both the

"major employer" and the "major source of income" in the Jaffna district. "The government paid monthly tax-free wages of approximately 5,200 teachers and close to 1,000 people working at Jaffna Teaching Hospital as well as paying pensions to over 18,000 Jaffna pensioners" (1997: 106–107). In the eastern districts, "the government continued to pay the salaries of almost 14,000 teachers and medical workers and the pensions of over 10,000 pensioners" (1997: 113).

18. By late 2001, the number of checkpoints in Colombo had been reduced significantly; presumably the memories will linger longer, particularly for Tamil Sri Lankans.

19. See the World Bank website devoted to social capital for an example of just how monolithic this notion has become in the development environment.

20. One is reminded of B. Traven's 1971 novel, *Government,* with his pithy description of how the state operated through networks of patronage (social capital) and violence to maintain a façade of democracy. Also, see Gramsci on the role of civil society in maintaining hegemony (1971: 206–278).

21. Of course, if rebellions threatened against rent-taking capitalist regimes, they would be more likely to be able to count on U.S.-backed military support (Chile comes to mind) than would a group of poor "rebels" trying to finance a fight for a more egalitarian economy by taking over, say, a copper mine; their rebellion would not (did not) become a civil war, and Collier's theory is supported.

22. The workshop participants included Francesca B. Bremner, John Conant, Swarna Kanthi Dharmawardena, Geraldine Gamburd, Michele R. Gamburd, Arjun Guneratne, Darlene Hantzis, Siri Hettige, Alan Keenan, Caitrin Lynch, Patrick Peebles, Sonali Perera, John Richardson, Nisala Rodrigo, John D. Rogers, Amita Shastri, Kevin Trainor, Robin D. Willits, Deborah Winslow, and Mike Woost.

23. Haraway's notion of situated knowledges is in the same vein as Gramsci's idea that people are enmeshed in contradictory sedimentations of "common sense" (Gramsci 1971: 323 ff.).

Part One: *Articulations of National Economic Policy and Ethnic Conflict*

Introduction

Deborah Winslow

When Sri Lanka (then known as Ceylon) obtained independence from Great Britain in 1948, many of the factors that would prove critical for the new country's economic and political health already were visible. Industrialization was so limited that it provided jobs for less than 8 percent of the workforce (Snodgrass 1966: 101). Therefore, the government depended on a few agricultural exports for revenue and foreign exchange,[1] even as it needed to continue an expensive social welfare system, symbolized by essentially untouchable food subsidies. Politically, the new country's unity was challenged from the start by a simmering division between a numerically dominant ethnic majority, the Sinhalese Buddhists who controlled the government, and a number of smaller minorities, the largest of them being Tamil by language and ethnicity, who had lost their bid for protective legislation in the new constitution.[2] Both the structure of the economy and ethnic relations are important for understanding economic policy. Never, in independent Sri Lanka, has economic policy been isolable from issues of ethnicity, because how the government has chosen to define and to resolve economic difficulties has consistently been informed by ethnic politics, just as ethnic politics has been informed by economic choices. Thus, while this section sets out some of the context for the sections that follow, it is not just "background" but part and parcel of the substance that constitutes the war.

This section begins with a brief sketch of the early years, from independence up to the major changes introduced in 1977. Then, we present two essays by political scientists, John Richardson and Amita Shastri, who look at the interaction between national economic policy and politics from 1977 through 2000.

The story of these early years is in part the story of how two Sinhalese political parties—the United National Party (UNP) and the Sri Lanka Freedom Party (SLFP)—alternated in office for 30 years, taking diametrically opposed approaches to national economic policy, but sharing a tendency to compete for the votes of the Sinhalese electorate by appealing to Sinhalese chauvinist sentiment. Sri Lanka's first prime minister was D. S. Senanayake, leader of the more conservative UNP. From independence in 1948 until the elections of 1956, the UNP government pursued economic policies similar to those that had prevailed during the final decades of British colonial rule. They promoted private enterprise and, outside of agriculture, the free play of market forces; they avoided creating state industries and sold off a few that already existed; and they concentrated government investment in infrastructure and peasant agriculture (Athukorala and Jayasuriya 1994: 9–10).

The latter was a personal passion of Senanayake, who had been minister of lands and agriculture from 1931 until 1947, the period covered by the interim Donoughmore Constitution, which transferred significant power from the colonial authorities to Sri Lankan leaders before independence. As minister, Senanayake's main goals had been to make the country self-sufficient in food and to relieve population and unemployment pressures in the densely crowded southeast. But the centerpiece of his economic development plan was not the economy of the south itself but the restoration of the ancient tanks (artificial water reservoirs) in the northern dry zone. In 1948, this region was sparsely populated, malarial, and poor. But British archaeologists had revealed that the region had been an important agricultural and political center of Sinhalese civilization until about AD 1200, when it was abandoned. Senanayake presented the expansion of peasant agriculture in this area (and, later, in the eastern dry zone) not only as an impetus to economic growth but also as an assertion of, and tool to rebuild, Sinhala pride and identity, a political counter to the commercial agriculture brought in by foreign colonial powers (Brohier 1955/56).

This proved to be a policy with major ethnic implications. By 1954, well over half of the "pioneer colonists" who had been relocated into the newly irrigated areas were Sinhalese (Farmer 1976 [1957], Table 20, opp. 172), while the populations of the northern and eastern areas into which they were being moved were either mixed Sinhalese and Tamil or predominantly Tamil.

Thus the settlement schemes effectively readjusted dry zone population balances in favor of the Sinhalese. Tamil politicians objected from the beginning that these schemes "confiscated their 'traditional homelands' " (Peebles 1990: 37), which they had hoped for decades would one day become the centers of "home rule" for Tamil provinces (Farmer 1976 [1957]: 302). What seemed a straightforward economic development plan, one that was endorsed by a visiting World Bank team of expert advisers with absolutely no mention of ethnic controversies (World Bank 1953: 384–398), actually put the full weight of national economic policy behind one community's vision of the island's past and future identity, at the expense of competing visions held by members of other groups.

The interest of Sri Lanka's first government in expanding peasant agriculture was also informed by the fact that it had inherited an extensive centrally funded welfare system, which had been negotiated by the country's leftist and worker parties in the 1930s and 1940s, when the island's economy was hit hard by the world depression. Sri Lanka's strong support for social welfare—including universal entitlements to health services, primary through university education, and subsidized food rations—is credited with giving Sri Lanka the lasting legacy of having by far the highest quality of life in South Asia (as measured by literacy rates, infant mortality rates, maternal mortality rates, and life expectancy). But without growth in industrial exports, the early governments had to rely on paying for the welfare system with the always inadequate income produced by tariffs collected on the export of the colonial commercial crops of tea, rubber, and coconut, which were also the country's major foreign exchange earners.

The Korean War (1950–53) raised world prices for rubber, which allowed the government to maintain the welfare system for a few years, but by 1952, the war boom had subsided and the cost of imports far exceeded the value of exports. Only by going into debt could the government continue, for example, to provide rice to its citizens at a price that was less than a third of what the government had to pay to acquire the rice on the world market. Soon the government was spending more on flour and rice subsidies than it was spending on development projects. When they tried to cut back on subsidies in 1953, there was an islandwide strike (*hartal*), the prime minister (now D. S. Senanayake's son, Dudley) had to resign, and the subsidies were reinstated (Athukorala and Jayasuriya 1994: 8).

This articulation of economy, cultural expectations, and ethnic politics would shape the way political leaders chose to allocate resources for at least another generation. Increasing agricultural productivity was, on the face of it, a practical matter. It would reduce the need for imported foodstuffs, saving not only money but also precious foreign exchange. But trying to alleviate poverty and achieve food self-sufficiency in this particular way—expanding irrigated agriculture and Sinhalese peasant colonization in the dry zone—also reinforced the image of the government as supporting the Sinhalese at the expense of the Tamils. However, the Sinhalese electorate was so dominant that Tamil votes were not needed to win national elections; therefore, the pressures that the UNP faced in the infamous elections of 1956 came not from Tamils but from the other major Sinhalese party, the SLFP.

A coalition called the People's United Front (MEP), which included the SLFP and smaller parties to its left, campaigned against the UNP on the platform that the elite and westernized leaders of the UNP—foreign educated, English speaking, allied with business—could not be trusted to provide adequately for the economic or cultural needs of the ordinary Sinhalese people. Reminding the public of the UNP's attempt to curtail subsidies, the MEP promised to expand the welfare system, protect workers, and make Sinhalese the only language of government, excluding both Tamil and English as "foreign" (Wilson 1977: 286). The MEP won decisively under the leadership of S. W. R. D. Bandaranaike, and one of their first acts was to pass the Official Language Act. An immediate nonviolent Tamil protest actually brought about a compromise agreement between Bandaranaike and the Tamil leader, S. J. V. Chelvanayakam, which would have given the Tamil language official status, ended Sinhalese resettlement in Tamil areas, and allowed Tamils some autonomy in administering those areas. But a counterprotest by Buddhist monks scuttled the agreement. The 1956 elections, particularly the branding of Tamils as somehow not really Sri Lankan, is now seen as a turning point where anti-Tamil rhetoric became firmly entrenched in Sinhalese political positioning and major Tamil parties abandoned hope for reconciliation.

The election of 1956 also ushered in far-reaching economic changes that broke with the direction established by the UNP, increased the size of the public sector, and thereby increased direct government intervention in economic practice. The MEP faced the same foreign exchange problems that the UNP had faced, but instead of trying to increase exports, they stepped up controls on imports (Abeyratne 1997: 351) and encouraged the development of domestic, import-substitution industries (Lakshman 1997a: 7). They also nationalized foreign oil companies, which resulted in a drop in foreign aid (especially from the United States), and took over locally owned enterprises, including the bus system, the ports, and the domestic banks (Athukorala and Jayasuriya 1994: 11–12). They did not curtail consumer subsidies, apparently unwilling to deal with the inevitable political fallout, particularly from the leftist and labor-oriented parties within the ruling coalition (Athukorala and Jayasuriya 1994: 12).

But in 1959, after only three years in office, Bandaranaike was assassinated by a Buddhist monk, apparently outraged by Bandaranaike's early attempt to compromise with the Tamils (Wilson 1977: 303). Elections were held in 1960; the UNP won, but they were unable to win a majority and new elections were called immediately. By July 1960, the SLFP had returned to power, this time led by Bandaranaike's widow, Sirimavo (Ross and Savada 1990: 46–47). Mrs. Bandaranaike proved even more pro-Sinhalese than her husband and actually carried out the official language policy implementation that her husband had avoided. Under Mrs. Bandaranaike, courts, even in Tamil areas, were instructed to issue decisions only in Sinhala; buses were lettered in Sinhala; even post office signs were only in Sinhala. By 1961, official policy was that Sinhala was the only language of government administration. There was substantial Tamil resistance, and Mrs. Bandaranaike responded by using state of emergency powers to curtail Tamil political rights (Ross and Savada 1990: 48).

Mrs. Bandaranaike faced opposition from all sides: the leftists, who wanted more concessions to workers and fewer controls on job-producing export commodities; the Tamils, who were incensed by the language policy, the threats to their political freedom, and the growing disparities in opportunities for jobs that arose when so many enterprises were controlled directly by Sinhalese bureaucrats and politicians (see also Gunasinghe, this volume); and the UNP, who objected to the increasing controls on business. The UNP also used Mrs. Bandaranaike's alliances with the communist and socialist parties, as well as her husband's agreement with the Tamil leadership, as fear-mongering tools to defeat her in the next election (Wilson 1977: 303–304).

So the UNP was back again in 1965, with strong support from the Buddhist clergy in a further escalation of ethnic politics. True to past form, the UNP acted to expand the private sector, sell off state enterprises, and promote capital-intensive "green revolution" agriculture (Lakshman 1997: 7). However, they met with serious bad luck. World prices for tea, rubber, and coconuts fell just as world rice prices rose; they were forced again to curtail the rice subsidies and, just as they had the last time they tried it, they went down at the next elections. Again, basic needs, the legacy of a colonial economy, and a politically defined sense of entitlement came together to limit the government's room for maneuver. This particular UNP period is also remembered for having rather desperately tried to promote Sinhalese Buddhist culture by changing the weekend. Instead of Sunday as a day of rest, this allegedly Christian tradition was replaced by the Buddhist one of recognizing the phases of the moon (Ross and Savada 1990: 48–49); it proved very awkward, especially for international business, and was soon rescinded.

After a campaign that was again characterized by Sinhala chauvinist rhetoric, Mrs. Bandaranaike returned to office in 1970, with a new coalition called the United Front. Winning in a landslide, she introduced a new constitution that enshrined Buddhism as the nation's foremost religion and denied any autonomy for predominantly Tamil areas. She also instituted policies that made it harder for Tamil students to gain university admission by lowering the admission standards for applicants who studied in Sinhala (C. R. de Silva 1984a). In her economic program, Mrs. Bandaranaike returned to the strict import-substitution and social welfare support policies of her earlier regime. But the 1973 oil crisis made this even more difficult to sustain than it had been in the past. Sri Lanka became more dependent on imports, especially petroleum and petroleum-related products, including the agricultural inputs needed for green revolution agriculture, and oil prices were now rising much faster than the country's relatively few exports. Economic controls became ever stronger, tariffs rose astronomically on imports, many goods—from batteries to automobiles to paper to bread—became scarce, travel abroad was almost impossible, and rich and poor alike stood in line to buy such basic commodities as cloth, sugar, and flour.

By the time the 1977 elections finally arrived, the economic austerities were so pervasive that UNP politicians were able, for the first time, to position themselves as the voices of the poor in addition to their usual claims to speak for economic pragmatism. They promised a total economic turnaround: open markets, free trade and travel, everything that the SLFP government had forbidden, and led by the charismatic J. R. Jayawardene, they won 83 percent of the vote, the most lopsided victory in Sri Lanka's history (Moore 1985: 242). The victory came with only limited support from Sri Lankan Tamils, most of whom voted instead for the Tamil United Liberation Front (TULF), which campaigned on the platform of a separate Tamil state, a measure of how large the rift between Sinhalese and Tamil people had now become (Ross and Savada 1990: 52).[3]

It is at this point of elevated ethnic tensions and the most significant economic changes in Sri Lanka's postcolonial history that our essays begin. The first essay, by John Richardson, examines the human consequences of the period from 1977 to 1982, the first years of Jayawardene's open economy reforms. Richardson introduces a quantitative assessment of incidents of violence over time to suggest that the open economy very quickly transformed what had been intermittent outbreaks of unrest between Sinhalese and Tamils to a new high of sustained and escalating conflict. He then presents extensive macroeconomic data to show that the Jayawardene reforms were not the economic success story that others have claimed. Instead, Richardson argues, there was an initial spurt of growth, financed primarily by increased foreign aid and borrowings from abroad, followed by rampant inflation, economic stagnation, growing debt, and worsening trade deficits. By 1982, many were worse off than they had been when Jayawardene came to power in 1977. Even more significant for understanding the civil war that broke out in 1983, however, was that the economic changes had increased the gap between rich and poor and heightened class and ethnic tensions.

In the next essay, Amita Shastri tells the different story of the 1990s. The boom times of the first years of the Jayawardene regime had been followed through the 1980s by lagging economic growth and climbing unemployment. In 1989, the voters brought in the more austere regime of Ranasinghe Premadasa, who, although also a member of the UNP, reined in spending, in part to increase support to the military, which now had to deal with the threat of revolts from a predominantly Sinhala JVP, as well as the LTTE. Premadasa also invested heavily in a new poverty alleviation program (called Janasaviya) and a massive housing construction scheme for both urban and rural areas (Athukorala and Jayasuriya 1994: 22). Premadasa promoted export zone industrialization; expanded the UNP policy of encouraging working-class Sri Lankans, especially women, to seek domestic employment in the Middle East; and undertook more of the privatization and stabilization measures recommended by the World Bank and the IMF. He also established a reputation for "crony capitalism" and widespread human rights violations (Lakshman 1997: 11), particularly in his suppression of the JVP. Premadasa's rule ended with his assassination on May 1, 1993. When elections were held the next year, the UNP was ousted, in large part because the ethnic conflict had become a full-fledged and very expensive civil war.

President Chandrika Kumaratunga came to power in August 1994, promising, as Shastri tells us, to negotiate peace with the LTTE, reduce defense spending, and use the resources saved to promote economic development. Kumaratunga's peace bid was unsuccessful. Instead, the war and its costs escalated. Nevertheless, the economy maintained positive rates of economic growth. This puzzle—how the country could maintain the war and still "prosper"—is Shastri's focus. She suggests that the answer lies in the fact that despite her leftist campaign rhetoric, Kumaratunga was caught by the fact that the country was now dependent on foreign capital, and to get that capital she could not deviate from the UNP's pro-market policies. Unemployment and inflation were kept in check by the same three that had dominated the Premadasa years: domestic work abroad, manufacturing jobs, and work in the armed services.

Each of these essays gives us a view from above. Together they help us see that the "post-1977 economy" is not monolithic, static, or a thing in itself somehow apart from Sri Lanka's historically produced ethnic relations. Like previous elections, the elections of 1977 produced a change but not a break with the past, which is, in any case, never possible. Richardson and Shastri show us that in many ways the economic practices, expectations, and understandings of the early years still had power, even as they were realized in and articulated with the changing national and international contexts of the 1980s and 1990s in Sri Lanka.

Notes

1. In 1948, 96 percent of all exports were crops, with tea providing 64.61 percent, rubber 12.39 percent, and coconut products 18.93 percent. Two-thirds of government revenue came from customs and excise taxes on exports (Peebles 1982: 215, 241).
2. In 1946, the Sinhalese made up 70 percent of the population; Sri Lanka Tamils (Tamils native to the island for centuries) made up 11 percent; and Estate or Indian Tamils, who had come in the late nineteenth and early twentieth centuries to work on estates, particularly tea estates, made up another 11 percent (Balakrishnan and Gunasekera 1977: 277). In 1948, Estate Tamils did not have citizenship or the right to vote.
3. In contrast to Sri Lankan Tamils, Estate Tamils voted primarily for the Ceylon Workers Congress, which entered into an alliance with the UNP just before the elections (Moore 1985: 233–34).

2　Violent Conflict and the First Half Decade of Open Economy Policies in Sri Lanka: A Revisionist View

John M. Richardson Jr.

Preliminaries

Setting the Stage

This chapter examines the human consequences of J. R. Jayawardene's open economy reforms during his first half decade in office. Three points of departure set the stage. First is a topology of conflict events data[1] that shows the period in question as one of intensifying violent political conflict. Second is an amalgam of political-economic theories, linking violent political conflict with economic processes, which suggests that worsening economic conditions, particularly those with significant adverse human impact, create a climate in which violent conflict is likely to intensify. Third is a body of conventional wisdom that characterizes 1977–82 as an economic success story and attributes the causes of intensifying violent conflict more to the policies of Prime Minister Bandaranaike's United Front government than to those of President Jayawardene.

The 1977–82 period surfaces as a focus of inquiry because of a disconnect between these three points. If United Front policies were principal causal agents, one might have expected violent conflict to reach a protracted stage earlier than it did. If 1977–82 was an economic success story, one might have anticipated a decline in conflict intensity, rather than escalation. This chapter does not seriously address the relative weight that should be given to United Front policies, but it does conclude that open economy reforms did not produce sustainable economic growth, that adverse human impacts of those policies were significant, and that those adverse human impacts contributed significantly to the escalation of violent political conflict in Sri Lanka.

Measuring the Intensity of Violent Political Conflict

Figure 2.1 maps the level of violent conflict intensity in Sri Lanka, along with major changes in governments, between 1948 and 1988. Versions have appeared in several previous publications.[2] Graphs like this are motivated by a methodological-

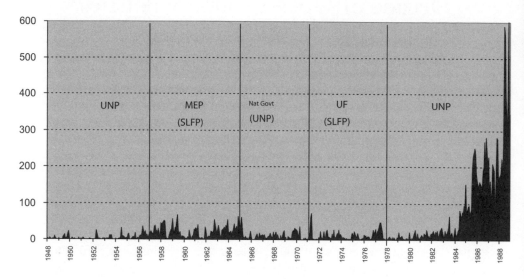

Figure 2.1. Violent conflict intensity.

epistemological stance which postulates that operationally defining a phenomenon as observable *problematic behavior,* unfolding over a relatively long period of time, is a useful starting point for analysis (Meadows and Robinson 1985: 17–90).[3] The analyst then seeks to identify other phenomena that cause variations in the problematic behavior. In the case of Sri Lanka's violent conflicts ("ethnic" and "nonethnic"),[4] the graph of problematic behavior was generated by collecting verbal descriptions of more than 5,000 conflict events, coding and aggregating them into monthly conflict intensity indices.[5]

Elsewhere, I have likened the intensification of violent conflict in Sri Lanka to the spread of an infection in a biological organism.[6] Were this a chart of infection, the period prior to 1984 might be labeled "relatively good health." The organism seemed resilient. Relatively severe outbreaks did occur, between 1956 and 1965 and again in 1971, 1977, and 1983, but they subsided. Either the disease was not virulent, there was an effective immune response, or appropriate treatment was provided.

Beginning in 1984, there was a qualitative change. High levels of infection appeared to be normal. Reduced levels were transient remissions. By 1986, an ominous metastasizing pattern is apparent. Were we to extend the plot for a decade or so, the added years would resemble the period after 1984, not before.

Edward Azar coined the term *protracted social conflict* to describe conflict patterns similar to those that have been present in Sri Lanka since 1984 (1990: 64–72).[7] Protracted social conflict means endemic conflict, largely dictated by militant group agendas. It has no clear termination point and produces negative sum outcomes in which virtually all participants lose. The economic spillover effects are widespread. A conflict mentality pervades the society's political culture and political economy, frustrating attempts to make peace. Conflict resolution without external intervention is rare. Protracted conflict, in Azar's words,

> reinforces and strengthens pessimism throughout the society and immobilizes the search for peaceful solutions. . . . Societies undergoing protracted social conflict find it difficult to initiate the search for answers to the problems and grievances. As the protracted conflict becomes part of the culture of the ravaged nation, it builds a sense of paralysis which afflicts the collective consciousness of the population. An environment of hopelessness permeates all strata of society and a siege mentality develops which inhibits constructive negotiation for any resolution of the conflict. (1990: 16)

Were we diagnosticians seeking causes for the spreading infection, we would scrutinize policies, processes, and outcomes in the political economy, focusing on the years immediately prior to 1984 for pathogens and preliminary symptoms. Our training would have provided theories and clinical experience to guide these inquiries.

Seeking Causes: Political Economic Theories of Conflict

Hypotheses about possible factors that might cause conflict escalation are found in a voluminous body of literature to which no brief essay can do justice.

With the caveats that any such enterprise requires, I have grouped this literature into five schools of thought labeled *relative deprivation, political-organizational mobilization, state competence, ethnicity-identity,* and *leadership shortcomings.* One would correctly infer from these labels that each school focuses on a somewhat different set of causal agents. Each describes the dynamics of an escalating conflict somewhat differently. In each, economic processes play a somewhat different role.

The *relative deprivation school* views conflict as a mass phenomenon—anomic collective action—which is evoked by a gap between the way individuals believe their lives should be and the way they are. Contributions to this school, particularly the influential writings of Ted Robert Gurr and his students, have given particular weight to measures of economic well-being in seeking to identify statistically significant relationships between deprivation and conflict (1970).[8] Economic factors recede in importance, although they are not totally ignored by contributors to the *political-organizational mobilization school.* Economic processes contribute to mobilization by creating a climate of discontent, especially through hardening class divisions, that facilitates the formation of militant social movements and groups (Tilley 1978).[9]

State competence is a term that I apply to a body of writing that begins with James C. Davies's seminal writings on the relationship between repression and violence (1962, 1969) but has been developed much more fully in state-centric comparative studies of social revolutions by Theda Skocpol and her students.[10] When bureaucratic institutions are corrupt, proponents argue, and when the security forces are unable to maintain public order, then credible revolutionary alternatives to the state may emerge and prevail. Thus proponents of this school view conflict itself quite similarly to organizational mobilization theorists—it is an organized phenomenon—but emphasize less proximate causes. The contribution of economic processes is even more indirect. A bad economy can create stresses and resource shortfalls that magnify institutional incompetence. Poor institutional performance can intensify social discontents and empower opposition movements.[11]

Recent work within the constructivist tradition, which I have labeled the *ethnicity-identity* school, gives much greater attention to the self-described motivations of conflict participants and their characterizations of the conflict process itself.[12] Proponents argue that studies of violent conflict need to "fruitfully combine reflections on the structural preconditions of violence with analysis of the ideological and symbolic repertoires that make violence possible" (Mehta 1998: 380).[13] Political-economic institutions are often sources of these socially constructed repertoires, which politicians strive to manipulate in self-interested ways.[14] Thus, the ethnicity-identity school's view of conflict is not incompatible with views that characterize conflicts as organized phenomena, but proponents see conflicts through a different lens. They maintain that it is more important to understand how conflict is rationalized than to understand how it is organized.

Scholars who emphasize *leadership shortcomings* do not ignore political-economic, organizational, and motivational causes of violence, but assert that shortcomings of top leaders cannot be ignored, especially bad decisions and divisive political rhetoric.[15] Political leaders seek to gain and keep power. Supporters, citizens, and interest groups expect them to deliver some mix of physical security, economic benefits, the promise of a better life, and other psychic satisfactions. Meeting these expectations is difficult. The problems that leaders face are complex, daunting, poorly understood, and caused by factors over which they may have little control. As time passes, institutional and popular support will almost inevitably decline. Facing loss of power, the temptation to engage in demagogic appeals, seek scapegoats for policy failures, and use state power to repress dissenting voices is almost irresistible.[16] These tactics often increase the potential for violent political conflict and intensify whatever level of conflict is already present.

Which factors proposed by these schools are *most important?* Scholarly debates between proponents of contending schools often resemble the parable of four blind men trying to describe an elephant. In fact, all of the factors described—economic processes, mobilization of groups, performance of state institutions, motivations, and leaders' decisions—can contribute to conflict escalation. They are interrelated in a complex system where the properties of interrelationship are as important as the properties of individual elements in determining the problematic behavior that the system generates.[17] Thus it is simplistic to assert that changes in economic processes can escalate violent conflict, but it is reasonable to assert that deteriorating economic circumstances will produce rising levels of deprivation. Rising deprivation levels will propagate through the system, impacting other elements that are more proximate causes of escalating conflict. This suggests that it would be useful to examine the political-economic circumstances of President Jayawardene's first term.

Two Pieces of Conventional Wisdom: The "Economic Miracle" and "Reaping the Whirlwind"

This is by no means the first article to critically review J. R. Jayawardene's open economy reforms,[18] but I think it is fair to say that the weight of conventional wisdom, at least regarding his first term, presents the following scenario.

> The United Front years were a period characterized by overtly pro-Sinhalese language and university admissions policies, economic stagnation, postponement of elections, and overt attempts to stifle dissent. Social reforms implemented after the JVP rebellion produced some benefits, especially for Sinhalese, but bleak economic circumstances, high unemployment, and repressive measures produced pervasive discontent. The UNP's overwhelming electoral victory and outpouring of popular support for J. R. Jayawardene reflected this.
>
> Jayawardene provided Sri Lanka with a more competent, economically reformist government that was at least rhetorically committed to communal reconciliation. It voluntarily implemented many structural adjustment reforms that later became integral to the conditionalities mandated by IMF and World Bank assistance packages in the 1980s. A period of rapid economic growth and improvements in well-being followed these reforms, contributing to President Jayawardene's overwhelming 1982 election victory, in a process judged relatively fair and free by most. The flawed referendum that followed did involve some overt repression by the government, but it was designed to serve a good purpose: preventing the oscillations in economic policy that

had retarded Sri Lanka's economic growth in the past. Had the economic momentum of the early 1980s not be derailed by "ethnic conflict," Sri Lanka would have become one of the next "Asian Tigers."[19]

An explanation of how conflict escalated, despite successful economic reforms and serious attempts at communal reconciliation, is suggested by the title of Kingsley M. de Silva's 1998 volume, *Reaping the Whirlwind,* his most recent among numerous books on post-independence Sri Lanka.[20] No brief summary can approximate de Silva's richly detailed historical scholarship, but the essence of his position appears to be this. Despite long-standing communal tensions and occasional violent outbreaks, "there was no full-blooded separatist movement among the Sri Lanka Tamils in the mid and late 1960s." Adoption of the 1972 "republican constitution" marked the critical starting point. Between May 1972 and the end of 1976, there was "a momentous shift in the political aspirations of the Sri Lanka Tamils, from demands for structural changes and constitutional reform, to an assertion of the right to self-determination on the basis of a Tamil State in Sri Lanka" (de Silva 1998: 154–155).

"A series of shortsighted policies and decisions" by United Front leaders produced this shift (de Silva and Wriggins 1994: 339). Some Sinhalese responded by viewing proponents of extremist views in their community more favorably. Post-election rioting, precipitated by a relatively minor incident in Jaffna on August 15, 1977, revealed the extent of the polarization. About this rioting, de Silva writes: "That such a seemingly trifling incident should have set off a chain reaction that culminated in the first major outbreak of ethnic violence in the island for nearly two decades was seen as unmistakable evidence of the sharp deterioration in relations between the Sinhalese and Tamils, that had occurred under the UF regime. Within two days of the clash in Jaffna, there was widespread rioting in many parts of the island as the Tamil minority came under attack. It could be truly said of the riots of 1977 that the UF had sown the wind and J. R.'s government reaped the whirlwind" (de Silva and Wriggins 1994: 340).

Following the riots, de Silva's analysis continues, President Jayawardene attempted to combine economic reforms with "policies of reconciliation."[21] His strategy was to maintain the UNP's Sinhalese political base and win the support of mainstream Tamils, while mollifying or marginalizing extremist elements in both communities. Ultimately, however, his well-intentioned efforts were torpedoed by intransigence, inexperience, and demagoguery on the part of top TULF leaders. This helped to strengthen the Liberation Tigers, who were increasingly able to dominate politics in the north after 1980. The Tigers were able to precipitate incidents that led to the "Internationalization of Sri Lanka's Ethnic Conflict."[22] Once India became involved, Sri Lanka's leaders increasingly lost the ability to control events. Escalating conflict not only polarized the society but stalled the economic revitalization that structural adjustment reforms and the Mahaweli project were catalyzing. Instead of becoming the next Asian Tiger, "Sri Lanka had the doubtful distinction of emerging as one of the most prominent centers of ethnic conflict in the world" (de Silva and Wriggins 1994: 339).

Despite de Silva's insights on the escalation of conflict, the questions posed at the outset of this chapter remain. If United Front policies were principal causal agents, why did violent conflict not reach a protracted stage much earlier? If 1977–82 was an economic success story, why did violent conflict not decline or remain at manageable levels, rather than escalating to a protracted stage in 1984?

My answer to the first question is that despite the August 1977 riots, Sri Lanka was relatively stable when J. R. Jayawardene assumed power, and peaceful development was still a realistic possibility. "Reaping the whirlwind" was not the only option. The Tamil United Liberation Front was still politically dominant in the north. Despite secessionist rhetoric, TULF leaders were open to conciliatory government moves on sensitive issues. Most Jaffna Tamils, even many young Jaffna Tamils, were not revolutionaries but social and cultural conservatives who respected hard work and authority. Although militants had grown in stature on the Jaffna peninsula, the total number of hard-core supporters was still miniscule—certainly less than 200. Militant groups lacked the popular support, the recruits, the international funding, and the foreign sanctuaries that were critical ingredients of their strength in the 1980s. Sri Lanka's warm relations with India, buttressed by Prime Minister Bandaranaike's close ties with Indira Gandhi, made it seem unlikely that the region's dominant power would foment rebellion in its small neighbor. In fact, these circumstances make it all the more puzzling that J. R. Jayawardene—arguably the most experienced and sophisticated politician of his generation—was unable to capitalize on the opportunities that overwhelming popular support conferred.

Before turning to open economy reforms and their consequences, we need also to remind ourselves that spillover effects from conflict events in Sinhalese majority regions—J. R. Jayawardene's home territory—and actions of the security forces who were at least indirectly under J. R. Jayawardene's command are key to understanding how conflict became protracted in Sri Lanka. K. M. de Silva is accurate when he concludes that internationalization of the conflict between Sinhalese and Tamils—India's involvement in particular—gave militants the resources necessary to sustain a protracted war. Anti-Tamil riots in the South, in 1977, 1981, and especially 1983, along with the burning of Jaffna's public library by police officers and pro-government thugs, were pivotal events that motivated India's intervention.[23] While there is evidence that pro-government thugs played roles in the 1981 and 1983 riots, these events have also been described as visceral expressions of mass alienation on the part of Sinhalese community members. This reinforces the intuition that we should look closely for adverse human impacts of open economy reforms. To this topic attention is now turned.

Open Economy Reforms: Overview and Macroeconomic Consequences

Goals and Philosophy

J. R. Jayawardene thought he understood the relationship between economic processes and ethnic conflict. He believed that economic development was a prerequisite to muting ethnic tensions and promised Sri Lankans capitalism with a Buddhist face. A central theme of the government's first budget message—that a just and free society required a just and free economy—was intended to respond to concerns that reforms emphasizing individualism and entrepreneurship would threaten Sri Lanka's traditional values (Ratnapala 1989: 24; Abeyesekere 1986: 291–292).[24] Broad goals differed little from budget messages of previous governments: economic growth, revitalization of industry and agriculture, new employment opportunities for youth, and improved balance of payments (Alailima 1997: 155; Columbage and Karunaratne 1986: 210). However, the proposed strategy for attaining these goals was fundamentally different. Between 1958 and 1977, government planners had often viewed market mechanisms as an impediment to rational development. Now, policy documents and government propaganda emphasized how market mechanisms would be the key to successful development.[25]

Specific reforms were designed to open Sri Lanka's economy to global trade, stimulate investment, allow private enterprises to compete with state-controlled ones and supplant bureaucratic distribution mechanisms with free markets. The state monopoly on imports was reduced to a few key commodities, and most other import controls were eliminated.[26] To make credit more readily available, state-owned banks were directed to expand branch banking in rural areas. Nominal interest rates were increased and made more flexible. Foreign banks were encouraged to compete in Sri Lanka.

UNP leaders did not believe, however, that regulatory reforms and liberalized credit would be sufficient to catalyze economic growth. Massive capital expenditures on agriculture, industry, housing, and infrastructure, financed with foreign aid, were also projected. These would eliminate infrastructure bottlenecks that had stifled productivity and discouraged foreign investment. Increased profitability would complement the incentives that had been put in place to attract investment (Jayasundera 1986: 56–57, 67–70). Thus they saw no contradiction between the open economy philosophy and a larger government role in capital formation. Three lead projects—Mahaweli irrigation and power generation, free trade zones, and housing construction were given top priority (de Silva and Wriggins 1994: 455ff.).

The Mahaweli Project

The massive "accelerated" Mahaweli River hydroelectric and irrigation project became one of the largest development projects in the world. It came to symbolize both strengths and shortcomings of the Jayawardene government's approach to development. Strengths were the ability to mobilize resources and expertise for initiatives that produced quick, highly visible results. Shortcomings were waste, neglect of longer-term social impacts, failure to deliver promised benefits to poor Sri Lankans, and heightening of ethnic tensions.

From an engineering standpoint, the "accelerated" strategy of building four large dam complexes simultaneously was at least a qualified success. However, completion of projects lagged far behind the government's ambitious timetable,[27] and there were destabilizing social and economic impacts. Meeting targets of an accelerated timetable required capital-intensive methods and large numbers of expatriate workers. Sri Lankan professionals and local residents resented the influx of highly paid (and sometimes culturally insensitive) expatriates who were viewed as taking up jobs that rightfully belonged to them. Massive inflows of foreign funds and lucrative contracts awarded without competitive bidding, coupled with weak accountability mechanisms, created opportunities for favoritism, kickbacks, and other corrupt practices. Inflationary pressures were created that finance ministry officials could not control (Karunatilake 1987: 413).[28] Further, the high priority given to building physical infrastructure was not matched by attention to creating a strong social infrastructure in the newly settled areas, causing a widening gap between rich and poor, political favoritism, and social unrest (Scudder 1995: 160–161; Nakamura, Ratnayake, and Senananayake 1997: 280).

Finally, Mahaweli development priorities and settlement schemes helped escalate ethnic tensions. Development priorities favored Sinhalese majority regions, and settlement schemes (called "colonization schemes" by Tamils) were viewed as a calculated attack by Sinhalese politicians on Tamil numerical dominance in the "traditional homelands." As we have seen, President Jayawardene's political plan was that distribution of benefits from successful economic development would help mute ethnic and class tensions. In the case of Mahaweli, however, political considerations shaped a development strategy that heightened tensions *before* benefits could be realized.

Housing and Urban Development

Apart from Mahaweli, Prime Minister Premadasa's housing and urban development programs represented the government's largest capital investment. Adjusting for inflation, nearly three billion rupees, about one-fourth of Mahaweli expenditures, were spent during President Jayawardene's first term. In housing and urban development, the government's primary role was direct intervention rather than stimulating the private sector. Paradoxically these programs, which were peripheral to the open economy reforms, came closest to achieving their goals during the UNP's first term.

Aided Self-Help Rural Housing, which was combined with a program of "Village Awakening" (Gam Udawa), proved to be by far the most productive and cost-effective. The program's philosophy harked back to an idealized view of rural life in the era of the great Sinhalese kings as "virtuous, cooperative, and free from exploitation and discrimination" (Brow 1990: 125–131). Most of the housing construction was done by the villagers themselves. Funds were provided for village infrastructure, including tubewells, public buildings, and in some instances electrification. Larger villages might be given a clock tower, said to symbolize the prime minister's strivings to make punctuality a norm in Sri Lankan culture. Despite funding cutbacks, beginning in 1981, more than 50,000 new houses had been completed by December 1982, with many more under construction.[29]

As in the case of Mahaweli, shortcomings lay in the area of social infrastructure, as an in-depth study of a single Gam Udawa village, Kukulewa,[30] by anthropologist James Brow emphasizes. The problems of political favoritism he identifies resemble those that complicated grassroots participation schemes in newly opened Mahaweli Areas. The Kukulewa program's principal beneficiaries were village leaders affiliated with the United National Party and their supporters. All of the 60 newly constructed houses were given to them. This had an unintended though foreseeable social impact: polarization of the village into bitter, resentful pro- and anti-UNP factions. Since the housing program, like most government programs, was used to reward loyal political supporters, there is good reason to believe that the pattern seen in Kukulewa was repeated in many Gam Udawa villages.

Investment Promotion and Industrial Development

While Mahaweli development, housing, and urban revitalization consumed the largest shares of government capital spending, investment promotion and industrialization, with an emphasis on export-oriented industries, were the heart of President Jayawardene's economic philosophy. His goal was to transform entrenched attitudes that viewed Sri Lanka's capitalist entrepreneurs as enemies of the people and repatriation of profits from foreign investments as a form of imperialism.[31]

Many of these policies were brought together in the newly established Greater Colombo Economic Commission, which was given authority to create export processing zones in a 160-square-mile area between Colombo and the international airport. The commission's export promotion program was designated as a top-priority "lead project." Plans were made to begin by attracting garment firms that would employ unskilled labor. Concurrently, improvements in zone infrastructures were undertaken in the hope of attracting electronic assembly plants and other "high-tech" factories (de Silva and Wriggins 1994: 460; Rabushka 1981: 57–58). Promotions touted Sri Lanka's labor force as docile, highly educated, and willing to work for some of the lowest wages in South Asia (Vidanapathirana 1986: 188).[32]

Overall, the industrial sector achieved mixed results. Between 1977 and 1981, the value of industrial output grew by nearly 80 percent, but deteriorating terms of trade produced a 35 percent decline in 1982 and a further decline in 1983. Capacity utilization, which had hovered around 50 percent during the United Front years, rose to about 75 percent. Data on value added, however, which takes into account an increased dependence on imported raw materials, show that this picture of a strengthened industrial sector was somewhat illusory. For the "boom" year of 1981, the value added contributed by Sri Lanka's industries exceeded 1977 levels by only 22 percent. In the "bust" year of 1982, value added fell *below* 1977 levels.

Nowhere was this truer than in the massive state sector, a United Front legacy that proved resistant to reform. In 1977, Sri Lanka's government managed 26 "state corporations," representing more that 60 percent of industrial output, which produced diverse products ranging from petroleum products and fertilizer to ayurvedic drugs and coconut whiskey (*arrack*). Political control over Posts and Telecommunications, the Ceylon Government Railways, and the Sri Lanka Transport Board (buses) was more direct and intrusive. A few state-run businesses were profitable, but most required both capital and operating subsidies. Wider availability of imported goods after 1977 made shortcomings in management and product quality more apparent.

UNP preelection promises had included selling off state industries to private investors, but political resistance, especially from Minister of Industries and Scientific Affairs Cyril Mathew, blocked this. Instead, a more modest goal was set of making state industries commercially viable while gradually eliminating government subsidies. Progress in attaining this goal was incremental at best and was as much impacted by international market forces as by domestic policies. In the areas of public transit and telecommunications, directly managed by the government, problems of inefficient management and bloated employment rolls went largely unresolved. By 1982, more than one-third of Sri Lanka's bus passengers were being transported in privately owned vehicles, but few workers had been laid off at the Ceylon Transport Board. That year 28,000 customers were waiting for service from Sri Lanka Telecomm, while the company posted a loss of 22.5 million rupees (more than $1 million).

International Trade and Finance

New trade and monetary policies—export promotion, trade liberalization and currency reforms—were intended to spur economic growth by linking Sri Lanka more closely with an expanding, diversifying global economy.[33] As in other areas, implementation of these policies produced mixed results. This was due to tensions between long- and short-term objectives, constraints on change imposed by political realities, fluctuations in international markets, and political leaders' inability to fully control (or even predict) economic behavior.

Open economy policies achieved their greatest success in expanding industrial exports, which increased in value by nearly 250 percent between 1977 and 1982. Overall, the percentage of Sri Lanka's exports represented by industrial products rose from 14 percent to an astonishing 40 percent. For the first time, industrial exports surpassed tea in revenues. Unfortunately, the major contributors to this growth were overseas sales of textiles and petrochemical fertilizers, both relatively low value-added products that depended heavily on imported materials.

Things would have been much worse were it not for the additional foreign exchange provided by remittances from Sri Lankans working abroad, tourism, and foreign aid. A measure of the contribution from these sources was Sri Lanka's current account deficit, which averaged only about 55 percent of its merchandise trade deficit between 1978 and 1982. Prior to 1978, the current account deficit had often exceeded the trade deficit.

Sri Lanka's status as a favored recipient of foreign assistance did have negative aspects. Increasingly, the government became dependent on foreign funds for shorter-term budget needs as well as capital improvements. Like other forms of dependence, reliance on assistance, once established, was difficult to give up. As dependence increased, Sri Lanka's budgets became more beholden to prescriptions imposed by foreign donors.[34] To receive additional aid, the government was forced to cut politically popular social programs, such as food stamps and housing construction.

Most severe in its long-term implications was Sri Lanka's rising burden of foreign debt. In 1976, Sirimavo Bandaranaike's last full year in office, Sri Lanka's foreign debt was about five billion rupees ($590 million). By the end of 1982, it had increased to more than 35 billion ($1.7 billion). Adjusted for inflation, Sri Lanka's obligations to foreign lenders had increased by nearly 150 percent in less than seven years. Even more worrisome, the rate of indebtedness was increasing faster than income from imports or GNP as a whole.[35] Borrowing to capitalize infrastructure development projects was predicated on the assumption that such projects would catalyze a larger, more robust, more export-oriented economy, making the repayment of large loans possible. But the slump in economic growth, beginning in 1980, raised doubts about this assumption.

Government Finance

The government's emphasis on capital investment meant that while reforms reduced bureaucratic economic controls, the government's economic role increased. Political commitments to simultaneously complete numerous major projects caused spending to balloon. In a single year, 1978, expenditures grew from 8.8 billion to 17.6 billion rupees, by far the largest budget increase since independence.[36] During Sirimavo Bandaranaike's second term, government spending averaged 31 percent of gross national product. For 1978–82, this jumped to 39 percent. In 1980, 43 percent of all economic activity was government spending.

While spending accelerated, growth in revenues lagged behind, creating a succession of increasingly severe deficits. In 1978, the first full year of open economy policies, deficit spending jumped by more than 200 percent, from 22 percent to 36 percent of expenditures.[37] Since UNP policies emphasized massive investments to jumpstart the economy and nearly two-thirds of the deficit was covered by foreign loans, this was not a matter of great concern initially. However, in almost every subsequent year, the problem grew worse, with current as well as capital expenditures contributing to deficits and domestic borrowing having to bear an increasing share of the burden.[38] In combination, heavy borrowing and scarcities created by multiple development projects caused an unprecedented inflationary spiral. Between 1977 and 1982, the rupee lost nearly two-thirds of its value, and its exchange value on international markets dropped from about 9 rupees per dollar to more than 20 rupees per dollar.[39] President Jayawardene's collegial, personalized governance style also contributed to high deficits (de Silva and Wriggins 1994: 468). The president preferred to work on budgets with individual cabinet members, making *ad hoc* decisions in which political priorities often outweighed fiscal ones. It was not until 1980, when both spending and the deficit soared to new record highs, that stabilization measures began to receive serious attention (Jayasundera 1986: 57–58). Modest tax increases and budget cuts produced some relief, but in 1981, a deteriorating balance of trade began to drag both government revenues and the economy downward. In 1982, the deficit rose again.

While capital expenditures rose, spending on "Social Services"—mostly devoted to health and education—remained stagnant in the face of rising demand. Over its term, the UNP government allocated slightly more per year than its predecessor to social services; however, the 1982 downturn pushed real values of social spending to 10 percent below 1977 levels. Another casualty was Sri Lanka's defense establishment, which saw its allocation fall from 2.5 percent of government expenditures in 1977 to 1.4 percent in 1982. The real value of the 1982 defense budget was 15 percent below the relatively meager allocation it had received in 1977. Thus, at a time when the armed services were facing increased demands to quell the ethnic unrest in the north, they were being given fewer resources to accomplish the task. While defense budgets shrank, spending on "civil administration" grew by 65 percent, and subsidies to Sri Lanka's notoriously unprofitable rail and bus transport services more than doubled.[40] These numbers suggest that military leaders had little political clout in the Jayawardene government.

Thus, as in so many areas, the Jayawardene government's effort to shift spending priorities exhibits a mixed record. It was most successful in targeting newly available funds to new economic development priorities, but had difficulty slowing the momentum of spending when funds became scarcer. Where domestic and governmental constituencies lacked clout, it was able to hold spending below inflation and even impose cuts. But despite chronic deficits, budget cutting in the politically well endowed transport sector, general public service sector, and some state corporations was successfully resisted.

Faced with similar circumstances in November 1971, Prime Minister Bandaranaike and Finance Minister N. M. Pererra had pushed an austerity program through Parliament that deferred many United Front campaign pledges. "We cannot continue to pay for food we consume with the savings of people in other lands; in other words of foreign borrowing which our future generations will have to pay long after we are dead and gone," Pererra said at the time. In 1981 and 1982, J. R. Jayawardene rejected both austerity and tax increases. Instead, he opted for deficit financing, hoping that an election victory and continued adherence to open economy policies would be followed by better times ahead.

Deficit financing, however, was not a long-term solution to Sri Lanka's fiscal problems. By 1982, borrowing to cover three years of record deficits had begun to push Sri Lanka's public debt toward unsustainable levels. Adjusted for inflation, public debt grew from about 25 billion rupees in 1977 to 31.6 billion in 1982. This rate of growth was no higher than under the United Front, which, too, had been forced to rely heavily on deficit financing. But two changes in the picture made things much worse. First, the percentage of debt held by foreign creditors nearly doubled, comprising 44 percent of the total in 1982. Since massive capital development projects were financed with foreign loans, this was not surprising. Beginning in 1980, however, Sri Lanka's government also began covering more short-term obligations with foreign loans. Large foreign debts, especially those owed to commercial lenders, created yet another vicious cycle for the nation's beleaguered financial planners to address. Foreign debts were denominated in foreign currencies, which meant that deflation of the rupee did not reduce them. Instead, inflation of the rupee and its resultant devaluation against foreign currencies meant that the rupee value of foreign debts increased. By 1982, Sri Lanka's government was spending more on debt service than on all of its social and economic support programs. Even more worrisome, the percentage of government revenues that needed to be set aside for debt service had more than doubled, from 11 percent in 1978 to 24 percent in 1982. Debt service now comprised nearly 38 percent of the annual budget deficit. If adverse trends continued, Sri Lanka would soon be faced with the prospect of taking out new foreign-currency loans simply to make payments on existing debts.

Appraisal

J. R. Jayawardene's government quickly demonstrated its ability to raise foreign funds, shift priorities from consumption to investment, and implement modest regulatory forms. But this did not guarantee that public sector projects would meet targeted goals or that Sri Lanka's private sector would become more productive and competitive. Like its predecessors, the UNP leadership achieved its greatest successes in areas over which the government could exercise direct control—constructing houses, government buildings, dams, power plants, and irrigation works. Where success required participation from domestic entrepreneurs and foreign private investors, achievements were more modest. Nor was J. R. Jayawardene very successful in overcoming entrenched political opposition to reforms in the plantations, state-controlled enterprises, and state corporations.

Economic reforms and increased government spending succeeded in unleashing an economic boom during 1978, 1979, and 1980, years when all things seemed possible. As 1981 drew to a close, however, economic portents were less promising. A combination of rising government debts, high inflation, worsening trade deficits, and stagnating economic performance were beginning to impact ordinary Sri Lankans and make cutbacks in popular programs inevitable. Adverse social impacts and a widening gap between the rich and poor received little attention in the rush to develop. These impacts are detailed in the following section.

Open Economy Reforms: Delivering Benefits to the People

An Economic Miracle?

Never had a change in ruling party produced such a visible economic transformation as the UNP's reform program initially delivered. Within weeks, previously barren store shelves were laden with imported goods.[41] Long queues for rice, wheat, milk, and other essentials disappeared as new marketing and distribution systems took hold. Infusions of capital plus availability of imported raw materials caused a surge in industrial production. In 1978, Sri Lanka's real gross national product grew by an astonishing 25 percent.

Whether or not growth could be sustained and its fruits widely shared were questions yet to be answered. Economic and administrative reforms helped produce the spurt of growth, but release of pent-up consumer demand, after years of austerity, also played a role. Imported consumer goods were now more widely available but priced beyond the reach of many. Open economy reforms weakened government social safety nets, placing the poor at greater risk. How did these changes impact the lives of ordinary Sri Lankans?

Economic Growth, Wages, and Income Distribution

For most Sri Lankans, tangible benefits were short-lived from the economic boom that transformed Sri Lanka's commercial climate in urban areas. UNP leaders touted high nominal growth rates as proof that reforms were succeeding, but after 1978, much of this growth was fueled by inflation. Prices rose 9 percent in 1978, 20 percent in 1980, and a staggering 38 percent in 1982. Adjusted for inflation, annual GNP growth averaged a respectable 5 percent between 1979 and 1981, but a 16 percent decline in 1982 erased those gains.[42]

As the economy boomed, migration from densely populated agricultural areas to Colombo and to newly opening Mahaweli lands became an attractive option. Among the migrants—mostly Sinhalese—were a very high proportion of mobile, newly literate young men who had completed some secondary schooling and felt frustrated by limited economic opportunities at home (Tambiah 1986: 51). Often, they blamed politicians and Tamils for their plight. Migration produced a higher than average male/female ratio in some parts of the island. The ratio averaged 103 for all Sri Lanka, but was 109 in urban areas and 113 in Colombo. In rural areas drained by the Mahaweli, this ratio ranged from 112 to 129. In some urban areas of northwestern Polonnaruwa District, bordering the Tamil-majority eastern province, the ratio of men to women was nearly two to one (Tambiah 1986: 51).[43] This demographic profile was fuel for social unrest, easily inflamed by bad economic conditions, perceived inequities, and chauvinistic political rhetoric.

During the boom years of 1977–80, however, economic conditions were more good than bad. Most sectors of the society appeared to be benefiting from growth. Real wages rose across the board, with the greatest gains—about 50 percent in three years—being posted for salaried agricultural workers. Well-to-do farmers, producing rice and tobacco for local markets, successfully capitalized on new government incentive programs. Members of a new entrepreneurial class—private tractor owners, traders, small shopkeepers, transport agents, and other middlemen—profited from the more open commercial environment (Bhargava 1987: 201). Industrial and commercial workers also achieved modest gains, averaging about 10 percent, and could still count themselves better off in 1980 than when the UNP had assumed power.[44] Government employees, too, received big increases initially that outpaced inflation. In 1981 and 1982, however, there was a slowdown in growth and then a decline in real GNP. On average, prices rose more than 20 percent in 1981 and more than 38 percent in 1982. Real incomes of many workers declined steeply. Schoolteachers were impacted most. Wage increases given in 1978 and 1979 barely kept pace with inflation. By the end of 1980, their purchasing power had already dropped 15 percent below 1977 levels.[45]

A vicious cycle, caused by deteriorating terms of trade and ballooning government budgets, was widening the gap between inflation and wage increases, despite policymakers' best efforts. Cost-of-living raises were necessary to maintain political support but could only be financed by government borrowing. Borrowing fueled inflation, which soon erased any real benefits from higher wages. Wage increases helped secure pro-UNP majorities in the fall of 1982, but this strategy was not sustainable. The inexorable outstripping of wage increases by inflation was particularly hard on middle-class government employees in urban areas who experienced erosion of status as well as purchasing power in the open economy era. High wages in new commercial enterprises were not uniform, but some were highly visible, especially in the booming tourist sector. Hotel doormen, restaurant waiters, and tour guides could earn more than department heads, university professors, and senior police officers (Manor 1984: 15–16).

Sri Lankan workers who lacked permanent formal employment fared worst of all (Lakshman 1997b: 181ff.).[46] They included landless agricultural workers outside the estate sector, small landholders who relied exclusively on family labor, self-employed craftsmen, those making a living from fishing or animal husbandry, small "cottage industry" workers, and casual laborers (Lakshman 1997b: 210). Men and women in these categories were most vulnerable to economic downturns. They were last to be hired and first to be laid off. They lacked the strong labor union representation that had helped tea-estate workers share the benefits of growth. Many of the economically marginalized lived in rural areas, but the more mobile among them, especially young men, were recent migrants to urban centers. In Colombo and other cities, they swelled the ranks of a frustrated lumpen proletariat whose members could not afford the tempting luxury goods newly displayed around them (Manor 1984: 16; Meyer 1984: 150).

Government Consumer Finances Surveys (Lakshman 1997b: 174–181)[47] documented a widening income gap between rich and poor. Open economy reforms did improve the lot of the affluent. In fact, for the survey periods 1973–78/79 and 1978/79–81/82, only the top decile increased their share of total income received. All others lost ground. In 1973, incomes of Sri Lanka's top-decile earners were 17 times greater than incomes of their counterparts in the lowest decile. By 1981/82, this ratio had more than doubled. The ratio for spending units, which assesses circumstances of multiple-earner poor and middle-class families more realistically,[48] grew from 10 to 17.

As noteworthy as the widening gap between rich and poor was the widening gap between the rich and the middle class. In 1973, the top 10 percent of income earners received less than twice the income of those immediately below them on the income ladder (in the ninth decile). By 1981/82, their share was more than three times as great.[49] The widening gap becomes even more apparent if one takes the share of fifth decile income recipients as a rough surrogate for the "middle class." In 1973, the income share of Sri Lanka's wealthiest was about four times as large as their "middle-class" counterparts. Less than ten years later, in 1981/82, the size of their share had grown to nearly eight times that of the "middle class." Belying visions of a *dharmistha* (righteous Buddhist) society, egalitarian norms of the 1960s and 1970s were now supplanted by a social Darwinist ethic that conferred merit on the fleetest in a new race for economic gain. One social critic pointed to "lower-middle-class pauperization" as a potentially more deadly problem than the nation's ethnic divisions (Wickremeratne 1995: 323–324).

Lower-middle-class pauperization was accompanied by an increase in the number of Sri Lankans living below the threshold of absolute poverty, though the extent of the increase is a matter of debate. Samarasinghe reports an increase in the number of "ultra poor" from less than 20 percent of the population in 1977–78 to about 25 percent in 1981–82. He cites government and official sources, which describe more than 30 percent of Sri Lanka's schoolchildren as "chronically undernourished" and more than 12 percent as "acutely undernourished" (1988: 75). Karunatilake provides statistics that show how inflation pushed growing numbers of families below the poverty line (1987: 213–215).[50] Tambiah concludes that the poorest workers and those "partly to fully unemployed" saw their living standards worsen after 1977 (1986: 35).[51] Lakshman's review of nine separate studies reaches broadly similar conclusions about increasing poverty levels, but notes that different definitions of poverty and measurement schemes were used to support both optimistic and pessimistic assessments of open economy policies (1997b).[52]

What did it mean to be "poor" in Sri Lanka during this period of economic and social transformation? A detailed, graphic picture emerges from investigations of Colombo sociologist Nandasena Ratnapala. Ratnapala obtained a self-definition of what it meant for family members to be living just above the poverty line from respondents in nine geographically dispersed communities:

1. They should have three meals a day (according to them, a light meal in the morning and two heavy meals necessarily rice at noon and for dinner) to keep them out of hunger.
2. Three pieces of clothing for each member of the family.
3. About two acres of paddy land and one acre of dry land with water or such other resources of employment which ensure a minimum of SL Rs. 500 per month.
4. Presence of some savings (say SL Rs. 500) to be used in an emergency (to keep them out of debt).
5. A house that shelters them from sun and rain. (1989: 26)[53]

Only a small fraction of the inhabitants in the nine communities had access to all these necessities on a reliable basis. More than half of the residents were functionally illiterate, and most had no marketable skill. Many of their houses lacked a bed or a chair to sit on. More than 80 percent of lactating mothers failed to receive even one nutritious meal per day. Average life expectancy for men was about 52 years. Women lived a little longer (Ratnapala 1989: 28–43, chap. 6).[54]

Ratnapala describes the impact of inflation on families living at this marginal level of existence:

> The present increases in prices, especially of food items, have robbed them of whatever nutrition they gained from their frugal meals. The rise in the price of sugar meant that 75 percent of the families have a cup of tea without sugar in the morning. The most pathetic side of this is that it has robbed the children of sugar in their tea, which they used to have earlier. A cup of tea was the least costly item in their life in the past being only about eight or ten cents. It cannot now be purchased with sugar even for 80 cents. Milk is completely out of the question. Bread or meals made out of flour, for example, were eaten in 98 percent of the houses at Chitra Lane [in Colombo]. But after the increases in price, only in four or five houses do they eat bread or meal made out of flour in the morning. In 14 houses they merely satisfy themselves with only a cup of plain tea and that too without milk. (1989: 43)

"The style of life in these villages," he concludes, "is punctuated not by leisure or festivals or celebrations, holidays, gatherings of friends, outings, parties, etc., but by the incessant struggle to eke out an existence" (1989: 32).

This was further complicated by another facet of open economy reforms, subsidy cuts. Cuts did not occur across the board. For example, rail and bus transportation continued to be heavily subsidized government enterprises that lost money (Karunatilake 1987: 235). Wheat continued to be imported by the government and sold at below world-market prices. However, inflation-adjusted allocations to social services, health, and education dropped between 5 and 10 percent. Cuts impacted repair and maintenance of government facilities, provision of essentials such as water and sanitation, and expenditures for consumable supplies and training (Alailima 1997: 158–160).

Elimination of the rice ration, long a goal of J. R. Jayawardene, was the most radical subsidy reduction. A first step was taken in 1978, when more than a third of the population saw their rice rations cancelled. In the following year, a food stamp program was implemented, replacing the rice ration entirely. Initially, it appeared that the new food stamp allocations might actually make poor people better off. Stamps were supposed to provide the same basket of goods that the food subsidy program had provided, and in fact, their initial market value was estimated at 112 percent of the subsidized food. However, food stamps were not indexed to market prices of staple foods, which were soon pushed upward by inflation. Increasing the value of food stamps required political action, which only came grudgingly. Between 1979 and 1982, government expenditures on meeting poor Sri Lankans' food needs dropped from 13.9 percent of the budget to 4.6 percent. By 1982, food stamps supplied poor families with only about half as much rice as in 1979 (Alailima 1997: 158; Samarasinghe 1988: 74).[55]

The impact on nutrition levels was predictable. A 1983 study by Harvard University's Institute of International Development reported that rising market prices for rice and wheat "tended to reduce the caloric intake of the lowest groups substantially, compared to their historical levels" (Tambiah 1986: 36).[56] According to another study, estimated calorie consumption of the lowest income decile fell from 1,335 in 1978/79 to 1,181 in 1981/82. In 1970, when a full ration of rice was available to all those in need, poor families were consuming more than 2,000 calories, per capita. Not only were poor families eating less but they were required to spend more of their discretionary income on food. In 1972, according to one estimate, 44 percent of their food needs were being met by government subsidies. By 1982, this figure had dropped to 20 percent (Alailima 1997: 165–169).[57]

Unemployment and Job Creation

Open economy reforms were more successful in creating jobs than in helping poor people. When the UNP government assumed office, a rising unemployment rate, surpassing 25 percent, was one of the nation's most pressing problems. Under Prime Minister Bandaranaike's government, despite creation of new public sector positions, the nation had experienced a net job loss.[58] More than 1.2 million Sri Lankans seeking regular work were unable to find it. Adding to the problem, open economy reforms motivated increasing numbers of women to seek employment, pushing labor force growth to an all-time high (Kiribanda 1997: 233–235, table 7-3).[59] By 1982, however, total unemployment had dropped to near 18 percent and perhaps even lower (Karunatilake 1987: 284, table 10.9).[60] If we accept the most conservative estimates, Sri Lanka's economy created at least 65,000 and probably more than 700,000 new jobs during J. R. Jayawardene's first term.

Creating more than half a million jobs in five years was a major achievement, but an 18 percent unemployment rate was still very troublesome. Nearly 1 million Sri Lankans who wanted to work could not find any employment. An even larger number were either underemployed or doing work they felt was beneath them. Much of this unemployment and underemployment was *structural*. It stemmed from a long-standing mismatch between skills that a modernizing economy needed and skills that workers seeking employment were able to provide (Kiribanda 1997: 241–246; Sri Lanka 1990: chaps. 4 and 5). Further, Sinhala-only education excluded many applicants from internationally oriented and tourist-sector positions that required English. Thus, in a new economic climate, language policies intended to break down class barriers wound up reinforcing the privileged position of elite government school and fee-paying private school graduates (Sri Lanka 1990: chap. 7).[61]

Some years later, following a second Sinhalese youth insurrection that nearly overthrew the government,[62] a Presidential Commission on Youth strongly indicted the mismatch between employment opportunities and the education being provided to the most volatile segment of the Sri Lankan community. "The majority of secondary school leavers," commissioners concluded, "find very little opportunities for self-employment as the education imparted to them in our school system does not equip them with the basic knowledge and the skills required for gainful employment" (Sri Lanka 1990: 30). Thus one of the great success stories of open economy reforms, job creation, still left many young Sri Lankans unemployed, disillusioned, and disaffected (Hettige, this volume). UNP leaders were aware of these concerns, but as the economy turned downward and deficits ballooned, their options for responding effectively became increasingly circumscribed.

Ethnic Disparities in Income and Employment

Economist S. W. R. D. Samarasinghe has attempted to sort out contending Sinhalese-Tamil claims of ethnically based employment discrimination and income disparity (n.d.). He found kernels of truth in simplistic perceptions of discrimination on both sides, embedded in a more complex reality. In the state sector, Tamils had steadily lost ground to Sinhalese, but retained a disproportionate share of highly visible administrative, professional, and technical positions. Low-country Sinhalese, on average, received higher incomes than Tamils, but Tamils did better than Kandyan Sinhalese.

UNP open economy reforms did little to change these patterns which, Samarasinghe reminds us, were based as much on political as ethnic ties. Since both political parties were Sinhalese-dominated, normal operation of the political spoils system tended to favor Sinhalese aspirants to government posts. J. R. Jayawardene expressed greater sympathy for Tamil aspirations than his predecessor, but was also attuned to perceptions and needs of his support base in the Sinhalese community. Widely shared economic growth, he continued to believe, was a far better way to mute ethnic tensions than affirmative action programs.

As the private sector assumed an increasing role in Sri Lanka's economy, ethnically based hiring practices in private companies became a matter of public concern and political discussion. Samarasinghe found that Sinhalese were somewhat overrepresented, while Tamils were somewhat underrepresented. Also, there was a clear relationship between ethnic identities of owners and employees. There is some evidence that Tamil businessmen benefited disproportionately from a more open economic environment, because administration of complex commercial licensing procedures under the previous government had favored Sinhalese (Gunasinghe, this volume).[63] Whatever the realities, it is clear that some Sinhalese businessmen felt they had lost out, as a result of open economy policies, and they resented the gains of Tamil competitors. These resentful Sinhalese businessmen had their counterparts among Jaffna vegetable farmers who, as trade restrictions were relaxed, saw profits wiped out by cheap food imports from India.

Whether in some "objective" sense open economy reforms helped to reduce discrimination and distribute benefits more equitably across ethnic groups may never be satisfactorily resolved. In an ethnically conflicted society, however, it is perceptions of relative deprivation rather than abstractions crafted by economists that matter. In the Sinhalese and Tamil communities, potentially disruptive elements *believed* they had been disadvantaged by open economy reforms. These elements viewed members of the "other" ethnic group and J. R. Jayawardene's government as legitimate targets for their resentments.

Health Care Services

The UNP philosophy of combining government-managed systems with private sector initiatives extended to health care. Here, the government had pledged "to restore the high standards of health and disease prevention that had existed earlier." Planning documents defined improved preventive and primary care as major goals for the government-run health care system. The private sector was given an increased role in providing curative care.

While improved care was touted as an outcome of health care reforms, reforms were also part of the government's across-the-board strategy to reduce spending on social entitlements. Thus, while there was an 80 percent increase in overall government spending during President Jayawardene's first term, allocations to health care remained nearly stagnant. When stringent spending cuts were imposed in 1982, government health care had no Dissanayake, Athulathmudali, or Premadasa to speak up,[64] and so it took a severe hit. Adjusted for inflation, 1982 spending was nearly 20 percent below 1977 (and more than 25 percent below 1971).

Budget cuts, heavier patient loads, and replacement of experienced doctors with a somewhat smaller number of inexperienced ones produced an overall degradation in the quality of service, with the impact bearing most heavily on the poor and in rural areas.[65] Like other open economy reforms, government-mandated changes in health care moved away from egalitarian norms that had long guided social service delivery in Sri Lanka. Establishing the fee-for-service system made it possible for doctors to increase their incomes, reducing pressures to migrate somewhat, but also reduced the quality of care given to public patients (Alailima 1997: 164–165).[66] Attracting good doctors to rural areas, never an easy task, became even more difficult. A two-tier health care system, with higher quality service given to those who could afford to pay, became the norm. The political spillover from this two-tier system reinforced and perpetuated it. Wealthy, politically influential Sri Lankans were less and less likely to experience the health care available to lower-class citizens. Thus healthcare system deficiencies were not a top political priority. Inexperienced physicians, deteriorating facilities, and long waits for service were primarily matters of concern for those whose political voices were weak.

While open economy reforms impacted health care services to the poor adversely, previously noted positive trends in overall public health indicators continued during J. R. Jayawardene's first term. Mortality rates fell by 18 percent, infant mortality rates by 24 percent, and maternal mortality rates by a remarkable 40 percent. These numbers, which helped maintain Sri Lanka's reputation as a development "success story," may have reflected payoffs from an increased emphasis on public health or simply the effectiveness of programs implemented by previous administrations. Whatever the explanation, Sri Lanka's continued strong showing provided ammunition for proponents of the new two-tier system and budgets that gave health care lower priority. Their views continued to shape policy in J. R. Jayawardene's government.

Primary and Secondary Education

A *de facto* two-tier system already existed in primary and secondary education—top quality schools for wealthy, politically influential Sri Lankans, inferior ones for most ordinary citizens—but the government made no attempt to extend open economy principles to the nation's schools.[67] A combination of increased demand for services and inflation-eroded budgets produced outcomes similar to those in health care.

Undoing Mrs. Bandaranaike's education reforms was the government's first priority. Students were now required to enter school at age five rather than six. At the other end of the educational cycle, GCE (General Certificate of Education) "Ordinary" and "Advanced" level examinations were reinstated. To meet these examination standards, years of post-kindergarten education were increased again from 11 to 12.[68] This two-year boost in education requirements contributed to an enrollment surge of more than 5,000 students (21 percent) in 1978.

A third new program—providing free textbooks for all students in grades one through ten—also targeted Sri Lanka's poorest students, in this case both Sinhalese and Tamil. Lack of sufficient income to buy textbooks had been identified as a major contributor to high dropout rates among poor children (Marga Institute 1978),[69] and it was hoped that government-supplied texts would help remedy the problem. Between 1980, when the program was initiated, and 1982, the government distributed 31.1 million texts costing nearly 192 million rupees. This new obligation represented more than 4 percent of current expenditures on education (Central Bank 1982: 87–88).

It would appear that J. R. Jayawardene's government began its term with a commitment to expand both educational services *and* funding for education. Inflation and competing budgetary pressures soon vitiated the latter commitment. Thus, while inflation-adjusted education expenditures rose by 11 percent between 1977 and 1980, they dropped by 14 percent between 1980 and 1982 to a level below 1977. The severity of these budget shortfalls becomes more evident when the government's increased obligations are taken into account. Between 1977 and 1982, expenditures per teacher declined 17 percent while expenditures per student fell by nearly one-third. After five years of UNP rule, Sri Lanka's pre-university education system was still among the developing world's best, but long-standing calls for reforms evoked little response from teachers and administrators who saw their facilities deteriorating, their workloads increasing, and the purchasing power of their wages decreasing simultaneously.

Widely differing school quality meant that poor children, especially those living in outlying areas, had little opportunity to improve their station through Sri Lanka's highly competitive educational system. For every 100 students who enrolled in kindergarten, only 51 would take the "O" level examinations, only 24 would enroll in "A" level courses, and only 2 would gain university admission. To enroll in advanced courses, not only did students need to pass nationally standardized examinations, but also the requisite schools needed to be available. In Colombo's educational district,[70] more than 66 percent of the schools offered advanced level courses and nearly 18 percent offered training in science. By contrast, less that 12 percent of rural Vavuniya district schools offered advanced training and only 3 percent provided science training. "Equalization of educational opportunity has continued to be a guiding principle," an Education Ministry survey noted, "but the education system has not been able to provide even basic facilities such as blackboards, sanitation, and water supply to about 20 percent of the schools. . . . Inadequate funding of the system as a whole and an imbalance in the allocation of resources between the prestigious schools and the rest of the system" were identified as the principal causes of this problem (Guneratne et al. 1983: 37).[71] Primary and secondary education, then, was yet another area where large numbers of Sri Lankans experienced deterioration in the quality of services they were receiving, after five years of J. R. Jayawardene's open economy policies.

Higher Education

United National Party higher education policies were a different matter. In this politically volatile area, reforms and organizational changes were combined with budget increases for staff benefits, library resources, support services, and equipment. A massive capital-spending program created three new university campuses and added new facilities to the existing ones. New continuing and technical education programs provided opportunities for students who were not admitted to traditional universities or were unable to pursue a full-time program of study in residence.

J. R. Jayawardene's first higher education priority, as we have seen, was to replace the communally divisive "media-wise standardization" university admissions policy with a merit-based scheme, designed to offer something to each interested party. Tamil applicants were once again given the opportunity to compete with Sinhalese for places on the basis of their GCE A-level scores, irrespective of the language in which they were examined. Less-advantaged Sinhalese and Muslim applicants benefited from a complex scheme of district quotas that could be adjusted to political realities and by an increase in the absolute number of places available (Wijetunga 1983: 139–140).[72] Other priorities, set forth in a new *Universities Act*,[73] were reversing United Front higher education reforms and establishing a more flexible system that could respond to the needs of Sri Lanka's expanding open economy.

While these reforms could be initiated quickly, UNP leaders knew that tinkering with admissions quotas, redrawing organization charts, and commissioning planning documents would not resolve two fundamental problems that had made higher education a catalyst for political discontent among Sri Lanka's youth. First was the declining percentage of qualified applicants who could reasonably hope to gain university admission (de Silva and Peiris 1995: 292).[74] Second was the mismatch between educational qualifications of most Sri Lankan university graduates and the employment needs of Sri Lanka's economy.

Attacking the first problem was easier for a government that had made capital investment the centerpiece of its development policies. Higher education capital spending increased nearly tenfold over 1977 levels. New campuses were created, and existing ones received new facilities (Wijetunge 1983: 122–125). Sri Lanka's technical institutes, which provided specialized education below the university level, grew to 26 in number (Central Bank 1983: 86–87).[75] An Open University was founded in 1980 to provide continuing education for adult and other nontraditional students. As in other areas, benefits from these investments had not been fully realized at the end of President Jayawardene's first term, but the total number of students enrolled in some higher education program had already more than doubled between 1977 and 1982. This growth by no means fully resolved pressures on admissions—less than 15 percent of those eligible were admitted in 1982—but held out the promise that higher education opportunities would increase further in the years ahead.

Reforming curricula to meet the needs of a more privatized, globalized, technologically sophisticated economy posed more difficult problems than upgrading physical facilities and creating new ones. The need for reform was well known. Indeed, providing job-oriented higher education had been the centerpiece of the United Front's flawed higher education innovations. In 1978, Sri Lanka's universities awarded nearly 1,300 degrees in arts and Oriental studies, but fewer than 500 in science and only 268 in engineering. A 1979 manpower study warned about shortages of engineers, science graduates, doctors, and commerce graduates. Applications for these specializations far exceeded the supply. But universities were resistant to change and ill prepared to compete with the private sector for qualified faculty who could teach technical subjects. Five years after the UNP took power, the percentage of science graduates grew by nearly 10 percent and commerce graduates by about half that much. The percentage of engineering graduates declined, however, and those receiving degrees in arts and Oriental studies still composed nearly half the total, as they had in 1977.

What prospects awaited these young men and women? A detailed review of *University Education and Graduate Employment in Sri Lanka*, completed in 1983, included an extensive survey of graduates' job market expectations and experiences (Sanyal et al. 1983: chaps. 7–11).[76] Study results reinforced widely held views about the greater marketability of professional and science degrees. Among those unable to find permanent employment, more than 90 percent had majored in an arts field. Typically, arts graduates also had to wait far longer to find jobs—often three years or more. Jobs they did land were frequently minor administrative or clerical posts that did not require a university degree at all. A survey of employers helped to explain this disparity. Their perception was that professional, science, and engineering curricula met high standards and were relevant to future employment. Employers of arts graduates, however, complained of poor preparation as well as a mismatch between examination standards and job requirements (Sanyal et al. 1983: 314–321).

Responses from a survey of university students in their final year communicated a similar message (Sanyal et al. 1983: chap. 7). Nearly half of the respondents reported dissatisfaction with their courses of study, due to "inadequate knowledge of the subject, poor practical skills . . . and course content that was irrelevant to their future needs and the needs of the country." "Inadequate knowledge of English" was also seen as a major problem, providing further evidence that Sri Lanka's official language policy had proved costly for many that were intended to be its beneficiaries. Students also expressed concern that despite efforts of several governments, higher education tended to reinforce rather than break down Sri Lanka's class hierarchy. Those in the top socioeconomic stratum were more likely to have the strong secondary preparation and English fluency that would enable them to compete successfully for the most coveted positions in the strongest universities. Having earned science, engineering, or professional degrees, they could then also capitalize on family, social, political, and caste connections to help them find employment (Hettige, this volume).

Less advantaged students who gained admission at all were more likely to meet the lower standards required for concentration in arts or Oriental studies. They, too, embarked on their careers as university students with high expectations, but those careers were more likely to end in frustration and disillusionment. Open economy rhetoric touted opportunities that an expanding private sector would provide, but the security of government employment in an administrative post not requiring specialized skills, remained the goal of many. For recruitment to these posts, political ties were often far more important than a strong academic record.

Open Economy Policies and the Escalation of Violent Political Conflict

In 1977, the potentially adverse social and political consequences of structural adjustment were less well understood than today. Just as Sri Lankan socialists believed central planning would allocate resources more efficiently and fairly, UNP reformers believed open economy policies would simultaneously promote economic expansion and the well-being of the poor. In Sri Lanka, as in many other developing nations, these expectations proved false. Achieving the massive capitalization and economic restructuring J. R. Jayawardene initiated could not be accomplished without pain and social dislocation. It proved impossible to control or fully cushion the impact of inflationary pressures produced by a volatile juxtaposition of generous foreign aid, high government deficits, and adverse movement in Sri Lanka's terms of trade. The turbulent economic and social climate that reforms created did provide new opportunities, but preponderantly for economically advantaged, socially privileged, and politically connected Sri Lankans. Belying President Jayawardene's campaign pledges, social norms were becoming more Darwinian than *dharmistha*.

We have seen in this section that most income groups benefited from the initial spurt of growth between 1977 and 1979, but that many saw these initial gains eroded by inflation, and by 1982 they were actually worse off economically than they had been when the UNP assumed power. As wage earners lost ground, the gap widened between the highest income groups and all other sectors of society. "Middle-class pauperization" is a term first heard during the open economy era. The quality of government health care and schools to which poor and middle-class Sri Lankans looked for education deteriorated. Those at the bottom of the income ladder, who bore the brunt of food subsidy cuts, fared worst of all. UNP leaders' plan to turn the economy around within a single electoral cycle and diffuse benefits throughout the society had proved unrealistic. While they were still optimistic about the longer-term future, they feared that voters might retaliate, giving a revitalized opposition the power to roll back open economy policies. This concern, rather than fear of a "Naxalite Threat," was probably the principal motivation for calling a referendum to extend the life of Parliament in December 1982.

Privations that became ever more visible in 1981 and 1982 differed in three respects from those of earlier years, with profound implications for levels of deprivation and alienation in Sri Lankan society. First, privations followed hard upon a three-year boom when nearly everyone appeared to be prospering. Before inflation gutted it, even the new food stamp program, it appeared, might improve the lot of the poor. Suffering under the UNP soured a climate of good times and heightened expectations. Second, privations were unequally shared, to a much greater degree. Especially in commercializing urban areas, the disparities were gaudily displayed for all to see. Under the United Front virtually everyone—poor and well-to-do alike—queued for basic foodstuffs at sparsely provisioned government outlets. Now the poorest Sri Lankans could see that foodstuffs were plentiful, but they had no money to buy them. Third, a widening gap between classes and displays of unaffordable opulence were coincident, in urban areas, with an invasion of material goods, cultural artifacts, and tourists that offended many Sri Lankans deeply. That some top UNP officials and pro-government businessmen, perceived to be corrupt, were among those who displayed their wealth most ostentatiously made things worse.

As we have seen, theories of conflict suggest that in a turbulent socioeconomic climate, those experiencing relative deprivation, alienation, and lack of control over their circumstances are likely to seek scapegoats. Irresponsible politicians will stoke the rage of the deprived to enhance their own power. Preelection campaigning is a particularly accessible forum for showcasing this tactic. Sri Lanka had two political campaigns, within three months, at the end of 1982. Ending the electoral cycle does not necessarily dissipate the hostile feelings that campaigning has aroused, especially in a climate of continued deprivation where campaign promises are unfulfilled. In such circumstances, some combination of provocations, reduced public civility, and diminished respect for public order can easily catalyze an explosion. All of these factors were present in Sri Lanka's major urban centers as J. R. Jayawardene's UNP government began its second term. In view of this, the explosion that did occur in July 1983 is not surprising.

Notes

Support is gratefully acknowledged from the U.S. Institute of Peace, the International Center for Ethnic Studies, and the American University School of International Service for the research leading to this chapter. Also, I should like to acknowledge the contributions of numerous doctoral students and research assistants, especially Dr. Deborah Furlong, Dr. Burcu Akan, Kenneth Friesen, Jianxing Wang, Kristine Herrmann, and Naren Kumarakulasingam.

1. The methodology of describing conflict using "events data" was first developed by political scientist Edward E. Azar (1987). A political conflict event is defined as a politically significant occurrence, involving strife and often violence, that falls outside the established legal procedures governing political life. Usually, political conflict events express some sort of protest against the government or the established order of things. For further elaboration, see Azar 1990: 2–8.
2. For example, see Richardson 1991 and 1999.
3. The methodology, called system dynamics, was first developed by Jay W. Forrester.
4. While I can distinguish between "ethnic" and "nonethnic" conflict events, I do not do so in this representation. At this level of aggregation, I think it is more useful not to distinguish between the two.
5. More specifically, the plot in Figure 2.1 has been generated in the following manner (see also Richardson 1990a, 1990b). First, verbal descriptions of "conflict events" were compiled from a variety of Sri Lankan sources. Second, each event was assigned four index numbers, denoting its time-duration, severity (extent of killings, injuries, and destruction of property), location, and size (number of people involved). Third, the four indices were aggregated into a composite by taking the geometric mean of the index numbers. Fourth, the values of event scores for each month were summed. This is a modification of a composite index developed by Pitrim Sorokin and described in 1937.
6. This metaphor owes something to Crane Brinton's 1965 classic. I develop the idea further, with specific reference to Sri Lanka in 1991.
7. Azar was working on Sri Lanka's conflicts shortly before he died.
8. For a more recent statement of his views, applied specifically to ethnic conflict, see Gurr and Harff 1994. The shortcoming of statistical analyses growing out of this school is that correlation coefficients are typically quite low.
9. A useful review article, critiquing both deprivation and mobilization theories, is Kerbo 1982.
10. Skocpol (1994) reproduces a number of these works, preceded by an original introductory essay. While the case studies focus on "social revolutions," many of the insights are generalizable to broader categories of violent political conflict.

11. Recently, governance has become a theme of importance among international development practitioners and scholars, as exemplified by World Bank 1997.
12. I am indebted to American University School of International Service doctoral students Burcu Akan Ellis and Naren Kumarakulasingam for a bibliographic essay on this school that contributed many of these observations.
13. The contributions to Spencer, ed. 1990 and his superb ethnographic study, 1990, also fall within this school, as does Tambiah 1996.
14. Paul Brass (1997) reminds us that the way events are contextualized, interpreted, and communicated matters far more than the "facts" of the event. Skillful politicians like J. R. Jayawardene understood this even better than postmodern theorists.
15. Carnegie (1997: 29) provides an unambiguous statement of this view.
16. Shinjinee Sen and I develop this argument more fully in our 1997 paper.
17. I develop this argument more fully in 1991. Systems analytic approaches look to biology and systems engineering, rather than economics and social psychology, for models of good theories.
18. For example, see Gunasinghe (this volume), Gunatilleke 1989, Moore 1990b, and Isenmann 1987.
19. This scenario is a composite of elements presented in a number of publications including Bhalla and Glewwe 1986, Lal and Rajapatirana 1989, Rabushka 1981, Samarasinghe 1988, and several of the contributions to Rasaputram et al. 1986.
20. Among the most relevant to this chapter are de Silva 1986 and 1993; also, of course, his definitive two-volume biography: de Silva and Wriggins 1988 and 1994.
21. "Policies of Reconciliation: Success and Failure" is the title of chapter 5 in K. M. de Silva 1998: 161–192.
22. "India and the Internationalization of Sri Lanka's Ethnic Conflict, 1983–1990" is the title of chapter 6 in K. M. de Silva 1998: 193–248.
23. This event was coincident with campaigning that preceded the Jaffna District Development Council elections in June 1981.
24. Entitlement programs were viewed as consistent with Buddhist Karmic law, which emphasizes sharing as a source of merit in subsequent lives. Providing essential needs identified by the Buddha—clothing (*cheevara*), food (*pindapatha*), shelter (*sensana*), and medicine (*gilanaprathya*)—had long been viewed as an obligation by Sinhalese rulers.
25. For example, see Liyanage 1997: 449–451.
26. The monopoly on petroleum products was retained.
27. All four dams were not completed until 1988, and even then, some nagging technical problems remained.
28. Inflation, fiscal indiscipline, and cost overruns eventually escalated rupee expenditures on Mahaweli by more than 300 percent over 1978 estimates.
29. By the end of 1984, data from the Local Government Ministry showed that the "impossible" target of building 100,000 houses had not only been attained but surpassed.
30. Kukulewa is an isolated dry-zone rural village in Anuradhapura District.
31. G. H. Peiris (1993a: 231) comments that industrial policy has never been center stage in Sri Lankan politics, in contrast to welfare and agricultural policies. For this reason, new governments have been more willing to make radical policy changes in this arena, reflecting differences in their ideological stances.

32. Also various promotional materials published by the Greater Colombo Economic Commission and the Foreign Investment Advisory Committee. One brochure characterized Sri Lankan workers as "intelligent and trainable, eager and productive, available and inexpensive."
33. While the initial impetus for structural adjustment came from within Sri Lanka, reflecting long-standing concerns of President Jayawardene himself, the government was later subjected to pressures from foreign donors to speed up and "rationalize" its policies. See Abeyratne 1997: 370–371.
34. Among the most severe critics of foreign aid dependence was economist H. N. S. Karunatilake (1987: chaps. 13, 14). Karunatilake served briefly as governor general of the Central Bank under President Jayawardene's successor, Ranasinghe Premadasa.
35. As a percentage of GNP, foreign debt increased from 103 percent in 1976 to 164 percent in 1982. As a percentage of imports, the increase was from 19 percent to 36 percent.
36. Adjusted for inflation, the increase was nearly 85 percent.
37. Unless otherwise specified, all rates of change from year to year are based on inflation-adjusted values to make numbers more comparable.
38. Borrowing from domestic sources to cover deficits increased from 38 percent of total borrowing in 1978 to 70 percent in 1980. It was 66 percent in 1982. As under previous administrations, Sri Lanka's Central Bank was the principal source of "loans" to the government.
39. During the United Front's seven years in power, the rupee depreciated in value by about 53 percent.
40. In 1977 constant rupees. Allocations to cover deficits in the Sri Lanka Transport Board and National Railways grew from 185 million in 1977 to 398 million in 1982 (the increase in current values was from 185 million to 1.18 billion). The deflated value of 1982 defense budget was 191 million rupees (486 million rupees in current values).
41. For example, see de Silva 1984b: 39. Between 1974 and 1977, Sri Lanka imported only 1,000 bicycles. There were 12,000 imported in 1978 alone. In 1979 and 1980, bicycle imports were, respectively, 33,000 and 98,000.
42. See Alailima 1997: 156 for a discussion of major trends in Sri Lanka's economy between 1980 and 1990.
43. The more detailed figures were Colombo District—urban: 113.6; rural: 112.4. Vavuniya District—urban: 124.5; rural: 111.1. Polonnaruwa District—urban: 142.4; rural: 112.4. Anuradhapura District—urban: 127.0; rural: 102.2.
44. Data are based on Central Bank estimates for "government employees" and "workers in wages boards trades" provided in *Annual Reports* and *Reviews of the Economy*. Other discussions of open economy reforms' impact on wages offering generally similar views are provided in Lakshman 1997b, Lal and Rajapatirana 1989: 30ff., and Samarasinghe 1988: 58ff. A somewhat more favorable assessment is offered in Peiris 1993b.
45. Data on the rupee value of wages in different sectors are readily available, but the impact of inflation on wage earners' purchasing power is a matter on which assessments differ. Central Bank estimates of real wages, to which I have referred when they are available, provide the brightest picture. According to these estimates, several categories of employees realized modest net gains for 1977–82, although most lost ground between 1980 and 1982. Independently compar-

ing wage increases with rates of inflation, rather than using Central Bank real wages estimates, produces a less-bright picture. Between 1977 and 1982, prices rose by more than 250 percent in Sri Lanka. Wage increases to government employees lagged price increases by more than 15 percent. Increases to industrial/commercial workers lagged by more than 20 percent. Teachers' raises lagged by more than 25 percent. Only agricultural workers, starting from a lower base, gained ground.

46. The author reports a 10 percent decline in the share of total incomes from wages and salaries between 1969/70 and 1981 and an additional 13 percent decline between 1981 and 1985. Casual labor as a percentage of total employment grew from 25.6 percent in 1978/79 to 36.2 percent in 1981/82.

47. Essentially similar conclusions regarding shifts in income distribution resulting from open economy policies are found in Samarasinghe 1988: 58ff. and Karunatilake 1987: 227–228. In the comparisons that follow, I use 1973 rather than 1977 as a base point. Because consumer finance surveys do not typically correspond to electoral years, no data for 1977 are available. I make the assumption that much of the shift in income distribution between 1973 and 1981/82 did result from open economy policies. In any case, the social consequences of this shift in income distribution toward inequality were likely to manifest themselves in the latter years of J. R. Jayawardene's administration.

48. Data based on spending units were more realistic for poorer families because such families typically had more than one wage earner.

49. The specific numbers are as follows: tenth decile: 30.0 percent of all income in 1973 and 41.9 percent in 1981/82; ninth decile: 15.3 percent of all income in 1973 and 14.9 percent in 1981/82.

50. The author notes that in 1979, 7.3 million (50.3 percent of the population) met the official definition of poverty that qualified them to receive food stamps.

51. Most of these, Tambiah adds, were Sinhalese.

52. For example, in a study not reviewed by Lakshman, G. H. Peiris concludes that while income distribution has become more unequal since 1977, the evidence that this has made the poor worse off in absolute terms is not convincing (1993b: 261).

53. Detailed descriptions of the nine communities are given in chapter 6 of Ratnapala 1989: 110–212. They were located in the following districts: Kurunegala (2), Gampaha (2), Pollonaruwa, Badulla (2), and Colombo (2). Researchers lived in each village for three months or more, collecting detailed data about the demographic traits, education, skills, employment, and economic circumstances of each family. Fieldwork began in 1978 and was completed in 1979. Ratnapala reports that most community residents lived below the self-defined poverty line.

54. Illiteracy rates, in particular, showed the contrast between the population surveyed and Sri Lanka's population at large, with a reported illiteracy rate of less than 20 percent (United Nations Development Program 1991: 122, 126). Ratnapala's researchers found that many community residents had not attended school, even when schools were available. In one, more than half of eligible children were not in school. In some villages, they tested samples of individuals who reported they could read and found that many were functionally illiterate.

55. Samarasinghe notes, further, that food stamps formed at least 20 percent of many family incomes and 50 percent or more of total income for a smaller

number. Thus, a reduction in food stamp values by half represented a very serious drop in family purchasing power.

56. Nakamura et al. (1997: 263) reach a similar conclusion.

57. The impact of food subsidy reductions on nutrition was confirmed by the Sri Lanka government (Sri Lanka 1988: 13–16).

58. This estimate is based on my own calculations. Between 1970 and 1977, the labor force probably grew by only about 1 percent annually, adding roughly 300,000 new workers. On the other hand, unemployment probably increased by 6 or 7 percent. If one accepts these numbers as reasonable order-of-magnitude approximations, then more jobs were lost than were created. All who examine employment issues in Sri Lanka point to the uncertainties surrounding *any* estimates, but the conclusion is inescapable that job creation under the United Front government was not robust.

59. Data on labor force size do not coincide with government terms in office but are revealing of changes during the Jayawardene years. Between 1971 and 1981, the estimated annual growth in the labor force overall was 1.2 percent, while growth in the female labor force was 0.9 percent. Between 1981 and 1985/86, the corresponding figures were 4.1 percent and 9.8 percent!

60. This rather pessimistic report of unemployment reflects estimates that take into account a special survey based on an islandwide sampling completed by the author in 1985. The *Labor Force and Socio-Economic Survey, 1980–1981* reported an unemployment rate of 15.3 percent. The *Census of Population 1981* reported an unemployment rate of 17.9 percent. The *Consumer Finances and Socio-Economic Survey* reported an 11.9 percent unemployment rate.

61. The elite government schools such as Royal College (Colombo), St. Thomas College (Mt. Lavinia), Trinity College (Kandy), Ladies College (Colombo), and St. Bridget's College (Colombo) were all located in urban areas. Fee-paying institutions such as the Colombo International School taught classes almost exclusively in English.

62. Once again, this insurrection, which intensified in mid-1987, was organized by Rohana Wijeweera under the banner of the Janatha Vimukti Peramuna (People's Liberation Front).

63. Samarasinghe (n.d.) cites a study by Gunawardena and Nelson (1987), however, which concludes that in Kandy at least, Sinhalese businesses improved their relative economic position after 1977.

64. Gamini Dissanayake, Minister of Lands and Mahaweli Development and Lalith Athulathmudali, Minister of Trade and Shipping, were, along with Prime Minister Premadasa, members of the president's inner circle and responsible for top priority programs. Minister of Health Gamini Jayasuriya, who represented Homagama constituency east of Colombo, was a respected senior UNP politician, but he had less influence with the president.

65. A large number of experienced doctors, especially Tamil doctors, migrated to the West during this period.

66. Alailima's assessment is supported by a wealth of anecdotal information about the health care system that I have heard during numerous visits to Sri Lanka over many years.

67. Fee-paying "international schools" were permitted at the secondary level, and a small number of wealthy Sri Lankans, who were preparing their sons and daughters for admission to U.S. and British universities, sent their chil-

dren there. However, elite government-funded secondary schools—Royal, St. Thomas, Trinity, Ladies, St. Bridget's, and others—continued to offer top quality educations and were a more typical choice, even of wealthy parents who could afford to send their children anywhere.

68. The system was similar to the one that Prime Minister Bandaranaike's reforms had supplanted in 1972. The school structure was Primary Level—Kindergarten and Grades 1 through 5; Middle School—Grades 6 through 8; Secondary School, First Cycle—Grades 9 through 10 and Secondary School, Second Cycle—Grades 11 through 12. O-level examinations were administered upon completion of Grade 10 and determined eligibility for further secondary schooling. A-level examinations, administered upon completion of Grade 12, also served as university entrance examinations.

69. Quoted in Diyasena 1983: 108.

70. Sri Lanka was divided into 30 educational districts with somewhat different borders than the island's administrative districts.

71. Cited in Alailima 1997: 164.

72. Thirty percent of the places were allocated on the basis of islandwide merit. Half of the places were allocated on the basis of comparative scores within districts, with an additional 15 percent reserved for applicants from "underprivileged districts."

73. The Universities Act 16 of 1978.

74. Paradoxically, university admissions were perennially contentious political issues because Sri Lankans valued university education highly, but Sri Lanka ranked near the bottom of developing nations in higher education funding and opportunities.

75. Polytechnic institutes, junior technical institutes, and affiliated technical units offered full-time and part-time diploma and certificate courses in engineering, technical crafts, commerce, and agriculture.

76. A total of 534 undergraduates in their final year, out of 3,622, were surveyed. The study of recent graduates surveyed 1,206 individuals who had completed their degrees between 1974 and 1979.

3 An Open Economy in a Time of Intense Civil War: Sri Lanka, 1994–2000

Amita Shastri

President Chandrika Kumaratunga was swept to power at the head of a center-left coalition of parties in August 1994 in Sri Lanka on the basis of widespread hopes raised by her electoral promises. In competition with the opposing major party, the United National Party (UNP), she promised to work for economic "globalization with a human face" and to negotiate peace with militant Tamil opponents of the system—the Liberation Tigers of Tamil Eelam (LTTE, or simply the "Tigers"). This would allow her, she promised a war-weary public, to cut war expenditure and channel the "peace dividend" to development and growth. These hopes were rudely shattered when discussions with the Tigers broke down and fighting resumed in mid-1995. The civil war in Sri Lanka was then fought with an intensity that surpassed all previous phases of the conflict.

In this phase of the ethnic conflict, or "Eelam War III" as it has often been called, the state diverted substantial financial resources to fighting the war. There were open military hostilities in the north and east of the island and a state of constant vigilance maintained in the rest of the island. The media and opponents of the regime regularly pointed to the decline and shortfalls in the performance of the economy and darkly predicted worse times ahead with the center-left People's Alliance (PA) government in power.[1] Yet a review of the economic data show that Sri Lanka's economy continued to grow at rates which are surprising in the context of a civil war—an average rate of real growth of just over 5 percent in the six years 1995–2000, the first term of the PA regime. This is especially noteworthy given the increasing openness of Sri Lanka's economy in recent decades and the Southeast Asian economic crisis that hit the international currency and trading markets in 1997–98.

This raises two interesting sets of questions. The first pertain to the empirical issue of how the small island-state of Sri Lanka managed to grow economically despite the surrounding military and economic crisis. What were the strategies and policies the regime adopted to overcome the resource constraint posed by the war? Did these policies and strategies differ significantly from those followed by the regime of the UNP which had preceded it? And how successful were they?

—>The second set of questions relate to the impact the economy had on the society and ethnic relations. Did the economic changes that took place contribute to or exacerbate ethnic cleavages? Did the "open" economy play a role in worsening ethnic group relations on the island? Various politico-economic analyses have pointed to a variety of causes linked with the opening of the market by the UNP in 1977 as responsible for the upsurge of ethnic violence in 1983. The severe dislocations experienced by different economic strata due to market opening (Gunasinghe, this volume), the impact of unprecedented and lumpy inflows of foreign aid (Levy 1989; Herring 2001); generous patronage channeled to favored constituencies, increasing inequalities in the society dramatized by an increasing consumption gap, and a growing sense of relative deprivation in significant parts of the population which could be displaced through mobilization by unscrupulous politicians in the direction of ethnic scapegoating (Manor 1984; Tambiah 1986; Shastri 1997: 504–509)—these are the causes mentioned most often. Several of these causes are investigated in some detail for the first tenure of Junius Richard Jayawardene in another chapter (Richardson, this volume). Given the continuation of the "ethnic" civil war through the 1990s, did the same lines of causality continue to apply?

In this essay, I examine these questions focusing on the years 1994–2000. The first section describes the economic policies and strategies adopted by Kumaratunga's regime in the context of the war. The trends and shortfalls of the regime with regard to economic growth and welfare are analyzed in the following sections. As the pros and cons of the performance of the regime have been clouded by an abundance of opposition rhetoric, it seems useful in the analysis to compare the policies and performance of Kumaratunga's center-left coalition to the previous regime of the center-right UNP, which was in power between 1977 and 1994, to identify differences in policy and performance between the two.[2] The last part of the article discusses the changes that took place in the economy under Kumaratunga with a view to assessing how they impacted ethnic relations on the island during this period.

The impact that trade and war have on states is taken as almost axiomatic in the field of international relations. The analysis in this chapter of the experience of Sri Lanka during this time highlights the tremendous impact that the forces of globalization have had on this small island economy and the manner in which these changes have been articulated in new ways into various aspects of the country's civil war. Along lines reminiscent of center-left regimes in advanced industrial states pressed by globalization, but even more impacted by external factors, Kumaratunga's regime was compelled to downgrade the importance of labor in the coalition under pressure from abroad. As I show below, her government continued on the path of economic opening launched by the center-right UNP in 1977. In their specifics, however, the policies of the People's Alliance were more in keeping with the "second phase" of economic opening followed by her predecessor, President Ranasinghe Premadasa, rather than the earlier profligate one of his predecessor, Jayawardene. A decline in foreign aid flows under Kumaratunga, as under Premadasa, compelled a greater emphasis on efficiency and downsizing the economic role of the government even while it propelled the economy toward greater global interdependence and growth. As identified below, these global linkages became enmeshed in the economics of the island and its internal ethnic conflict in ways that fueled the conflict and generated serious concern about the longer-term prospect.

Economic Policies and Strategies

In the elections of 1994, to differentiate her coalition's orientation from the ruling UNP, President Kumaratunga promised the people "globalization with a human face" if voted to power. In doing this, her center-left coalition of five parties accepted the direction of economic policy that had been instituted by the UNP in the preceding years, but sought to reshape policy to fulfill the basic needs of a broader segment of the population.

On coming to power, President Kumaratunga promised the attentive public that her government, which included the two leftist parties, the Lanka Sama Samaja Party (LSSP) and the Communist Party (CP), would not overturn the open economy policies of the previous UNP regime. She gave assurances to business that her government was committed to building a strong economy within the market framework in which both domestic and foreign capital would serve as engines of growth. In a break with the policies of past regimes led by the Sri Lanka Freedom Party (SLFP), she clarified that her government had no plans to nationalize or expropriate private property, that it would honor all bilateral investment protection agreements and relevant international treaties, and that there would be no restrictions placed on repatriation of dividends and capital.

However, international and domestic big capital interests remained skeptical of her assurances and were slow in resuming investment. The situation was not helped by the numerous strikes that the trade unions who had supported the PA launched to demand pay increases, after having been suppressed over the previous 17 years by the UNP regime. Led by the two leftist parties, the unions demanded the institutionalization of the "workers' charter" that had been promised before the election. Some 200 labor disputes demanded resolution in 1995 alone, with several of them turning violent and taking employers hostage.[3]

With both capital and labor represented within the ruling PA coalition, it was subject to acute tensions in its first two years. The president, her deputy finance minister G. L. Pieris, and certain segments of the SLFP were more pragmatic in their approach to economic issues in the context of an open economy and liberalization. Ranged against them were the two leftist parties and segments of the president's own party, including Kumaratunga's mother and prime minister, Mrs. Sirimavo Bandaranaike, who remained committed to socialist ideas.[4] The leftist parties particularly emphasized the need to protect the wages and conditions of work for labor in the course of globalization. There was initially an attempt to forge a compact on democratic-socialist lines, as in the corporatist societies of northern and western Europe, between the government, capital, and labor. This was to be spelled out in the form of a "workers' charter." Efforts to reach agreement, however, broke down due to differences about the principles on which the charter would be based. Representatives of workers argued that raises in pay should be linked to inflation while employers argued for pay raises to be linked to increased productivity.[5] The leftist parties also remained opposed to the privatization of public-sector enterprises that was being urged by the IMF and World Bank. These policy disputes caused a decline in investor confidence, a low inflow of foreign capital, and a drop in the level of activity in the economy.

To compound the difficulties faced by the leadership, the IMF proved unwilling to disburse the final installment of $87 million of Enhanced Structural Adjustment Facility (ESAF) funds, which it feared would be used by the PA to fulfill its consumerist electoral pledges made to win popular support. Consequently, the more generous of these pledges promising an increased allocation of funds to the poor and unemployed had to be cut back. Still, the new government was able to increase some consumer subsidies and refurbish President Premadasa's Janasaviya welfare and employment program as the new Samurdhi program that would cover one-third of the country's population. It was anticipated that 1.1 million families would receive sums ranging from SL Rs. 500 to 1,500 per month to help supplement their incomes.[6]

Faced with a crunch in resources created by the war and declining rates of growth and investment, Kumaratunga was compelled to shift the emphasis of her regime more clearly to the right in a pro-business and management direction in late 1996.[7] She reshuffled her cabinet and proceeded to follow the advice of the IMF and allied international actors more closely, earning their approval and additional ESAF funds in two tranches. In the following period, her government sought to encourage a more market-oriented pattern of economic growth even while it attempted to protect the economic system from the adverse effects of the international market. It reduced tax rates and set up a simplified tariff and tax structure. In particular, it introduced a general sales tax (GST) to replace a series of indirect taxes which had had a cascading effect on the rest of the economy. It offered attractive fiscal incentives, including tax holidays and concessionary rates of tax for 15–20 years to foreign and domestic investors. It carried out reforms in the financial sector to improve its efficiency and strength, provided greater operational autonomy to state-owned banks, and set up a more flexible system to manage the exchange rate. The process of debt management was made more market oriented. It stepped up privatization to increase the efficiency of the economy as well as to help ameliorate the budget deficits. Toward this end, it carried out the privatization of publicly owned gas, plantations, telecommunications, and airline units. It also sought to rationalize the welfare program and tax luxury goods.

The regime was compelled to undertake further belt-tightening measures with the escalation of the war in the year 2000. The budget that had been passed belatedly in February, after the presidential election, had optimistically visualized that the costs of the war would be manageable and helped by remittances from abroad. It had projected a growth rate of 5 percent, with inflation running below 8 percent, and allocated SL Rs. 52.4 billion ($706 million) for defense expenditure. To help pay for this, the national security levy on all goods and services had been raised from 5.5 percent to 6.5 percent. The government had cut consumer subsidies further and raised the price of diesel and liquefied gas, transport fares, electricity, water, and telephone service (Economist 2000; AFP 2000a). Yet these proved insufficient. Following on the heels of the failure of the government to evolve a new constitutional consensus with the opposition UNP and to open channels of communication with the Tigers, there was a sharp escalation of the conflict on April 22, 2000, when the LTTE captured the military base in Elephant Pass and raised the possibility of taking over the Jaffna peninsula once again. The government moved to speedily purchase numerous sophisticated arms and equipment to repel the threat. It also got a $100 million trade loan from its neighbor, India. In July, the parliament approved new revenue measures, such as taxes on liquor and tobacco, to raise SL Rs. 24 billion. In early August, supplementary estimates for an additional SL Rs. 28 billion ($356 million) were rushed through for urgent military requirements. The shortfalls in the revenue raised to pay for this expenditure was largely to be financed by domestic borrowing.

Defense spending consequently surged to over 6.1 percent of GDP (AFP 2000), a level of spending which was closer to that of 1995 and 1996 at the onset of Eelam War III. The increased expenditure inevitably increased the budget deficit, encouraged inflation, and adversely affected economic growth.

This surge in spending was accompanied by other expenditures undertaken by the government to improve its electoral prospects in the parliamentary elections that were due in November 2000. In late July, the government decided to raise the pay of nearly 2 million employees in the private sector by SL Rs. 400. By mid-August, other supplementary measures of SL Rs. 8.6 billion were approved by the government to increase the allowances of public servants, pensioners, Samurdhi beneficiaries (welfare recipients), and graduate trainees, as well as to increase the fertilizer subsidy and unforeseen defense expenditures (Kannangara 2000; Ladduwahetty 2000).

Economic Achievements

The economic policies of the PA worked to produce numerous noteworthy results—several of them surprisingly positive. Despite the economic constraints, the economy did better in many respects than during the first period of UNP rule under Jayawardene, but not as well as under his successor, Ranasinghe Premadasa.

Despite the war, the economy continued to demonstrate significant real growth. It grew at an average rate of 5.1 percent overall, a figure which compares favorably with the average for the decade of 1980–89 of 4.2 percent when Jayawardene was in power (Table 3.1). It falls slightly short of the growth generated in the more stable period under President Premadasa between 1990 and 1994 of 5.3 percent when the economy experienced significant expansion after the JVP rebellion had been forcibly put down and the fighting in the northeast was being conducted at a lower pitch. The PA average also compares very favorably with the average growth of the developing countries of 3.3 percent. However, it falls far short of the rate which the regime had been aiming for, of at least 8 percent per annum, a level estimated to be necessary if Sri Lanka's youth unemployment problem was to be eliminated. The overall growth of the population meanwhile was at a barely re-placeable level of 1.1–1.4 percent per annum.

This level of economic growth was not maintained primarily through a generous inflow of foreign assistance, as had been the case under the UNP. Indeed, the PA was a less favored recipient of foreign aid than the UNP had been. Compared to an average sum equivalent to 13.3 percent of GDP that came in as foreign assistance in the 1980s, a figure which fell to 10.3 percent in the first half of the 1990s, the level of foreign aid under Kumaratunga dropped further to average 8.5 percent between 1995 to 2000.

Yet it is noteworthy that, in proportionate terms, gross domestic investment in Sri Lanka did not fall commensurately. It had fallen from the higher level of 26.2 percent of GDP in the 1980s to 24.1 percent in the first half of the 1990s from which it surprisingly picked up to average 25.8 percent between 1995 and 2000—so that while it was lower than much of the Jayawardene period (a period notably flush with foreign funds), it compares quite favorably with the more austere Premadasa period.

A study of the data shows that this investment was financed primarily from a higher level of domestic savings generated by the economy. Gross domestic savings had risen from 12.9 percent of GDP in the 1980s to 14.4 percent in the early 1990s. These rose further to average 17.3 percent between 1995 and 2000 (see Table 3.1). It is noteworthy that the overwhelming proportion of these savings were generated by the national private sector, largely through the high inflows of private remittances from abroad. It is also worth noting that the bulk of domestic investment came from domestic private investors. The Central Bank of Sri Lanka reported in 2000 that 89 percent of the total investment was private, underlining the growing role of the private sector in the economy (Central Bank 2000: 4, 21).[8]

Government Revenue and Expenditure

Along with a drop in foreign funds and assistance, there was pressure by international agencies like the IMF for the government to engage in more effective budgetary and financial management to encourage growth. The PA regime seems to have followed this advice after a reluctant start. In contrast to the UNP regime under Jayawardene but similar to the period under Premadasa, this was largely done through the maintenance of a tight fiscal and monetary policy to gain greater control over prices and to maintain an effective real devaluation rate. In doing so, the PA regime sought to avoid the central pitfall of the UNP regime's economic policy in the 1980s of spawning an overheated economy through a very high level of public spending, runaway inflation, and speculation (Levy 1989; White and Wignaraja 1992; Shastri 1997). This was an important and favorable development made possible by improved monetary controls and fiscal discipline, by moving toward a more rationalized tax and tariff structure, increased agricultural production, and the positive effect of low world market prices on import items. As a result, for instance, the Colombo Consumers Price Index (CCPI), a commonly used measure of inflation, which rose at an average rate of 12.8 percent annually in the 1980s

Table 3.1. Economic Indicators

	1980–89 avg.	1990–94 avg.	1995	1996	1997	1998	1999	2000	1995–2000 avg.
GDP growth (real) (at factor cost, constant prices, % change)	4.2	5.3	5.5	3.8	6.3	4.7	4.3	6.0	5.1
GNP growth (real) (constant prices, % change)			6.0	3.2	6.8	4.6	3.8	5.8	5.0
Population growth (% change)		1.1	1.1	1.1	1.2	1.3	1.5	1.4	1.3
Colombo consumers price index (1952 = 100) (% change)	12.8	13.1	7.7	15.9	9.6	9.4	4.7	6.2	8.9
Unemployment rate (%)	n/a	14.4	12.3	11.3	10.5	9.5	8.9	7.6	10.0
as percent of GDP									
Gross domestic investment	26.2	24.1	25.7	24.2	24.4	25.1	27.3	28.0	25.8
Gross domestic savings	12.9	14.4	15.3	15.3	17.3	19.1	19.5	17.4	17.3
Foreign savings*	13.3	10.3	10.4	8.9	7.1	6.0	7.8	10.7	8.5
Balance of payments, current acct	-8.1	-6.3	-6.0	-4.9	-2.6	-1.4	-3.6	-6.4	-4.2
Budget, current acct	2.7	-1.6	-2.7	-3.8	-2.2	-2.4	-1.0	-3.4	-2.6
Budget, overall balance	-12.4	-9.8	-10.1	-9.4	-7.9	-9.2	-7.5	-9.9	-9.0
Public debt			93.3	92.2	85.8	90.8	95.1	96.9	

Note: *Net import of goods and non–factor services.
Source: Central Bank of Sri Lanka, Annual Reports.

and 13.1 percent in the early 1990s, rose more slowly, by about 8.9 percent every year between 1995 and 2000.[9] At the same time, the Sri Lankan rupee depreciated more moderately. As against the annual depreciation of 9.1 percent which was the norm in the 1980s, the Sri Lankan rupee fell at the rate of about 8 percent per year under the PA. This was, however, higher than the figure of the Premadasa years of the early 1990s when it fell by 4.4 percent.

The overall budgetary deficits the PA ran were also lower than those which had been the norm under the UNP. In contrast to overall deficits which were equal to 12.4 percent of the GDP in the 1980s and 9.8 percent between 1990 and 1994, the PA's deficits averaged 9.9 percent between 1995 and 2000. This was despite the higher deficits it ran on the current account, largely due to the war (see below). At the same time, it is important to note that it could only do so *and* follow a path of greater budgetary discipline by implementing cuts in subsidies and at the expense of overall long-term capital and development expenditures, as pointed out below.

In keeping with the PA's new emphasis on pro-market reforms, the overall weight of the state in the economy was reduced. This is evident in both the size of the revenue acquired by the government and the level of expenditure incurred by it. While this was a trend which was begun under Premadasa (Shastri 1997), it continued to be evident under the PA. Measured as a proportion of the GDP, the revenue raised by the government, which had declined from levels of 22.3 percent in 1985 to 20.4 percent in 1995, fell further to 16.8 percent by 2000. Expenditure and net lending by the government, which had been brought down from 41.8 percent of GDP in 1980 to 30.5 percent in 1995, was brought down further to 26.7 percent in 2000 (Table 3.2).

Within the public expenditure and lending categories, current expenditure levels were generally held down, but defense spending rose overall. Current expenditure, which was equal to 22.3 percent of GDP in 1990 and 21.9 percent in 1994, rose to 23.1 percent in 1995 but was then brought down to 18.7 percent by 1999. Mainly due to increased defense spending, it rose up to 20.3 percent of GDP the following year. Expenditure on security, which had been as low as 1.3 percent in 1980 and had fluctuated somewhat above 4 percent for much of the 1980s and early 1990s (it was 4.6 percent in 1994), averaged 5.4 percent of GDP under Kumaratunga. Payment of interest on debt, a large proportion of which had been incurred under the UNP in the 1980s, was equal to another 5.4–6.4 percent of GDP between 1995 and 2000. Interest repayments, which had been as low as 3.4 percent in 1980, had reached their highest levels with debt maturation under Premadasa—being equal, for example, to 6.4 percent and 6.6 percent of GDP in 1990 and 1994, respectively. Continuing the emphasis on better financial management and effort to retire old debts which had been insisted on by the IMF during the Premadasa period, interest payments averaged 5.8 percent under the PA. As a result, in what was a positive development, medium-term and long-term debt came to dominate in Sri Lanka's liabilities under Kumaratunga, equal to 94 percent of its total debt.[10] Nondefense wage expenditures remained much the same proportionate to GDP under the PA, but subsidies and transfers were cut from 6.1 percent of GDP in 1995 to 4.2 percent by 2000. This was also a policy which had been started under Premadasa and which stood in contrast with the significantly higher figure of 8.4 percent of GDP, which had been characteristic of Jayawardene's regime in 1980.

Capital expenditure and net lending declined because of the war. Capital expenditure and net lending, which had been cut to 7.5 percent by 1994 (Table 3.2), were cut further to average 6.4 percent for the six years under the PA. This situation stands in dramatic contrast to the phenomenal years of J. R. Jayawardene's first term when capital expenditures (including large construction projects) ranged as high as 23.3 percent of GDP, as they did in 1980. Public investments, acquisition of real assets, and capital transfers were all correspondingly cut from the much higher levels characteristic of the early 1980s.

The administration sought to curb budget deficits, again continuing a trend established under Premadasa. The overall budget deficit exclusive of foreign grants and proceeds earned from privatization averaged 9 percent between 1995 and 2000. Contrast this with the years of high living during the first term of Jayawardene when budget deficits had ranged as high as 22.2 percent of GDP in 1980. Still, as the Central Bank of Sri Lanka noted, in comparative developmental terms, the fiscal deficit remained too high. In 1999, for instance, while Sri Lanka had a budget deficit equal to 7.6 percent of its GDP, the developing countries *as a whole* averaged 4.4 percent (Central Bank 1999: 23).

The budget deficits were to be covered by financing from foreign and domestic sources, both of which were available at far lower levels than had been true in the early 1980s. Foreign financing, which had amounted to 9.2 percent of GDP in 1980 but had been cut to 5.7 percent by 1990 and 3.5 percent in 1994, was further cut to average 1.9 percent in the years 1995–2000. Within this, the proportion of public long-term capital inflows declined and that of long-term private inflows increased—again a trend begun under Premadasa and in keeping with central long-term IMF objectives and interests of developed capitalist states to make economies such as Sri Lanka's more market dependent and integrated with the circuits of private international capital.

Overall, the government's total wage bill was maintained at levels between 5 and 5.5 percent of GDP. Gross defense expenditure (which included the settlement of deferred payments) averaged 5.8 percent in the PA's six years. It rose from 4.6 percent in 1994 to 6.5 percent in 1995 when Eelam War III broke out. This increased expenditure was largely covered by the "national security levy," which was increased from 3.5 percent to 4.5 percent of GDP in late 1995, to 5.5 percent in 1999, and further to 6.5 percent in 2000, as well as by increases in the excise tax on cigarettes and hard liquor. The diversion of resources to the war severely restricted the possibilities for the mobilization of financial resources by the government for investment in the economic and social infrastructure to increase productivity and growth in the longer term.

As a result of the PA's economic policies, the sectoral changes in the economy that had been initiated by the UNP's liberalization policy continued apace. The importance of the agricultural sector in the GDP continued to fall—from 30.3 percent in 1978 to 19.4 percent in 2000—even while 40 percent of the population remained employed in agriculture. Despite all claims that the purpose of opening

Table 3.2. Summary of Fiscal Operations as a Percentage of GDP

Item	1980	1985	1990	1994	1995	1996	1997	1998	1999	2000[a]
1 Revenue	19.6	22.3	21.1	19.0	20.4	19.0	18.5	17.2	17.7	16.8
2 Expenditure and net lending	41.8	34.1	31.0	29.5	30.5	28.5	26.4	26.3	25.2	26.7
2.1 Current expenditure	18.5	20.1	22.3	21.9	23.1	22.8	20.7	19.6	18.7	20.3
2.1.1 Security	1.3	4.5	4.1	4.6	6.5	5.8	5.1	5.0	4.4	5.6
2.1.2 Interest	3.4	4.6	6.4	6.6	5.7	6.4	6.2	5.4	5.6	5.7
2.1.3 Wages[b]	4.5	3.6	3.9	3.1	3.4	3.3	3.1	3.0	3.0	3.2
2.1.4 Subsidies and transfers	8.4	5.5	6.5	5.9	6.1	6.0	5.1	4.6	4.2	4.2
2.1.5 Others	0.9	1.9	1.4	1.8	1.4	1.3	1.3	1.6	1.4	1.6
2.2 Capital and net lending	23.3	13.9	8.7	7.5	7.4	5.7	5.7	6.7	6.5	6.5
2.2.1 Public investments	18.5	13.8	8.3	7.0	7.9	6.0	5.8	6.7	6.5	6.4
Acquisition of real assets	7.9	4.5	3.7	2.9	3.4	2.7	2.9	3.2	3.0	2.6
Capital transfers	9.4	8.6	2.3	2.4	2.9	2.2	2.1	2.2	2.5	2.8
On lending	1.2	0.6	2.2	1.7	1.7	1.1	0.8	1.4	1.0	1.1
2.2.2 Other	4.7	0.2	0.4	0.6	-0.5	-0.3	-0.1	—	—	0.1
Restructuring cost	0.0	0.0	0.0	0.6	0.5	0.0	0.2	0.4	0.4	0.3
Others	4.7	0.2	0.4	-0.1	-1.0	-0.3	-0.3	-0.3	-0.4	-0.2
3 Current account balance	1.1	2.2	-1.2	-2.9	-2.7	-3.8	-2.2	-2.4	-1.0	-3.4

4 Overall deficit before grants and excluding privatization	-22.2	-11.7	-9.9	-10.5	-10.1	-9.4	-7.9	-9.2	-7.5	-9.9
5 Financing	22.2	11.7	9.9	10.5	10.1	9.4	7.9	9.2	7.5	9.9
5.1 Foreign financing	9.2	6.4	5.7	3.5	4.5	2.3	1.9	1.7	0.7	0.4
5.1.1 Loans	5.3	4.4	3.6	2.0	3.2	1.3	1.1	1.0	0.1	0.0
5.1.2 Grants	3.5	2.0	2.1	1.4	1.4	1.0	0.8	0.7	0.6	0.4
5.2 Domestic financing	13.0	5.3	4.2	6.5	5.1	6.5	3.4	7.1	6.8	9.4
5.2.1 Banks	9.8	2.9	0.1	0.2	1.1	1.7	-0.2	1.9	2.4	4.3
5.3 Privatization	0.0	0.0	0.0	0.5	0.4	0.6	2.5	0.4	—	—
Memorandum items:										
Total wage bill	5.0	4.2	4.9	5.1	5.2	5.0	5.0	5.3	5.3	5.5
Gross defense expenditure [c]	1.3	4.5	4.1	4.6	6.5	6.0	5.4	5.6	4.9	6.1

Source: Central Bank of Sri Lanka, *Annual Reports.*
[a] Provisional.
[b] Excluding those paid to defense staff.
[c] Including settlement of deferred payments.

Table 3.3. Sectoral Composition of the Economy as Percentage of
GDP at Current Factor Cost Prices

Sector	1978	1988	1998	2000
Agriculture, forestry, and fishing	30.3	26.3	21.1	19.4
Mining and quarrying	2.2	2.7	1.9	1.9
Manufacturing	18.4	15.4	16.5	16.8
Construction	4.7	7.3	7.6	7.3
Services	44.4	48.3	52.9	54.6
Of which: Transport, storage, and communication	10.7	10.8	11.1	11.7
Wholesale and retail trading	19.7	19.9	21.5	22.6
Banking, insurance, real estate	2.2	4.5	7.6	8.1
Ownership of dwellings	3.7	2.6	1.9	1.8
Public administration and defense	3.6	5.4	5.3	5.2
GDP	100	100	100	100
Net factor income from abroad	−0.6	−2.6	−1.3	−2.0
GNP	99.4	97.4	98.7	98.0

Source: Central Bank of Sri Lanka, *Annual Reports.*

the economy was to industrialize, the share of manufacturing in GDP, which had fallen from 18.4 percent in 1978 to 15.4 percent by 1988 (Table 3.3), rose only slightly to 16.8 percent by 2000. Instead, the major share of growth was experienced by the services sector—a sector which had grown from 44.4 percent in 1978 to 48.3 percent by 1988 and which grew further to 54.6 percent by 2000. Within this sector, the largest growth was experienced by the banking, insurance, and real estate sector, which grew from 2.2 percent of the GDP to 8.1 percent over the two decades.

Viewed in structural terms, the Sri Lankan economy continued to go through a process of transformation by which it became more closely integrated into the global market, which provided the momentum for its growth. This was manifestly evident in 2000 when, despite the escalation of the war and its impact on the state budget, the economy grew at 6 percent due to a favorable growth trajectory in the international market (Central Bank 2000: 1).

Mass Welfare

How well did the regime protect the interests of the people? In the popular oppositional rhetoric of the media and critics of the regime, it was frequently alleged that the costs of the war were overwhelming, the cost of living had "gone through the roof," and corruption (especially in arms procurement) and incompetence within the government were rampant. While these allegations were true to a point, the aggregate quantitative information available shows that the situation was not as negative as the opposition made it out to be.

Seeking to protect its political interests and assert a more independent position, initially the regime did not consistently follow the advice of powerful international actors. For a while its actions even helped partly to keep inflation in check in a manner keenly disapproved of by the IMF. Following up on promises made in the 1994 election, the government lowered the price of bread, flour, diesel fuel, and fertilizer when it came to power.[11] However, it was hard put to maintain these subsidies once defense expenditures escalated with resumption of the war, and it was compelled to remove the subsidies after 1997.

Due to the tighter economic policy of the government, as mentioned earlier, there was a lower rate of inflation under the PA than in the 1980s or early 1990s of about 9 percent per year. Indeed, as Table 3.1 indicates, consumer prices seem to have increased more slowly in this period (see also Central Bank 1999: 10, chart 1.5). This was most true for clothing but least so for food—a situation which had the most deleterious effect on the lower socioeconomic strata of society in whose budget food counts for a greater proportion of family expenditure.

According to the Central Bank, while wages rose in nominal terms during this period, they declined slightly in real terms (Central Bank 1999: 10, chart 1.6). The lack of improvement in the plight of workers was a source of dissatisfaction to the leftist parties within the ruling coalition. Still, it was better than the time under the UNP when the real wages of several categories of workers had declined markedly (Shastri 1997: 501).

It is particularly noteworthy that despite the lower level of activity in the economy compared with the early 1990s, the unemployment rate continued to fall. It dropped from the average characteristic for 1990–94 of 14.4 percent of the workforce to 12.3 percent in 1995 and further down to 7.6 percent in 2000. This occurred largely due to the new open and militarized economy, which had already come into being under the previous UNP regime (Shastri 1997: 499–500).

Given the climate of war and fearing instability, foreign investors remained reluctant to come in, and there was limited capital investment by the government. Instead, the three major avenues of employment which proved to be most important were export manufacturing, the armed services, and domestic work abroad. Two-thirds of the jobs gained at home were in the export manufacturing sector, dominated by the garments industry, to which young women gravitated in large numbers (Lynch, this volume). The major avenue of employment for young men was perforce the armed forces (Gamburd, this volume). And, lacking employment opportunities at home, young unemployed women migrated in even larger numbers as domestic workers to the Gulf countries and even to Southeast Asia. According to the Central Bank report for 1999, due to the growth of both the public sector (mainly the army) and the private sector, 85,000–95,000 jobs were created within the country, but double that number of Sri Lankans, about 178,000, departed for jobs abroad (Central Bank 1999: 11).

Although unemployment was declining, it remained highest among the youth. Two-thirds of those who were unemployed were between ages 20 and 29, and the proportion of those unemployed increased by level of education. In political terms, this contributed to the resurgence of the nationalistic JVP, which focused renewed criticism on the government.

Anecdotal evidence based on personal observations and discussions as well as the press suggests that in the continuing conditions of war the situation deteriorated for a large number of Sri Lankans. Many of the goods commonly mentioned by critics—such as diesel fuel, transport fares, electricity rates, tobacco, bread, and sugar—were precisely the ones on which the government had cut subsidies.[12] Doubtless, the rise in the prices of these goods contributed to the more general increase in prices across the board and a declining popularity of the regime.[13]

The Cost of War

The story of the overall growth masks the cost the war had for the society and its economy. While it is not possible to quantify with precision the overall cost of the war during this period separately from the preceding period, in cumulative terms the cost of war had been massive for the country as a whole. On the basis of the limited data that are available, one can get some idea of the immense cost in the form of death and destruction that has been suffered by the country and its people.

Reported in an almost routine fashion, death and displacement of persons continued to undermine society. More than 60,000 Sri Lankans were killed in the war between 1983 and December 2000.[14] Close to 20,000 may have been killed in the six years under the PA. In addition, according to one source, some 493,000 were displaced in the north and east by the fighting in the two years after December 1994 alone. Between 1983 and December 1996, 1,017,000 Sri Lankans were displaced by the war (National Peace Council 1998: 13). It is hard to imagine the impact that this loss of life and displacement of persons has had on the fabric of society and on everyday social and cultural relations.

The search for security and employment acquired its own compulsions in these circumstances. Official counts estimated that around a quarter of a million Sri Lankans emigrated after 1983, with India receiving 150,000 and Europe and North America receiving 90,000.[15] Seeking opportunities for employment and security, more than half a million Sri Lankans had migrated to work in the Middle East by 1995. As these statistics cited by the Central Bank indicate, migration abroad remained the leading avenue for employment throughout the war.

Property and assets destroyed or damaged by the war constitute another staggering cost. The total cost of replacement and repair of private property and infrastructure was estimated conservatively to be SL Rs. 75 billion in 1995 (National Peace Council 1998: 18). Further damage was caused after that by the actions of the armed forces and the rebels. For instance, the damage caused by the explosion at the Central Bank of Sri Lanka alone was estimated to be worth SL Rs. 1.85 billion (National Peace Council 1998: 13).

Each major incidence of violence and damage brought lost productivity and investment, decline in investor confidence (especially of foreign investors), and a drop in tourism. The number of tourists, for instance, reached a peak figure of 407,000 in 1994 (itself a peak reached again only after 1982), but dropped once more to 305,000 in 1997 due to the resumed conflict (National Peace Council 1998: 20).

The larger real cost of the war has to be calculated in terms of the opportunities foregone by all Sri Lankans since 1983. Sri Lanka attained the status of a low-middle-income country (like Philippines, Indonesia, Thailand, and China), when its average per capita income rose to $753 in 1996. The Central Bank calculated that had there been no conflict, Sri Lanka's annual investment would have been 2–3 percent higher per year than it has been due to the fact that higher private investment, both domestic and foreign, as well as more public investment would have been forthcoming.[16] It was estimated that this higher level of growth over the previous 16 years of the conflict would have raised Sri Lanka from a low-income country to low-middle-income status by 1994, with a per capita income approximating $800 in 1994 and $1,200 in 1999, rather than $829 in 1999, as proved to be the case. In concrete terms this would have meant that the monthly average income of Sri Lankans in 1999 would have been SL Rs. 7,040 rather than the sum of SL Rs. 4,875 that it attained (Central Bank 1999: 22).

The opportunities lost in these years gain an added edge when measured in international comparative terms. In contrast to the developing economies of Asia (including China and India), which grew at an average rate of 6.9, 9.1, and 6 percent per year in 1982–91, 1992–96, and 1999, the Sri Lankan economy grew only at 4.2, 5.2, and 4.3 percent in the three periods. Thus, while in relative terms the Kumaratunga regime did no worse than the earlier UNP regimes and indeed, if anything, seems to have done better, given the larger international context (as measured by the average performance of the other developing economies), the situation still evoked deep concern. As the Central Bank urged, "These approximate figures underscore the paramount need to take all steps to end the senseless conflict. If allowed to continue, the conflict could seriously drain the resources and energies of the people and marginalize the country in the international community" (Central Bank 1999: 22).

The Economy and Ethnic Conflict

What impact did the economy have on ethnic relations during this civil war? Did economic changes contribute to or exacerbate ethnic cleavages?

As seen above, while all regimes after 1977 had been moving toward a more open market economy, the changes that took place under Kumaratunga were different from the process of transition launched by Jayawardene. If we accept the arguments made in earlier analyses about the causal relationships between the opening of the market by the UNP in 1977 and the ethnic violence that erupted in 1977, 1981, and 1983, we find those conditions did not occur in the 1990s. The factors of the severe dislocations experienced by different economic strata caused by market opening, the impact of unprecedented and lumpy inflows of foreign aid, generous patronage to favored constituencies, increasing inequalities of the society dramatized by an increasing consumption gap, and the growing sense of relative

1977 NOT 1990s

deprivation in significant parts of the population which could be displaced through mobilization by unscrupulous politicians in the direction of ethnic scapegoating are not as applicable to the 1990s.

In large part this would be because many of the changes initiated by the earlier regime, involving a radical switch to a pecuniary moral economy and subject to popular resistance at the time, had effectively been made and their impact had been broadly accepted. Kumaratunga's regime in the late 1990s carried out policies and faced an economic conjuncture that was similar to Premadasa's but very different from Jayawardene's. It continued to reduce the state's role in the economy and sought to build up the state's capacity to manage and regulate the economy better. The process of privatization encouraged by external agencies was accompanied by a constrained resource situation created by the decline in foreign aid and investment as well as the war. The sharpening of disparities in income and consumption was slower in pace, and migration abroad to the Gulf for employment and to raise one's consumption had emerged as an option that was available to and perforce accepted by a wider segment of the population.

In contrast to the excesses of the UNP's arbitrary use of political power, the PA regime adhered more closely to democratic norms and did not engage in belligerent rhetoric directed against the minority communities. This made for a situation in which the regime was generally perceived as one with a better record of governance than the preceding UNP. Indeed, with the market increasingly becoming the arbiter of individual economic fortunes, the contracting role played by the state in the nonmilitary economic realm, as well as the efforts by the regime to promote a package of constitutional reforms that would treat members of all communities in a fair manner, there were fewer occasions for allegations of ethnic partisanship to be raised.[17]

It is encouraging that both the government and the opposition seemed to have learned from the past. From its position in the opposition, the UNP also expressed itself with greater restraint on ethnic issues. To the degree that political rhetoric engaged in by elites provides ideological structures of meaning to the understanding of mass publics, mobilizing them to political action, the situation under Kumaratunga was a clear improvement on the past. This period contrasted sharply with the Jayawardene period.

Yet the economic changes had become enmeshed with the ethnic cleavages and the war. The increased openness of the Sri Lankan economy provided new sources of funds to fuel the armed conflict. The increasing dependence of the economy on the international market for growth and employment highlighted the fact that as long as the global economy was growing, the national economy could also continue to grow *despite* the war. Indeed, labor remittances from abroad had emerged to constitute important sources not only of foreign exchange but also of domestic investment, enabling the government in turn to mobilize and channel more revenues for the war effort. On the opposing side, the LTTE was also funded by its own networks and resources from abroad: voluntary or involuntary donations by expatriates, affiliated businesses, clandestine arms shipments, and allegedly the drug trade (Gunaratna 1997: 23–31). As long as these conditions obtained, lacking a political solution to the conflict, it was difficult to envisage an early end to the war due to a lack of resources on either side.

Aggregate data illuminate important trends but in a simplified form. The story of the overall growth of the Sri Lankan economy was, in essence, the story of the island's relatively more stable southwest. Although hurt by the periodic bombings and suicide attacks of the Tigers, the low inflow of foreign investment, and the lack of public capital investment, the damage suffered by the southwest did not approach the death and devastation suffered by large parts of the north and east, especially the Jaffna peninsula, where much of the fighting occurred. Large areas of the northeast had been laid waste.[18] While no specific figures can be given showing the ethnic breakdown of those affected, large numbers of those killed or displaced came from this region and consequently belonged to the minority communities (Tamil and Muslim). Teenagers and children had been drafted by the LTTE to fight or perform other functions in the war. Seeking to flee the depredations of both sides, an overwhelming number of emigrants to the developed Western countries and to India were drawn from the minority Sri Lankan Tamil population in this region. In the uncertain economic and military climate, little productive activity was possible (Kelegama 1999: 76–77). Most of the population remaining there survived on checks sent by relatives living elsewhere or on doles of food and meager essential supplies from the government or international nongovernmental organizations. It remains to be seen what impact these developments would have on the minority population in the northeast.[19]

There were also reports of the growth of a "war economy" on the island, which had created groups who had a vested interest in continuing the war. These ranged from reports of commissions and kickbacks being earned in high places in the award of defense contracts and arms purchases to illicit profiteering by official and private interests who were accused of trading at exorbitant prices goods that were in short supply in the war zone of the northeast (Rajasingham-Senanayake 1999). While it would be an overstatement to say that the state and society were captive to such interests and their designs to continue the war for their private benefit, there is no doubt that their activities increased the harsh burdens of the war and promoted cynicism and alienation toward the regime.

How far the cleavages that defined the conflict by the close of the millennium were "ethnic" in character is an elusive question. As a closer look at local alignments reveals, the politics of representation manifested as a grim struggle for dominance, and group identities were charged with diffuseness due to the society's fluid and fragmented character. In the war zone of the north and east, where the writ of the state ran only unevenly or not at all, different groups of Tamil militants (the LTTE-TELO in the LTTE-held territories, the EPDP or PLOTE in areas not run directly by the Sri Lankan army) asserted their claims of being the rightful representatives of the region's population. Each attempted to assert exclusive control over and extort "taxes" from the people in return for "protection." Efforts by the regime to restore normalcy by establishing elected administrations were repeatedly and violently foiled by the LTTE.[20] To guard against possible guerrilla attacks, the southwest, especially Colombo, looked increasingly like an armed camp, through which travel was characterized by delays caused by stops and searches at military check-points, especially of anyone suspected of being a Tamil. Those belonging to the Tamil community had to be registered at the nearest police station and were apt to be detained until they could pay their way out or were cleared of any suspicion harbored toward them. While the intra-ethnic fighting between Tamil militants undermined the claim of each group to serve as the legitimate voice of the "Tamil community" and its interests, the inability of the government to legislate meaning-ful constitutional reform even while it energetically prosecuted the war against the most militant of the Tamil groups only added grist to the mill of diffuse Tamil alienation with the regime and validity to separatist sentiment.

Thus in the gap between what Sri Lanka achieved and what was possible in the global economic conjuncture of the 1990s lay the costs of the war in the northeast in particular and on the island in general, the growing militarization of the state and economy, and the marginalization of a segment of its (Tamil) citizens from fully participating in the economy and its growth.

Conclusion

Under the People's Alliance, Sri Lanka continued to grow economically de-spite the civil war, which was fought with heightened intensity, by moving to pro-market policies very similar to those of the preceding UNP regime. Its economic policies illustrated the limited margin for maneuver that was available to center-left regimes in the developing world in the context of growing integration with global trade and capital. With its constraints compounded by the challenge to the country's internal unity, the class and sectoral cleavages represented in the coalition were subordinated to the challenge of containing the separatist movement. The regime was able to get a certain level of foreign financial support and investment in exchange for a continued opening of the market, more thrifty management and spending policies, and privatization of state-held enterprises.

The policies and experience of the PA were more like those of the Premadasa period of the early 1990s than the high-spending Jayawardene years of the 1980s. By following a strategy of more careful monetary and fiscal management of the economy, the government was able to keep its expenditures, budgetary deficits, in-flation, and public debt in check. Private domestic investment, based on individual remittances from abroad, provided the main engine for growth, with the privatiza-tion of inefficient public sector undertakings providing added momentum. In the given context of globalization and war, the major sources of employment and earn-ings were migration for work abroad, production of garments for export, and the armed forces. With this configuration of policies, Sri Lanka was able to register higher levels of economic growth than the developing countries taken as a whole, but not as high as those in the Asian region of which it was a part.

There is no denying that its growth was affected by the costs of the war, which were immense in both direct and indirect terms as well as in terms of opportunities foregone. The diversion of resources for military purposes and the death and de-struction that ensued in the wake of the fighting were accomplished at the cost of investment in capital and social infrastructure. The burden of the conflict was also felt in the dissolution of social ties and cultural relations, be it through displacement and migration of large numbers of people within the country and abroad or the continued exposure to violence, death, and destruction, especially in the northeast.

The regime's management of the economy and prosecution of the war had implications for the manner in which ethnic cleavages perpetuated themselves in this period. As argued here, the impact of the dislocations caused by the introduction of the open economy and the uncontrolled expenditure policies of the Jayawardene regime no longer obtained. However, the greater linkage with and dependence on global economic networks provided resources for both the state and the separatists in the conflict, which continued with all its attendant costs. Lacking the implementation of a constitutional and political solution, these costs increased a sense of alienation toward the regime in the minds of its Tamil citizens. The tremendous human and economic costs of a conflict which seemed to have deteriorated into a stalemate of continued fighting to the detriment of all concerned made it urgent that the government seek a viable political solution to the conflict.[21]

Notes

1. In the months before the elections in late 2000, these critiques became particularly sharp in the opposition newspaper, *Island.*
2. I have used both primary and secondary sources for the study, including the annual reports of the Central Bank of Sri Lanka, data put out by the Department of Census and Statistics, periodicals, and news reports. I have also drawn on personal observations, interviews, and printed materials collected on recent trips to Sri Lanka.
3. EIU 2nd quarter 1996: 14.
4. EIU 2nd quarter 1995: 6.
5. See Kanes 1998; Amerasinghe 1998; and EIU 3rd quarter 1996: 4.
6. EIU 2nd quarter 1995, 6, 13, and 4th quarter 1995: 11–13.
7. For details see EIU 2nd quarter 1997, 12–18; 3rd quarter 1997: 12–15; 4th quarter 1997: 11–14.
8. Also see Central Bank 1999: 9, chart 1.4.
9. This is at variance with the commonly heard opposition complaint, made just before the 2000 elections, of there being an inordinately sharp rise in prices due to the war.
10. EIU 3rd quarter 1999: 28.
11. EIU 1st quarter 1995: 12.
12. See, for instance, Hettiarachchi 1998.
13. Beyond this, on the basis of the data available, it is difficult to say to what degree economic burdens increased on the poor or inequality increased in the society. Some data relating to the initial period of the regime indicate that the increase in inequality characteristic of the Jayawardene years had been reversed slightly. According to one survey, income shares for the poorest 20 percent

of the population had increased from 5.1 percent of the national income in 1986/87 to 5.5 percent by 1996/97. In contrast, the incomes of the richest quintile in the population had fallen from 52.3 percent to 50.2 percent in the same period (Central Bank of Sri Lanka's Consumer Finances and Socioeconomic Survey for 1996/97, cited in Kanes 1998: 18).

14. Compare this with the total number of 3,400 persons estimated to have been killed by the conflict in Northern Ireland since the "troubles" began in 1967.

15. Unofficial estimates put the figure at double the number—at over a half million people. Those working with refugees in Germany give the following distribution for the Sri Lankan Tamil diaspora: Canada, 200,000; India, 165,000; Germany, 60,000; France, 40,000; Switzerland, 35,000; and the United Kingdom, 35,000. My thanks to Christian Wagner for this information, personal communication, November 14, 2001.

16. Sri Lanka's per capita GDP moved to US$856 in 2000 (Central Bank 2000: 3).

17. There were some small outbreaks of violence along ethnic lines between elements in the Sinhalese and Muslim communities, as in Puttalam and in Mawanella. Allegedly, these incidents involved volatile rivalries relating to political and criminal cliques associated with certain politicians of the ruling party versus established minority interests.

18. It was shocking to see the devastation when I visited the Jaffna peninsula in August 1998. In what had clearly been vibrant communities, buildings lay smashed, cracked, and pockmarked by shrapnel, roads were riddled with potholes, and gardens and fields were unkempt and grown over, many of them lying deserted and silent. Although under government control and functioning under some semblance of normalcy, with the numerous road blocks and armed personnel, even the city of Jaffna looked like a war zone.

19. The last complete census taken on the island was in 1981. Widespread instability caused by the JVP and the LTTE insurgencies prevented the 1991 census from being taken. The census completed in July 2001 did not cover the six minority-dominated districts of the north and east on the plea of minority representatives that conditions of normalcy did not exist in those districts.

20. As evident in the killing of two elected civilian TULF mayors in 1998.

21. The human and economic costs of the conflict were explicitly put forward as the reason for acceptance of a cease-fire by Prime Minister Ranil Wickremasinghe, leader of the UNP, soon after he was elected in December 2001. The escalation of the fighting and defense expenditure along with political instability after mid-2000 contributed to a rise in the budget deficit (10.8 percent of GDP), inflation (14.2 percent), and a negative rate of growth (of −1.5 percent) in 2001. For this subsequent period, see Shastri 2002: 179; Shastri 2003: 220; Central Bank 2002.

Part Two: *Articulations of Class,*
Ethnicity, and Violence

Introduction

Michael D. Woost

In the last week of July 1983, the people of Sri Lanka went through some of the worst rioting and ethnic violence in their history. It was surely the worst episode of anti-Tamil violence since independence in 1948. Even before the fires burned out and the dust began to settle on this catastrophic moment, there was an understandable rush to explain and analyze. These efforts were multiple, contentious, and positioned politically. They ranged from government pronouncements, newspaper editorials, and social science analysis, to everyday discussions among ordinary people, from all walks of life, trying to help each other understand and explain and/or legitimize what had occurred.

As I recall from that time, many people with whom I spoke were dumbfounded at what had happened, unable to fathom how Sinhalese could do such things to Tamils or how Sinhalese could do such things (such as destroying places of employment) to themselves. In other cases, public debates about the emergent conflict appeared to be aimed at reconstituting Sinhala and Tamil identities. For example, Serena Tennekoon (1987) examines the way in which debates in local newspapers became part of a process of reconstructing Sinhala identity in post-1983 Sri Lanka. As these public and private discussions indicated, there was a good deal of doubt about identity. If one had not taken part in the rioting and violence, how could one say that it was the Sinhalese who carried out this pogrom, if not all such people felt compelled to join in the mayhem? And Tamils whose lives, homes, and businesses were left untouched by the violence, more or less, how was it that they were spared? And what would be their fate now in this violent rearrangement of social relations among identities? Their lives were affected even if they had escaped physical violence.

Social scientists, too, tried to answer the many questions

about the causes and effects of the violence.[1] Probably the most prominent and influential of these many social science interventions was the 1984 essay that we reprint here, "The Open Economy and Its Impact on Ethnic Relations in Sri Lanka," written by Newton Gunasinghe. Gunasinghe lays out a provocative analysis of the moment of violence, one that draws heavily on notions of class and class fractions. What he attempted to do was to map connections between the increase in inter-ethnic violence and the open economic policies introduced by the United National Party in 1977.

Gunasinghe hinged his explanation on the contention that prior to 1977, certain fractions of the Sinhala business class had enjoyed state patronage and safeguards for their respective businesses. Under the open economic policies, these arrangements were collapsing, producing disaffection among a large sector of the Sinhala business class. In contrast, many Tamil-run businesses began to thrive, since they had always operated without the benefit of state safeguards and already knew how to operate effectively in these new conditions of production and exchange. For their part, the urban poor had to contend with the removal of many of the welfare programs that had provided support for their families. Their new situation, Gunasinghe argued, left them feeling deprived, making them vulnerable to exploitation by other classes for violent ends. Furthermore, Gunasinghe added, all of this occurred in a context in which ideological barriers between ethnic communities were being drawn more starkly in public and private rhetoric. What we had then was a very volatile conjuncture, with all the elements needed for an eruption of ethnic violence.

Gunasinghe maintained that what occurred in July 1983 was an articulation of these various disgruntled elements into a force ready to wreak havoc on those whose advantages seemed to derive from the disadvantages of others. His analysis thus represents one of the first and most considered attempts to understand how people in class fractions, experiencing policy changes in very different ways, were linked through a principle of ethnicity rather than class. These were not necessary linkages but articulations made in a specific conjuncture, by specific groups of people, all acting on their own interests, yet funneled through the channel of ethnicity. What the essay also represents is an attempt to map out the significant groupings in society and how their interests were affected by the shift in economic policies.

Siri Hettige's contribution similarly attempts to chart the structure of opportunities and interests in Sri Lankan society, but he does so 20 years after Gunasinghe's essay was first published. Hettige contends that while Gunasinghe's interpretation is provocative, the empirical evidence upon which it is drawn is rather sketchy. Hettige draws on two surveys of Sri Lankan youth. One of these was conducted as a pilot survey in 1998, and the other was a much broader survey covering the entire island. Drawing on this large data base, Hettige outlines the very complicated and contradictory experiences of Sri Lanka's youth as they struggle to make an adequate and acceptable living. The current conditions of production and employment are now very different from what they were after 1977. Categories of identity and interest seem to have multiplied in the intervening years.

Hettige's mapping of the opportunity structure should also make us look again at the class and interest structure of the immediate post-1977 period.[2] The situation was probably even more complex than Gunasinghe allowed in the space of his essay. As Hettige contends, militarization of Tamil youth had begun before the policy changes of 1977. The changes also opened up many opportunities for advancement in the expanding private sector for all ethnic groups. So, like Gunasinghe's analysis of the processes of identity leading up to the riots of 1983, Hettige's chapter indicates once again how tentative are the articulations of identity around the poles of ethnicity.

In today's economy, Sri Lankan youth face many obstacles to bettering their lives. These obstacles are no longer so easily reducible to an ethnic differential. Identification on the basis of gender, class, status, rural versus urban, and so on are important intervening factors in youth experience of their position in Sri Lanka's economic formation. For that reason, while not denying the continued dominance of ethnicity in material struggles for hegemony, Hettige maintains that the data collected in the survey speaks to the utter contingency of articulations of conflict around the pole of ethnicity. Given the experience of present-day youth in the country, a very different articulation of identities and conflict is possible, one that could lead to a complete redirection of violence. As noted in the introduction, no articulation of identity and practice should be thought of as the necessary one, the only one possible.

In Part I we saw the outlines of connections between economic policy changes and episodes of violence. The two articles by Shastri and Richardson provided the ground into which we must dig deeper to find ways in which these connections are actually articulated in social life. Hence, what both Gunasinghe and Hettige provide are technologies of vision that allow us to look deeper into the connections between economic policies and conflict. They both demonstrate that the connection should never be conceived in any sort of linear fashion. People's responses to policy change may be affected by their abstract class position in some fashion. Yet this is not a historical necessity. Agency in any conjuncture is articulated out of many possible formations of identity already in motion and always potentially in collision. Mapping agency is much more complicated than it may appear when proceeding from abstract categories of interest. Consequently, the essays by Gunasinghe and Hettige remind us that should the ethnic war subside or even end, the contradictions that spawned it, although historically transformed by war and other global shifts, will still remain. The calm of peace after war's end may only be a moment of shock, a gasp of relief, before conflict articulates around some new, unexpected principles of identity and interests.

Notes

1. Given the wide range of publications referred to here, I can only note a few of the more prominent. Considerations of space also prohibit any attempt to reference a wide variety of articles that came out in Sri Lanka in weekly and monthly publications shortly after the violence, though a number of the more prominent of these are to be found in some of the edited collections cited below. A more extensive and detailed bibliographic essay is clearly needed: Abeysekera and Gunasinghe 1987; Dunham and Abeysekera 1987; Social Scientists Association 1985; Gunasinghe, this volume and 1976, 1986; Gunawardana 1985; Manor 1984; Gombrich and Obeyesekere 1988.
2. Others have already engaged in this reassessment of identities and interests in the post-independence period. See, e.g., a recent analysis by Siri Gamage (1999). In the volume containing Gamage's essay, one can find a number of contributions relevant to this discussion (Gamage and Watson 1999).

4 The Open Economy and Its Impact on Ethnic Relations in Sri Lanka

Newton Gunasinghe

Although the anti-Tamil riots of July 1983 stand out for the sheer magnitude of devastation, the recent history of Sri Lanka is not devoid of other instances of mass violence directed against ethnic and religious minorities. The year 1915 witnessed widespread anti-Muslim riots; islandwide anti-Tamil riots and Sinhala-Tamil clashes occurred in 1958. However, from 1977 onwards, anti-Tamil riots have become more frequent, with many instances of localized violence and two instances of islandwide rioting, finally culminating in the holocaust of July 1983. Ethno-religious contradictions and rivalries have always been present in the modern body politic of Sri Lanka, with roots spreading back into the historical past; it is only occasionally, however, that these contradictions have erupted into open rioting. Thus, after the 1915 anti-Muslim riots, no ethno-religious riots occurred for a period of more than four decades, and after the anti-Tamil riots of 1958, there was a period of relative calm for nearly two decades. It is only from the year 1977 that ethno-religious riots have become frequent.

A number of political and ideological factors contributed to the intensification of ethnic tensions during this period.

a. The government's failure to evolve a political solution to the secessionist demand advised by the Tamil United Liberation Front and the consequent emergence of armed militant groups who embarked on the path of armed struggle to achieve a separate state.

b. The violent skirmishes between state security personnel and the armed militant youth groups being interpreted by the broad Sinhala masses as a facet of Sinhala/Tamil conflict, under the guidance of chauvinistic elements both within the regime and outside it; the hysterical chauvinistic propaganda carried out by the popular Sinhala press is of cardinal importance in the formation of ideology among the Sinhala masses during this period.

c. The general breakdown of law and order and the rule of law during this phase witnessed the emergence of goon squads under the patronage of important political personalities. They operated with impunity against workers on strike, political dissenters, dissident intellectuals, students boycotting classes, and even against independently inclined judges of the Supreme Court. A high point in this rule of goon squads was the referendum held in December 1982. During the holocaust of July 1983, the rule of goon squads attained its zenith and consummation with the state security forces either being oblivious or actively encouraging the mobs on the rampage.

d. Organized attempts on the part of certain chauvinistic elements both within and outside the regime to ignite an anti-Tamil pogrom with the expressed intention of breaking the economic base of Tamil entrepreneurs, resulted not only in attacks against small Tamil shopkeepers but also attacks against major industrial establishments.

While not denying that the general deterioration of political relations between the Sinhala and Tamil ethnic groups has contributed to the frequent occurrence of riots, it is now proposed to concentrate on the economic context of these conflicts.

The period 1977–83, as pointed out earlier, is one of incessant ethnic rioting; it is simultaneously a period during which the country's economic structure was overhauled with the introduction of an open economic policy. Is it possible to establish a correlation between the open economic policy and the frequent occurrence of rioting? If such a correlation could be established, what are its specific forms and manifestations as far as ethnic relations are concerned? Within this context, how far could the open economic policy be implemented without causing irreparable damage to ethnic relations, whose deterioration may emerge as a fundamental barrier to any policy of rational economic development?

The economy of Sri Lanka during the period 1955–77 could be called a state-regulated economic system. There were a number of facets to this process of state regulation. The state, through the establishment of a number of industrial and commercial corporations, started performing an important economic role. A number of private enterprises were nationalized, expanding the public sector of the economy, culminating in the nationalization of the plantations, the foundation of the export-import economy. The private sector, basically consisting of light industrial and commercial enterprises, came under strict state regulation; the system of quotas, permits, and licenses, a product of the policy of import-substitution, made state patronage essential for any industrial or commercial venture in the private sector. Given the elaborate system of political patronage that has grown within the context of party politics, it can be assumed that the quotas, permits, and licenses without which one could not do business were handed over to favorites of the politicians of the ruling party. And the ruling parties were, of course, Sinhala parties. If a regulated economy exists, irrespective of the regime being SLFP or UNP, state patronage becomes essential for the survival and expansion of any private enterprise; as this patronage is exercised not on the basis of rational criteria but on the basis of political favoritism, it is reasonable to assume that those business groups closer to political circles in power stood to gain most. It is well known that the period of state regulation and import substitution provided the background to the upliftment of a fair section of middle-level Sinhala entrepreneurs to the position of captains of industry.

The public sector, consisting of newly established corporations and nationalized enterprises, came under the control of a bureaucracy. Political patronage became a key necessity in the process of recruitment to this bureaucracy. By this time, the universities had started instruction in the national languages, and a fair section of rural, lower-middle-class youth had graduated from the higher education institutes with degrees and diplomas. The system of recruitment on political patronage also favored the Sinhala youth. Irrespective of the regime being UNP or SLFP, opportunities existed for Sinhala youth to build up patron-client linkages with local politicians and press themselves forward. The Tamil youth, especially those of the north and the east, did not enjoy this advantage, as their local politicians represented regional ethnic parties, enjoying no power at the center. Thus the expansion of the public sector was not merely an increase in the state regulation of the economy; it was, simultaneously, an area of expansion of job opportunities for Sinhala youth. The emerging Sinhala management stratum in the public sector also established good relations with the Sinhala entrepreneurial groups, and this reinforced the advantages that the Sinhala entrepreneurs already enjoyed.

It is possible that this situation did not apply to the large enterprises in the private sector, and in these enterprises, political patronage was probably not an important factor in recruitment and formal criteria would have been more valued. Therefore, it is likely that Tamils would not have suffered any specific disadvantage in the private sector.

Under the conditions of a state-regulated economy, the private banking sector also came under strict control and their expansion was limited. The local credit market was dominated by the two state banks. The directors of these two banks were also persons appointed on the basis of political patronage and were closely linked to the political parties in power. Given this situation, the same conditions that applied to the issuance of quotas, permits, and licenses applied to the granting of bank credit. Here, too, Sinhala entrepreneurs linked to the ruling political party stood to gain, whereas Tamil entrepreneurs, especially the middle-level ones who enjoyed no upper-class social status and lacked political patronage, did not enjoy any specific advantage.

In 1977, with the introduction of the open economic policy, most of the elements of the regulative mechanisms were dismantled. The system of quotas, permits, and licenses was abolished. The import-export trade was liberalized. The public sector monopoly in the distribution of some commodities was abolished; some enterprises were denationalized, but, more importantly, the management of some public sector enterprises was handed over to the private sector. Foreign private capital was allocated a major role in bringing about export-led growth. Banking in the private and foreign sectors was encouraged, and limits to their expansion were removed. A number of "sacred cows" in the meanwhile were slaughtered. The subsidized rice ration that the people had been used to since the days of the Second World War was discontinued; the free health scheme was subverted, with doctors in government hospitals being granted the right to engage in private practice. The free education scheme was affected by teachers in the government schools being permitted to give private tuition. The objective of the government was not merely to remove the bottlenecks of the state-regulated economy but to ensure the uncontrolled free-play of market forces in all areas.

But to the degree that this uncontrolled free-play of market forces was assured, the degree to which political patronage could be converted into economic resources too became contracted. Formerly, within the context of the state-regulated economy, some sections of Sinhala entrepreneurs could expect to obtain special concessions as a mark of political patronage. With the dismantling of state regulation, the possibility of obtaining such concessions vanished; if import-export trade is unrestricted, what one needs to engage in trade is not a permit but capital or the availability of credit.

Thus if, within the open economy, certain sections of Sinhala entrepreneurs were no longer able to enjoy the special concessions to which they had become accustomed during the period of state regulation, it was not because the government was against Sinhala mercantile interests but as an inevitable consequence of the removal of controls. Non-Sinhalese entrepreneurial sections who had not enjoyed special patronage during the period of controls did not stand to lose when the controls were removed. Thus something akin to "fair competition" commenced in the field of business, especially in the middle rungs; those with capital, resources, business contacts, and acumen forging ahead of those less endowed with these factors.

The removal of restrictions on the private banking sector also contributed to this atmosphere of "fair play." If political patronage was a crucial element in obtaining credit during the period when the credit market was dominated by the two state banks, the expanding private banking sector provided an avenue to those who did not necessarily enjoy political patronage but who could establish their creditworthiness on commercial criteria. Thus the expansion of the private banking sector reduced the importance of political patronage in obtaining loans and in fact provided a sector where politically weak, non-Sinhala entrepreneurial sections could compete equally with the politically dominant Sinhala entrepreneurs.

During the period of state regulation of the economy, a section of Sinhala merchants who started life as petty traders were able to rise up to the top as industrialists. By the mid-seventies, these groups were well established in business, often exporting their products to the international market. The introduction of the new economic policy did not adversely affect these well established enterprises, but immediately below this stratum was a fairly widespread stratum of Sinhala entrepreneurs who were adversely affected. Small industrialists who were manufacturing light industrial products for the domestic market, among whom Sinhala businessmen predominated, were badly affected by the liberal import policy which opened up hitherto captive markets to foreign competition; many of these small enterprises were compelled to close down. It is possible that in the field of trade, which was subjected to a generalized licensing system, as distinct from the specialized licensing system applicable to industry, non-Sinhala interests predominated. With the introduction of the open economic policy, commodity circulation accelerated, and the volume of trade grew together with the profits to be earned in this sector. Conversely, many of the small industrial enterprises had become bankrupt. If our assumption relating to the diverse ethnic composition of these two sectors holds, it is possible that Sinhala entrepreneurial groups in the middle rung suffered, while the non-Sinhala sections in the same social stratum improved their position.

The operation of the open economic policy, with its attendant cuts in social welfare and subsidies, assumes as its social base a political system where opposition, dissent strikes, etc., are kept at a bare minimum. During the course of the last six years, the state attempted to quell all forms of legitimate protest and create a social system that was exclusively geared to the attainment of high rates of economic growth. The "safety valves" that were present in the body politic earlier to express frustration and aggression from those sections of society who felt deprived were deliberately closed. It is possible that within this context, the sense of relative deprivation felt especially by the urban poor contributed to anti-Tamil chauvinism.

It is possible to examine the correlation between the frequent occurrences of anti-Tamil and antiminority riots and the operation of the open economic policy in relation to a number of hypotheses:

The state-regulated economy of the 1956–77 period, rather than being a "socialist" phase as is sometimes asserted, is actually a period during which the state

a. through political patronage helped a stratum of Sinhala entrepreneurs to rise to the level of industrialists;
b. protected a section of predominantly Sinhala entrepreneurs of the middle level engaged in light industrial production; and
c. created extensive job opportunities mainly for the Sinhala people through the expansion of the public sector.

By the mid-fifties, a stratum of mainly Sinhala entrepreneurs who were petty merchants in social origin, but who had undergone a period of initial capital accumulation in the war years and the Korean war boom, had come to the fore. They had amassed capital primarily through trading and light industrial production and were eager to move into new areas of profit-making. The state, through the import-substitution policy and credit supplied from the state banks, encouraged them to move into industrial production and granted liberal tax holidays for these new enterprises. Making use of the protected domestic market, the Dasa and Piyadasa groups moved into textile manufacturing; the Maliban group moved into confectioneries and food items; the McCallum group moved into brewing and manufacturing beverages; the Sri Ramya group moved into assembling sewing machines and making other consumer durables; the Wettasinghe group moved into the area of plasticware and electrical accessories; the Gunasena group moved into large-scale printing and publishing. Some entrepreneurial groups who were well established by the mid-fifties, such as Richard Pieris and the de Soysa group, also made use of the new opportunities and moved into industry, the former into rubber products and the latter into consumer durables.

During the same period, some Tamil entrepreneurial groups, notably Gnanam and Gunaratnam, also moved into industry, the former into the area of textile and hardware production and the latter into the area of textile and film production. But the proportion of local Tamil entrepreneurs who were successful at making use of the new economic opportunities seem to be smaller when compared with their Sinhala counterparts. Confronted with the import-substitution policy, the big export-import traders, among whose ranks Sinhala representation was small, initially reacted with local assembling and packaging of these imported items. But as the pressures of the state to increase the proportion of locally manufactured components in the final product became greater, those firms assembling commodities with prestigious brand names found it harder to comply with these regulations, as there were difficulties in obtaining licenses from the foreign parent companies under these new conditions. The local entrepreneurs, on the other hand, found it easier to comply with the pressures of the state in the absence of any such linkages with foreign firms.

Immediately below this level of operation, where the required levels of capital were comparatively high, there was the level of the light consumer market. Within the context of a near total ban on the importation of light consumer items (soap, edible oil, matches, sweets, pencils, brushes, etc.), a totally protected domestic market for these items was created. Here an entrepreneur relying on a small quantum of capital could carry on production with reasonable profits, if he had the necessary political patronage to obtain the iniquitous licenses. It is possible to cite the composition of the matchmaking industry in this period as an example.

The matchmaking industry was dominated by two firms, Ceylon Match Company Ltd. and Lanka Lights; the former, a subsidiary of the Don Carolis group, was a substantially larger producer than the latter. However, due to the policy of state regulation the match production in both these firms was controlled by government quotas, which allowed enough room for the functioning of small enterprises in the same field, as the amount of capital needed to establish a matchmaking plant based on labor-intensive methods was rather low. More than a dozen small entrepreneurs supplied the market with their products, protected by the government-imposed quota system. The quota, at this level, did not help expansion; indeed, it is possible to argue that it was anti-expansionist in character and also helped maintain the status quo. However, it ensured the survival of small entrepreneurs who had ventured into the production of light consumer items.

Differential Impact on Entrepreneurs

The expansion of the public sector, although perceived as a noncapitalist path of development by certain sections, was actually a process through which the state subordinated a significant proportion of the country's economic resources to itself. These economic resources then could be distributed among the supporters of the regime on the basis of political patronage. Both entrepreneurs as well as nonentrepreneurs who were Sinhalese were better placed to exercise pressure on the UNP and SLFP politicians. As such, they stood to gain most from the expansion of the public sector. The large public sector corporations and their factories thus got located primarily in Sinhala areas, with only a small minority of plants going to the northern and eastern provinces. Once this discriminatory locating was accomplished, it was possible to argue for preferential recruitment for the workforce from the local area, which automatically ensured Sinhala preponderance. Even at the supervisory and administrative levels, jobs were allocated on political patron-

Table 4.1. State Personnel Classified by Major Occupational Groups and Ethnicity, 1972

	Sinhala	Tamil	Muslim	Burgher	Others
As a % of population in 1971	72.0	20.5	6.5	---	1.0
Administrative, Professional & Technical Grades	67.7	28.5	2.5	0.9	0.35
Middle Grades	81.2	15.3	2.2	0.8	0.4
School Teachers	81.5	11.6	6.6	0.01	0.06
Minor Employees	86.4	10.6	1.9	0.5	0.27
Labor Grades	85.5	11.6	2.0	0.3	0.23
Total %	82.63	12.93	3.53	0.46	0.47

Source: Statistics of Personnel in the State Services, 1972.

age. Well-known SLFP supporters and their kith and kin may be denied access to the job pool during UNP rule, and vice versa, but they had their chance once the SLFP returned to power; but the Tamils, especially those of the north and the east, were more and more permanently excluded from this complex network of Sinhala political patronage. As Table 4.1 above establishes, this discrimination was most pronounced in the middle and lower grades of occupations, where the majority of employees were concentrated.

As far as the non-Sinhala ethnic groups are concerned, this was a phase during which:

a. the top entrepreneurial stratum, especially the Tamil section within it, found the avenues opened up through import substitution more or less closed to them, as they did not enjoy sufficient political patronage from either ruling party;

b. the middle-level entrepreneurial stratum found itself confined to trade and commerce due to the difficulties encountered in obtaining special licenses required for light industrial production in the absence of political patronage; and

c. the Tamil people in general benefited much less from the new job opportunities created in the public sector, both due to lack of political patronage and the paucity of public sector development activities in the north and in the east.

From a historical perspective, the growth of a top entrepreneurial stratum from the Tamil people of Sri Lanka occurs much later than the growth of a similar stratum from within the Sinhala people. The first generation of Sinhala entrepreneurs accumulated their capital through the liquor trade and arrack renting[1] as far back as the mid-nineteenth century, and later invested their capital in graphite mining and coconut plantations. Similar avenues of accumulation were not present in the north and the east where liquor sales were rather low due to the widespread consumption of homemade palmyrah toddy. Further, the absence of plantations in these areas possibly prevented the emergence of a group of entrepreneurs who could earn profits by servicing the plantations. Thus the Sri Lankan Tamil entrepreneurial stratum, when it made its appearance, had to emerge through trading. Thus it is from these ranks that a local Tamil entrepreneurial stratum emerges. By the mid-fifties, a top Tamil entrepreneurial element had already come into existence and they exercised partial control over the export-import trade. There was a relative absence of middle-level Tamil entrepreneurs involved in light industries. The expansion of the public sector covered export-import trade as well. The founding of the Co-operative Wholesale Establishment and the State Trading Corporation as government-controlled monopolistic institutions in the field of export-import trade severely restricted an area of operation of the top entrepreneurial stratum located in wholesale foreign trade. Trade with India and Pakistan, in particular, was dominated by Indian and Sri Lankan Tamil entrepreneurial groups. The Co-operative Wholesale Establishment gradually established a virtual monopoly over trade with India and Pakistan exercising an exclusive monopoly over importation of dried fish, lentils, onions, etc. This should certainly have reacted adversely on those entrepreneurial groups who formerly controlled import-export trade, among whose ranks Tamil entrepreneurs were significantly represented.

The middle-level Tamil entrepreneurs too were mainly involved in trade, transport, and services rather than in light industry. They were scattered all over the island, centered in provincial townships as well as in Colombo. The founding of the CWE at the level of foreign wholesale trade was paralleled by the establishment of cooperative stores at the village level, and the entire country was covered by an elaborate network of cooperative stores. These stores were subsequently organized into electorate-level administrative units, on whose boards of directors sat nominees of the local member of Parliament. The cooperatives gradually obtained monopolistic control over distribution on certain commodities, which the private sector was prohibited from trading in. Shopkeepers and traders, irrespective of their ethnicity, were badly hit in the process, but the Sinhala trader was better placed to diversify his activities by moving into light industrial production on the basis of political patronage, an avenue more or less closed to the Tamil trader.

As Table 4.1 indicates, the Tamil proportion in the administrative, professional, and technical grades in the public sector in 1972 was 28.5 percent. However, this is somewhat misleading, as administrative, professional, and technical occupations are grouped together and as the annual pattern of recruitment is not given. The Tamil proportion in the recruitment to the administrative services, for instance, progressively declined during the sixties and the seventies. It is possible that Tamils enjoyed an advantageous position in the professions (as doctors, engineers, etc.) due to the availability of better secondary education facilities, especially in the north. At the level of the middle-level occupations as well as that of the workers, it is clear that Tamil representation is nearly half of their proportion in the population. In terms of employment generation, it is the middle and the lower grades that are of crucial statistical significance, as for every job created at the administrative/professional level, 15 jobs are created in the middle-level grades and 20 in the manual grades.

Within this context:

a. the Sinhala entrepreneurs, those who had graduated to the export market as well as those who remained in the middle level, manufacturing light industrial products for the domestic market, felt more or less content;
b. the urban poor, covered by the state welfare system to a certain degree, though dissatisfied, were less inclined to direct their aggression against minority ethnic groups.

Hence ethnic contradictions, although present and even intensifying, did not frequently erupt in the form of widespread antiminority riots.

By the mid-seventies, the top industrial stratum of entrepreneurs, among whom the Sinhala predominated, had already accumulated substantial amounts of capital. They had already discovered overseas markets for their industrial products: the Maliban group exported confectioneries to the Middle East, the Dasa and Piyadasa groups exported garments to the western countries, and Richard Pieris found markets for their rubber products in Europe and in Asia. In other words, their exclusive dependence on the protected domestic market came to an end. They were able to compete in the overseas market, especially in those commodities which required labor-intensive methods of production, as they could afford to pay low wages and keep the production costs down. However, in order to expand further, they needed foreign capital and technical collaboration, which was not encouraged under the policy of a state-regulated economy.

In contrast, the middle- and small-level entrepreneurs who had moved into light industry continued to rely on the protected domestic market, which guaranteed their survival if not expansion. Those entrepreneurs of the same level who had not moved into light industry and who continued their exclusive reliance on trading operations, had to establish various covert and overt links with the state trading agencies and the cooperatives. As the economy was one of utter commodity scarcity, black markets in various scarce items flourished, operated by middle- and small-level traders who illegally siphoned off the scarce commodities from the public sector to private shops. If it were not for the lucrative trade in the black market, many middle- and small-level traders would have found it difficult to continue their operations, as the public sector was already dominating the vital areas of trade. Thus the middle- and small-level industrialists found their niche to be protected by state regulation, while the middle- and small-level traders found an avenue of operation in the black market; these strata felt more or less content with the status quo.

The condition of the urban poor by the mid-seventies was characterized by low wages, high rates of unemployment, deterioration of living standards, and rather low levels of internal differentiation. They were dissatisfied with the status quo, and within the context of a state-regulated economy, the state seemed to be responsible for all the economic problems. The rate of inflation was low, and so was the annual increase in monetary wages. The essential items distributed through the state and semi-state agencies, on the basis of an elaborate system of rationing, were cheap, but due to commodity scarcity, the queues for obtaining them were long. As the state was seen as being responsible for this bad state of affairs, the frustration and aggression felt by the urban poor took an anti-state direction. The strike wave in late 1976, which primarily broke out in the public sector organizations, was one such occasion when protest was directed against the state. To the degree that protest was directed against the state, it appeared to take a class direction, the urban poor in general and the working class segments within it in particular protesting against the state on economic issues. To that degree, the divisive lines that demarcated the ethnic groups became blurred, people from different social strata and ethnic groups finding a nonethnic target to direct their aggression against. Hence the period of state-regulated economy was simultaneously a period during which ethnic contradictions did not erupt in the form of open rioting.

The open economic policy, by abolishing controls, also eliminated the system which enabled the Sinhalese entrepreneurs to obtain special concessions.

a. At the level of those who had already graduated to the export market, the removal of controls is unlikely to be adversely felt, while it is possible that some benefits actually accrued to them.
b. Middle-level entrepreneurs, those producing light industrial goods for the domestic market, were very badly affected by the liberalization of import-export trade.
c. The urban poor lost their welfare facilities; the real income of certain layers increased, but within the context of expanding consumerism, their real and imaginary needs grew to an extent which they were unable to satisfy. The sense of relative deprivation they felt was intensified to a level that could be utilized by a different social stratum for violent ends. The UNP regime, that was voted into power with a massive majority in 1977, felt that state-regulated economic policy—which was followed by an earlier UNP regime in the period 1965–70—had outgrown its usefulness. The state-regulated economy was seen to be associated with economic stagnation, commodity scarcity, high levels of unemployment, and institutional corruption. As private capital, both foreign and local, was allocated the role of the prime mover in the economy, the system of state regulation had to be dismantled as a system, so as to permit the maximum area of operation for the market forces.

The top industrial entrepreneurial stratum that had already graduated to the export market stood to gain from the introduction of the open economy. The open economic policy presented itself as an export-led model of growth in contrast to the state-regulated economic policy which was associated with import substitution. The top industrial stratum looked with enthusiasm at the export-led model of growth, as they were already exporters of industrial products. Further, the open economic policy gave them all the necessary encouragement to enter into collaboration with foreign capital, which they needed for their next phase of expansion. For this purpose, two new areas of operation where partnerships between local and foreign capital could take place, were established—the Export Promotion Zone, under the Greater Colombo Economic Commission (GCEC), and the Foreign Investments Advisory Committee (FIAC). To promote middle-level local entrepreneurship, the Local Investment Advisory Committee (LIAC) was also created.

The top industrial entrepreneurial stratum is in the process of making use of these new investment opportunities to establish joint ventures with foreign capital.

In the GCEC area, the proportion of local capital in joint ventures increased from 33 percent in 1980 to 39 percent in 1981. In the FIAC area, the proportion of local capital increased from 44 percent in 1980 to 58 percent in 1982.

With the removal of import controls in 1977, the protected market for home-made light industrial products came to an end. Every conceivable item was imported from the industrial centers of the world, as a result of which domestic manufacturing of light industrial products was seriously hit. The middle-level entrepreneurial stratum which was engaged in light industrial production for a protected domestic market found it difficult to continue production as they could not successfully compete with the imported products. Due to the specific characteristics of the state-regulated economy and the importance of political patronage in economic enterprise, the overwhelming majority of the industrial entrepreneurs at this level were Sinhala businessmen.

It is possible to substantiate the ruination of small industries by taking the case of the matchmaking industry. Immediately on the aftermath of the removal of import controls, large quantities of boxes of matches were imported from China and India. The quality of these matches was superior to those manufactured locally, but there was no significant price difference. Consequently, the imported matches captured the domestic market, driving away the local product. The dozen or so small manufacturers had no choice but to close down their work places. But the Ceylon Match Company Limited, which was the only firm in this line of business with a substantial capital base and foreign support, was able to fight back. This company reinvested capital, modernized its manufacturing plant, and turned out a product which, in terms of quality, compared well with the imported products. This improved box of matches successfully competed with the imported products and reconquered a substantial area of the market, probably a larger slice than it had during the period of import-substitution. The second large company in the field of match manufacturing, Lanka Lights Limited, found its capital base insufficient for modernization. It was obliged to become a subsidiary of a major company, Delmege Forsyth Limited, which provided the necessary capital for modernization. This company too now turns out a box of matches, the quality of which is superior to its former product, but which has not yet reached the level attained by the products of the Ceylon Match Company Ltd.

The Urban Poor

The recent history of the matchmaking industry demonstrates, in a microcosm, the structural alterations that have taken place in the light industrial sector exclusively dependent on the domestic market:

a. In the period of state regulation, the market was shared by two relatively big firms and a dozen small manufacturers who were not necessarily competing against each other, as the level of production of each manufacturer was controlled by state quotas;

b. With the removal of import controls, superior imported products equivalent in price to the local products reached the domestic market and drove all the local products away from the market;

c. The small manufacturers were driven to the wall and were compelled to close down their plants.

d. The big manufacturer modernized the process of production, reentered the market, and recaptured a bigger slice of the market than it had controlled earlier;

e. The middle-level manufacturer was compelled to turn into a subsidiary of a major firm in order to continue production in competitive conditions.

The condition of the urban poor during the period of the functioning of the open economic policy is not devoid of contradictions. As evidenced by the moderately high rates of economic growth, economic stagnation came to an end. There was a substantial increase in the job opportunities available. In the informal sector, wages rose; for instance, the daily wage of a carpenter or mason, rising from SL Rs. 15.00–20.00 in the early 1977 period up to SL Rs. 60.00–70.00 in early 1983. In the formal sector, too, monetary wages increased, but it is possible that these increases were insufficient to offset inflationary pressures. At the same time, the increase in job opportunities meant that, at the household level, the number of income receivers increased, contributing to a significant increase in the household income, which probably helped to dampen the inflationary pressures. In the meantime, the urban poor were subject to substantial cuts in the social welfare benefits which they had enjoyed for decades. The subsidized rice ration, together with certain other subsidized food items and consumer items which used to be distributed through the network of cooperative stores, were discontinued, to be replaced by food stamps, the real value of which progressively declined as inflation increased. The erosion of state welfare facilities, especially in the fields of health and education, probably contributed to the lowering of their quality of life. Although economic opportunities increased for the urban poor, their sense of economic insecurity too increased, as the state was abandoning its self-proclaimed ideological position as the "provider for the poor folk."

Of crucial importance is the accelerated process of internal social differentiation among the urban poor that sets in with the opening up of the economy. The urban poor, which consisted of certain layers of the working class, the lumpen proletariat, itinerant workers, vendors, and carters, which in the earlier period suffered an equality of poverty, were subject to a process of internal economic differentiation, as economic opportunities expanded. The mass exodus to West Asia from the ranks of the urban poor strengthened the economic position of these households from which the migrant workers emerged, as a substantial proportion of their income was repatriated to the country. Certain households boasted of three or four individuals employed in West Asia and the repatriated income, though absolutely insufficient for capital formation, still was quite sufficient to permit these households to engage in conspicuous consumption to the great dismay of other, less fortunate households from the same social background. This process, which could be termed "the color TV in the slum tenement" syndrome, increased the relative sense of deprivation suffered by the majority of the urban poor who had not partaken of the Dubai bonanza.

Increasing economic disparity between the new rich elements of speculators, contractors, bookies, gem merchants, and Middle East job recruitment agents who had no qualms about engaging in ostentatious display further strengthened the sense of relative deprivation felt by the bottom layers of the urban poor. At the level of mass communication, for instance, the TV advertisements of all kinds of consumer items occurred in a background of vulgar ostentation, which contrasted sharply with the living conditions of the state-regulated economy. When the conditions of social existence for the urban poor became difficult, the resultant hostility was directed against the state as the state was regarded as being responsible for all things good and bad. With the open economic policy, the state abandoned its image as the provider of the poor folk and, rather than controlling the economy, appeared to be handing over its economic responsibilities to the private sector. Thus at the level of mass psychology, the perceived "guilt" of the state for the difficult conditions the urban poor were experiencing substantially lessened. Nevertheless, the frustration and oppression generated by the sense of relative deprivation mounted and, by the latter phase of the open economy, converted the urban poor into inflammatory material.

The open economic policy, by removing controls, enabled

a. the top entrepreneurial stratum, both Sinhala and Tamil, to link up with foreign capital,
b. the middle-level non-Sinhala entrepreneurial group to expand within trade, commerce, and services; they were less affected by the collapse of the domestically oriented light industries; and
c. through the expansion of the private sector in general, the creation of job opportunities where political patronage was unimportant and, consequently, better opportunities for people from the minority ethnic groups to obtain employment.

The benefits that accrued from the open economic policy to the top industrial entrepreneurial stratum, both Sinhala and Tamil, among whose ranks the Sinhala businessmen predominated, has already been discussed. But at the middle level, it is possible that the impact of open economic policy was discriminatory. As it was pointed out earlier, in the light industrial sector of the middle-level entrepreneur, it was the Sinhala businessman who was dominant. This implies that the Tamil and Muslim entrepreneurs were basically concentrated in trade, commerce, and services. With the opening up of the economy, the light industrial sector was seriously hit. But the converse holds true for the sector that consists of trade, commerce, and services. The importation of various consumer items, after a relatively long period of commodity scarcity, pushed up the volume of trade to hitherto unprecedented heights and accelerated the velocity of commodity circulation in the market, both of which resulted in an enormous increase in the volume and rate of trading profits. Numerically vast sections of small and middle-level traders stood to accumulate substantial amounts of profit, among whom the Tamil and Muslim businessmen were overrepresented in relation to their proportions in the population. The state-sponsored development activities, such as the Mahaweli Development Project, and other river valley development projects, the construction of roads and buildings, and rural integrated development programs contributed to an enormous expansion in the service sector, and it is precisely the middle-level entrepreneurial stratum that stood to gain from this expansion. The middle- and small-level industrialists who were being ruined by the operation of the open economy perceived the profits accruing to the traders as an unduly large slice of the cake.

As the representation of Sinhala businessman in the strata of middle- and small-level traders is not as high as their population proportion, it was ideologically possible to interpret the rise in commercial profits as "Tamil entrepreneurs getting rich at the expense of the Sinhala." This is precisely what was expressed by a number of Sinhala merchants who contributed articles to the Sinhala newspaper, *Divaina,* in August 1983. For instance, on August 28, 1983: "Our merchants rarely had an opportunity to import essential commodities. Up until now, trade in these commodities in Pettah has continued to be a monopoly in the hands of people who are not citizens by descent. Our people had no room in the Pettah market, which covers an area of one square mile." Further, an editorial comment in the *Divaina* of September 18, 1983, states: "Although it is said that an open economy functioned in this country from 1977, in the Pettah market for a long time a trading monopoly of a limited group has continued. As consumer trade depends on the price levels in the wholesale market, these merchants were able to determine the prices of a large variety of commodities on an islandwide basis." The president of the Sri Lanka Small Industrialists Association, who was interviewed by the same newspaper (September 11, 1983), said, "As a society which allocates first place to commerce evolved, commercial power got alienated from the majority Sinhala and went to the minority national groups." All these comments testify to the deep sense of frustration felt by middle-level Sinhala entrepreneurs.

As the private sector expanded, the job opportunities in this sector also increased. Unlike in the public sector, these jobs were not allocated on the basis of political patronage. At the level of major companies, the working language continues to be English. In the public sector, the working language continues to be Sinhala. In addition to political patronage, the Sinhala youth also benefited from the fact that the public sector required its employees to possess a working knowledge of Sinhala. The youth from other national groups had to learn Sinhala in order to obtain confirmation in their public sector appointment. In the private sector, especially in the major companies, no language hurdle confronted the non-Sinhala employee. Hence it is possible to assume that the expansion of the private sector did not introduce any specific disadvantages to the non-Sinhala communities as far as job creation is concerned.

The frequent and incessant ethnic hostilities and anti-minority riots in the 1977–83 period are in the last analysis linked to certain unexpected economic results of the operation of the open economic policy, where

a. the Sinhala entrepreneurs of the middle level are either adversely affected or find themselves, in the absence of direct political patronage, in a situation of unequal competition with Tamil and Muslim entrepreneurs of the same level.

b. the dissatisfied sections of the urban poor constituted a volatile social base, capable of being mobilized for their own narrow ends by the ideologists of Sinhala dominance as well as by frustrated sections of Sinhala entrepreneurs.

An entrepreneurial stratum that accumulates and rises due to state patronage acquires a social and ideological character distinct from an entrepreneurial group that emerges in a society subject to the free play of market forces. Such an entrepreneurial stratum expects state patronage at every operation that it undertakes and expects the state to step in and protect them if it faces a difficult situation. The middle-level entrepreneurial stratum that was engaged in industrial production hopes the state would take some steps to protect them from "unfair" competition, which, of course, runs against the principles of the open economic policy.

The dissatisfied sections of the urban poor no longer directed their hostility against the state, as they did during the phase of state regulation. As the economic role of the state appeared to them to be marginal, some other object of hostility had to be discovered to be held responsible for the current malaise. It is precisely here that the Sinhala chauvinist ideology, which initially emerged from the ranks of the middle-level traders, found a fertile ground, engulfing numerous social strata among the Sinhala.

It is necessary once again to reiterate that this is not to underplay the important political and ideological aspects of the ethnic conflict in Sri Lanka. Our attempt here was to identify some salient elements relevant to ethnic conflict in general and the July 1983 riots in particular within the economic infrastructure and especially the transformation of the economy from a state-regulated economy to an open one.

There are many studies of ethnic relations and ethnic conflicts in Sri Lanka. Some of these studies have also attempted to establish linkages between the intensification of ethnic contradictions and economic causes. But almost all of these studies tend to correlate the tempo of ethnic conflict with the "boom" and the "depression" in the business cycle, with the general underlying assumption being that ethnic conflicts are more likely to erupt into open violence during phases of economic depression.

We, however, laid emphasis on the linkages between economic structure and ethnic contradictions, in relation to the discontinuance of a particular model of economic growth—i.e., state-regulated economy bent on import substitution—and the implementation of a radically different model of economic growth—i.e., an open economy bent on export-led growth. What is important in an analysis of this type is not merely the ups and downs of the business cycle but the structural alterations that have occurred in an economy and how these alterations affect the ethnic relations in a multiethnic society. We attempted to demonstrate the manner in which different social strata emanating from different ethno-religious communities compete with each other in a social context of differential factor endowment, how this competition occurs within a fabric of ideology, political patronage, and state intervention, and how suddenly the rules of competition break down, giving rise to open mob violence. Not only is this line of investigation likely to shed fresh light on the social and economic background to frequent occurrence of ethnic riots during a specific time period, but it is also likely to identify social structural limits to the successful operation of an open economic policy within the context of a multiethnic and multireligious society.

Note

Originally published in three parts as "The Open Economy and Its Impact on Ethnic Relations" in *Lanka Guardian* 6, no. 17 (January 1, 1984): 6–8; no. 18 (January 15, 1984): 15–17; and no. 19 (January 29, 1984): 10–12. Colombo: Lanka Guardian Publishing Co. Copyright is now held by the Social Scientists Association (Colombo). Reprinted with permission.

1. Editors' note: Arrack renting was the British colonial government practice of farming out the collection of liquor taxes, usually through a system of competitive bidding. Arrack is an alcoholic beverage distilled from coconut sap.

5 Economic Policy, Changing Opportunities for Youth, and the Ethnic Conflict in Sri Lanka

Siri T. Hettige

Many researchers and commentators have examined the causes and consequences of Sri Lanka's ethnic conflict. Some have attempted to trace the conflict's origins to ancient times while others have confined themselves to more recent developments (Spencer, ed. 1990), particularly the Tamil community's real and perceived grievances in relation to economic, social, political, and cultural rights. These grievances are usually discussed with reference to the postcolonial Sri Lankan state which, it has been widely argued, evolved in such a manner as to enable the majority Sinhalese community to shape state policies and programs and derive undue benefits at the expense of the Tamil constituency.

However, empirical evidence shows that the situation is considerably more complex than simply the Sinhalese community being favored at the expense of the Tamil community. State policies and programs have varied widely over the past 40–50 years, and they have not always benefited some communities at the expense of others. In fact, some policies and programs have benefited all ethnic communities.[1] Moreover, Sri Lanka's ethnic communities are not monolithic entities with no internal tensions and differentiation. For instance, intracommunity discrimination based on caste is identified as a major issue by Tamil youth in the north and east, according to the National Youth Survey of 1999.[2]

Changing state policies and programs do shape opportunity structures and influence the distribution of livelihood opportunities in society. But opportunities and life chances also depend on one's relative position in the social hierarchy and other collective and personal attributes. Therefore, the key problem should be formulated as follows: First, what policies and programs shape which opportunity structures? Second, how do the changes in opportunity structures impact on different social groups and classes? In this chapter, I outline the broad policy changes that took place after independence and their implications for certain important political constituencies with a view to explaining why these political constituencies responded in the way they did. Empirical data supporting the assertions made here are drawn from several surveys and studies conducted by the author (Hettige 1998, 1999b, 2000), supplemented by secondary sources.

Changing Policy Regimes after Independence

One of the major outcomes of colonial rule was the establishment of a modern centralized state that functioned through an elaborate public bureaucracy guided by a set of codified rules and regulations. Rapid economic, social, and political changes, induced largely by the interventions of this state, produced varying public reactions. While some considered the colonial state to be the most important source of repression, others felt that it was the main source of relief and opportunity. Public service became the most prestigious and lucrative form of employment for youth belonging to middle and upper social strata. At the same time, the promotion of free enterprise, particularly in the areas of plantation production and related activities, opened up business opportunities for enterprising natives who, in turn, amassed considerable wealth and joined the colonial elite. Expansion of educational opportunities also gave young people the chance to obtain formal qualifications that would help them to secure administrative and professional employment in both state and private sectors. These changes loosened up traditional social structures, which in turn facilitated social and spatial mobility, often within a single generation.

Social and spatial mobility of a sizable segment of the population toward the latter part of the colonial rule raised expectations and aspirations of many people, including those who belonged to lower social strata. Yet, given the dual system of education that persisted throughout the British colonial period and the limitations of the country's economic structure, those who had access to English-medium schools were relatively advantaged with respect to desirable employment opportunities (Wickremasuriya 1978). The vast majority of youth who were Swabasha (vernacular, in either the Tamil or Sinhala language) educated were left out of the competition for lucrative and prestigious white-collar employment in the state sector. This situation became worse after the introduction of free education in the early 1940s.

A representative form of government was introduced in 1931, which led to an intensification of political competition among various ideological and interest groups engaged in national politics. These groups became more sensitive to the grievances and demands of their respective constituencies. This, in turn, formed the basis for the emergence of a welfare state in the country even before political independence in 1948. Increasing public investments in rural infrastructure, including irrigation facilities and alienation of state land to landless peasants, also became integrated into the welfare agenda.

The social welfare orientation of the postcolonial state did not appear to contradict the liberal economic policy orientation of the first postindependence regime in the country. The postcolonial native elite, which comprised the landowners, urban merchant capitalists, westernized professionals, and top public servants, succeeded in bringing into existence in 1948 an elected government that was committed to a liberal economic policy. But it was not long before this policy regime was challenged by left-leaning parties that mobilized marginalized rural peasants, urban workers, and other aggrieved groups seeking economic and social reform. In 1956, this political mobilization culminated in the electoral triumph of the Mahajana Eksath Peramuna (MEP) led by S. W. R. D. Bandaranaike, which was the first radical shift in economic and social policy since independence.

Bandaranaike's government embarked upon a state-led development program, which not only set in motion a process of nationalization of private enterprises but also established many new state enterprises. One result was that more and more economic resources came under the control of the state. The state, in turn, became the leading player in the production and distribution of wealth as well as the main source of employment, particularly the white-collar employment valued by upwardly mobile youth. State-led development continued to control the economy until 1977, even though there were changes of government during this period. Only in 1977 did the situation change drastically again. Before we make an attempt to analyze the significance of the 1977 policy shift, it is necessary to examine, first, the impact of state development strategy on the opportunity structures and, second, how different constituencies were linked to these opportunity structures.

Opportunity Structures under State-Led Development

The social welfare programs already in place before the 1956 elections were expanded over the following two decades. Public investments in rural infrastructure development and various subsidies benefited almost all segments of the country's population. As Gunatilleke (2000) has demonstrated, although there were some regional imbalances, they reflected the persisting rural and urban disparities rather than any deliberate discrimination against a particular ethnic community. This is evident from the comparative district data on literacy, employment, infant and maternal mortality, life expectancy, and the general Physical Quality of Life Index (PQLI). The relatively more developed, mostly Tamil district of Jaffna in the north is favorably placed in comparison with an equally developed, predominantly Sinhala district like Galle in the south. On the other hand, the more backward northern district of Vavuniya with a mostly Tamil population is comparable to Hambantota, one of the less developed districts in the south with a predominantly Sinhala population.

If we first take the two more developed districts of Jaffna and Galle between 1971 and 1981, the literacy rate increased in Jaffna from 82.7 percent to 93.4 percent. For Galle, the change has been from 82.7 percent to 89.8 percent. The maternal mortality rate has declined from 0.7 to 0.2 in the Jaffna district, while the rate in the Galle district has remained virtually unchanged, around 0.9; the infant mortality rate in the Jaffna district declined from 51 to 18, whereas in Galle the rate declined from 41 to 38. Life expectancy for women increased in Jaffna from 67 to 75 years, while the increase in Galle has been from 70 to 73 years. The PQLI increased from 83.8 to 91.7 in Jaffna and from 84.4 to 88.5 in Galle. The pattern of change over time with respect to all the above indicators in the two less developed districts of Vavuniya and Hambantota in the north and the south, respectively, has been similar. In both, there has been a significant improvement over the above period. If we look at the communities, the most significant exception has been the community of Tamil plantation workers. This has been largely due to the fact that they were perhaps the most oppressed community during the British period, and they continued to be deprived of their citizenship rights for many years even after independence. They did not benefit equally from the wide-ranging social welfare programs, and their living conditions continue to leave much to be desired.[3]

Nevertheless, economic and social policies adopted after 1956 shaped the opportunity structures in the country in a decisive and differential manner because the increasing concentration of productive resources in the state sector made access to such resources dependent on the political process. In this regard, the nature of public policies as well as access to seats of power became decisive factors. It is also necessary to distinguish between generalized social services, on the one hand, and more specific public goods such as land, employment, and education, on the other. This is an important distinction because it is access to, and distribution of, these specific public goods that formed the basis of many well articulated minority grievances.

In other words, post-1956 economic policy and its consequences did constitute a critical factor in the evolving ethnic conflict. What should also be noted here is that the impact of economic policy on specific constituencies was mediated by a number of factors ranging from language policy to the aspirations of young people. Before we examine these mediating factors, it is necessary to look at the structure of the postcolonial economy as it was within the limitations of this economy that the growing aspirations of different constituencies had to be satisfied.

Colonialism and the Postcolonial Economy

The colonial mode of production in the British colony of Ceylon produced what was later referred to as a dual economy, comprising an export-oriented plantation economy and a growing smallholder peasant economy, the latter largely producing subsistence food crops (Snodgrass 1966). The country did not undergo a process of urban industrialization. Thus the only large city in the country, Colombo, did not become a center of industrial production providing employment opportunities to prospective migrants from rural areas. This helped curb rural-urban migration.

As Sri Lanka's plantation sector employed mostly South Indian immigrant labor, it was the smallholding peasant sector that was open to the rapidly growing rural population. Sri Lanka's rural population increased from 1.8 million in 1871 to 7.2 million in 1959. Even though new land was cleared and made available to peasant families, per capita availability declined in absolute terms. The population ratio per acre of land increased from 1.9 to 3.1 during the same period. In other words, the average size of agricultural land parcels decreased steadily. Increasing population pressure led to continuing fragmentation of existing smallholdings, and landlessness emerged as a major issue even before independence, compelling successive governments to embark upon land redistribution programs, tenurial reforms, and peasant resettlement schemes in sparsely populated regions like the north-central and eastern parts of the country. Although many rural families benefited from these initiatives, rural agriculture remained unattractive to upwardly mobile youth belonging to all communities, largely due to declining profitability, lack of pensions, and low social status. Even if some youth wished to get into agriculture, increasing landlessness among rural families made this an unavailable option for them. With the rapid expansion of education in the country after the introduction of free education in the early 1940s, rural youth in large numbers acquired educational qualifications and aspired to white-collar employment in the state sector.[4] This was equally true for both northern Tamil youth and southern Sinhalese youth.[5] However, according to available data, from the 1970s on, unemployment among educated youth was a major problem. The rate of unemployment has been the highest among youth with a secondary education or above. For instance, the rate of unemployment in 1996 among those with no schooling was 2.2 percent. In the same year, unemployment for those with a secondary education was as high as 46 percent.[6]

Even though the native colonial elite was not divided along ethnic lines at the beginning of the twentieth century, signs of ethnic polarization emerged over the next four decades. Ethnic identity became an important aspect of preindependence elite politics. Prospects for a centralized parliamentary democracy that would give the majority community an overwhelming dominance in national politics persuaded the Tamil political elite to ask for safeguards to protect minority rights, but the parliamentary system of government that was established at the time of independence did not provide such safeguards.

The northern Tamil constituency had a major stake in the country's professions, educational system, and public service during the colonial period. Since the official language was English, those who had a good command of English had easier access to government jobs, which were considered to be prestigious, stable, and lucrative. In regional towns, including Jaffna on the northern peninsula, missionary schools made English-language education available to children even from nonelite families. In the major cities, fee-levying private schools were open to the affluent. Meanwhile, the vast majority of nonelite, rural children had to be content with a basic education in their native languages.

With the expansion of the education system from the early 1940s, the polarization between the English-educated and the Swabasha-educated became quite obvious. An English-educated minority continued to dominate the public service, modern professions, and higher educational institutions, relegating Swabasha-educated people to lower-rung occupations. Pressure was building up against the status quo. The demand for the change of the official language was one of the manifestations of the growing popular resentment. The thorny issue, however, was whether to make Sinhala the official language or to adopt both Sinhala and Tamil as official languages.

It is important to note that both Sinhala and Tamil were spoken in rural schools. While Sinhala was the language of instruction in most parts of the country, Tamil students in rural areas in the north and east were taught in Tamil. Although many Tamils in the north had attended English-medium schools, by the time of inde-

Table 5.1. Languages in Which Respondents Can Read

	Can read in Sinhala (%)	Can read in Tamil (%)	Can read in English (%)	Other (%)
All respondents (N=9,901)	9,062 (91.5)	1,341 (13.5)	1,456 (14.7)	93 (0.9)
Sinhalese respondents (N=8,582)	8,582 (100)	76 (0.9)	1379 (16.1)	48 (0.6)
Tamil respondents (N=1,261)	446 (35.4)	1,261 (100)	61 (4.8)	2 (0.2)
Burgher/Eurasian respondents (N=15)	9 (60.0)	3 (20.0)	15 (100)	0 (0.0)
Other respondents (N=43)	25 (58.1)	1 (2.3)	1 (2.3)	43 (100.0)

Source: S. T. Hettige 1999a.

Note: Some respondents can read in more than one language; therefore, the percentage totals will be more than 100.

pendence many more had become Swabasha-educated. This trend continued after independence, and the vast majority of educated youth, both Sinhalese and Tamil, soon became Swabasha-educated and monolingual. The National Youth Survey of 1999 found that 78.3 percent of rural youth and 56.6 percent of urban youth spoke English poorly or not at all (see Tables 5.1 and 5.2). Even though they hailed from ordinary village families, most of these youth aspired to white-collar employment in the state sector, which guaranteed regular salaries, job security, social prestige, and pensions, even without English proficiency. Such employment was important for them not just from an economic point of view. Given the lowly social background of many upwardly mobile rural youth, regular employment in the state sector amounted to significant social mobility, which would not have been possible outside that sector.

As mentioned before, no significant industrial sector emerged in the country before independence. What private sector did exist was composed mainly of service sector firms and plantation companies, which were organized largely on the basis of social networks such as those linked to family, kinship, and "old boy" (alumni) associations; these were not necessarily open to Swabasha-educated, rural youth who did not speak English and did not have access to urban elite networks. A clear case in point is the plantation sector, which recruited its executives and middle-level managers from the same social circle to which the owners of plantations belonged. Given this situation, it is doubtful whether the northern Tamil youth had easy access to white-collar jobs in the plantation sector even if they spoke English. This sector was opened up for educated rural youth only when the

Table 5.2. English Language Proficiency by Social Background

	Very Good	Good	Poor	Not at all
Total	2.5	22.3	45.0	30.1
Urban	7.8	31.6	40.4	16.2
Rural	1.1	20.6	45.7	32.6
Estate	3.0	13.6	37.9	45.6
Sinhalese	2.0	21.6	44.2	32.2
Tamil	3.1	21.7	49.6	25.5
Moor	6.2	31.0	43.8	19.0
Malay	—	50.0		50.0
Burgher	25.0	12.5	62.5	—
Western	5.6	27.0	42.1	25.2
Central	2.9	17.8	42.3	37.0
Southern	0.8	19.7	49.5	30.0
Northern	3.8	24.1	58.9	13.3
Eastern	1.5	27.3	59.3	11.9
Northwestern	0.6	25.7	41.9	31.8
North-central	0.6	16.6	39.2	43.6
Uva	0.6	14.4	42.8	42.2
Sabaragamuwa	0.7	19.1	41.5	38.6

Source: Hettige 1999b.

plantations were nationalized in 1972. In fact, following the nationalization of hitherto privately owned plantations, many university graduates hailing from ordinary rural families moved into managerial positions in this sector.

Thus, even though the state-led development strategies that were adopted following the election of the left-leaning MEP coalition in 1956 led to the expansion of state sector, rather than private sector, employment, not all segments of society benefited equally from this expansion, in part because of national language policy. As mentioned earlier, one of the key elements in the political agenda of the newly elected MEP coalition in 1956 was the abolition of English as the official language. The Sinhalese nationalist groups supporting the MEP coalition were successful in prevailing upon the latter to replace English with Sinhala. This naturally angered the Tamil constituency and led to open resentment and protests. Although legislation was introduced later to provide for the use of Tamil for official purposes in predominantly Tamil areas, a sense of injustice and discrimination remained in the minds of the Tamils.[7] Moreover, non-Sinhala-speaking minority groups tended to feel that their future prospects were bleak in a state-dominated economy. Many English-educated members of the minority groups began to migrate to other countries looking for better prospects.

Sri Lanka's economy remained highly regulated from the late 1950s until the late 1970s. During this period, productive assets were nationalized and state monopolies were established in a number of fields. Several import substitution industries were established in different parts of the country. Although some new jobs were created, they still were not adequate to meet the demand for regular state sector employment. The growing political pressure on the leaders to provide employment to the unemployed led to the creation of unproductive jobs. The result often was overstaffing in many public sector institutions.

Furthermore, non-Sinhala-speaking, monolingual Tamil and Muslim youth were excluded from the competition for white-collar jobs in the public sector institutions located in the predominantly Sinhala areas. As a result, the favorable position that the Tamils occupied in relation to public sector jobs during the British period was converted into a disadvantaged position in the first three decades after independence. The state sector jobs that monolingual Tamil youths could get were mostly concentrated in the northern and eastern parts of the island. The result was that they remained spatially and linguistically segregated from the predominantly Sinhala areas in the south and west. This no doubt reinforced their ethnic and regional identity, which is a critical factor in the present conflict.[8]

Tamil access to higher education was reduced in the early 1970s when a scheme of standardization was introduced to reduce regional imbalances that had persisted from the colonial times (C. R. de Silva 1974; Jayasuriya 1979). The proportion of Tamil-speaking students in professional courses like engineering and medicine at Sri Lankan universities was reduced from a very favorable to a substantially lower level. Since these courses offered the greatest opportunities for upward social mobility, a substantial reduction in university places due to state intervention was not taken lightly by those who were adversely affected. Lack of opportunities for employment and social mobility both within and outside the state sector no doubt frustrated non-Sinhala-speaking Tamil youth. It is noteworthy that the first political assassination against the Sri Lankan state was committed by militant Tamil youths in the mid-1970s,[9] several years before the state-dominated, protected economy was liberalized and opened to the outside world.

From State-Led Development to Economic Liberalization

By the mid-1970s, Sri Lanka faced serious economic difficulties (Hettige 1996, 1997). The unemployment rate reached crisis proportions, particularly among educated youth. The worsening foreign exchange situation compelled the incumbent government to reduce imports, which led to widespread shortages in basic commodities, including food. Many state enterprises were overstaffed and running at a loss. This situation offered a great opportunity for the advocates of economic liberalization. The main opposition party, the United National Party (UNP), which had long been committed to free enterprise, campaigned on a liberal economic platform and won a landslide victory in the 1977 general elections. This was the beginning of the present era of economic liberalism in Sri Lanka. Since then, there has been a gradual but steady decline in state domination and control over the economy and life chances. Today, market forces dominate almost all spheres of economic activity. Most state monopolies have given way to private enterprises operating in a state of relatively free market competition.

The private corporate sector, stagnant during the decades when the state dominated the economy, expanded rapidly after 1977 but did not change its recruitment practices. The effects of Swabasha-medium schools have continued to affect employment and have led to the virtual segregation of the country's school population on ethno-linguistic lines. Although children in ethnically mixed communities have continued to learn each other's languages in informal settings, the vast majority of children in the country did not have such opportunities (and, as Gamburd shows in this volume, such opportunities have declined during the civil war). Most children remain monolingual until they leave school or universities and look for jobs. Most private sector establishments conduct their business transactions in English and, therefore, are reluctant to open their doors to monolingual, Swabasha-educated youth, even if they have educational qualifications. The private sector employers argue that these "educated youth" do not have the skills and outlook necessary to fit into a modern business or office environment; therefore, employers prefer less-educated but English-speaking urban middle-class youth. The establishment of private and international schools in the country over the past two decades has created a large pool of English-educated urban youth, so there is no dearth of potential recruits to the private sector. Children attending better equipped public schools also find their way into the private corporate sector. As a result, unemployed Swabasha-educated youth, particularly from rural areas, allege that, due to their social class background, they are being discriminated against by the private sector.

Even though the private sector has expanded in recent years, at the expense of the public sector, it has not accommodated the continuing demands of rural youth for white-collar employment. The National Youth Survey found that while less than 5 percent perceived discrimination on the basis of race or religion, almost half of those surveyed thought that personal connections mattered in getting employment and 20 percent thought that low-income groups were discriminated against. It is this experience which perhaps produces their perception that the private sector discriminates against youth hailing from ordinary village families (Hettige 1999a, 1999b).[10] Given this situation, it is not difficult to understand why educated rural youth continue to be preoccupied with state politics and state sector employment. In our surveys, over 50 percent of respondents overall and close to three-fourths of respondents from Tamil-dominated northern and eastern regions said they preferred government jobs.

As the responses in Table 5.3 indicate, half of the respondents feel that private sector employers favor known groups and personal acquaintances. Many of them also state that lower-class applicants are discriminated against by the private sector. As Table 5.4 shows, more than half of youth in all parts of the country prefer state

Table 5.3. Forms of Discrimination in Hiring by
the Private Sector, as Perceived by Sri Lankan Youth

	Frequency	Valid percentage
Favoritism toward known groups and acquaintances	664	48.6
Bias against low-income applicants	269	19.7
Religious bias	10	0.7
Racial bias	63	4.6
Political bias	185	13.6
Other	174	12.7
Total	1,365	100.0

Source: Hettige 1999b.

sector employment, and only one-fifth have expressed a preference for private sector employment. This pattern is more pronounced in the northern and eastern provinces where the Tamil-speaking youth are concentrated. There are also significant variations between male and female as well as rural and urban respondents. Differences among educational groups are also noteworthy. For instance, many more women than men prefer state sector employment (nearly 67 percent as against 43 percent, respectively). Only 18 percent of rural youth prefer private sector employment, whereas 27 percent of their urban counterparts prefer this sector. The response pattern reverses in relation to the state sector. It is highly significant that university graduates have the greatest preference for state sector jobs. The proportion is as high as 72 percent as against less than 50 percent among those with a primary education.

Therefore, even though the private sector is expanding, it does not yet play a major part in facilitating upward social mobility for rural lower-class youth.[11] The expanding private sector has been the largest single employer of youth over the past two decades. Free Trade Zone factories, urban construction sites, and tourist hotels have attracted thousands of rural youth. On the other hand, the actual jobs that rural youth find in the private sector are only in lower-level, unskilled, or semiskilled occupations. This is not the kind of work that either northern or southern educated rural youth are seeking, and this contributes to their feeling that they are discriminated against by the private sector.

Thus it was not surprising that in our 1998 survey of nearly 300 middle-level executives drawn from 12 public and private sector companies, we found that the public sector continues to be the main employer of educated rural youth and facilitator of their upward social mobility (Hettige 2000).[12] The same survey, however, revealed that the public sector also continues to be heavily biased in favor of the majority Sinhalese community. In contrast, the private sector has become more ethnically inclusive.[13] As is evident from Table 5.5, minorities are underrepresented in the public sector, whereas they are better represented in the private sector.

Table 5.4. Sector of Employment Preferred by Sri Lankan Youth

	Government	Private	Self-employed	Other	Unknown
Total	53.4	20.0	24.8	1.5	0.3
Male	43.2	21.7	33.3	1.5	0.4
Female	66.8	17.9	13.5	1.6	0.2
Urban	44.7	27.1	26.1	2.0	0.2
Rural	55.8	18.1	24.2	1.5	0.3
Estate	52.7	19.5	27.8	—	—
Western	40.5	28.8	28.0	2.6	0.1
Central	55.9	22.1	22.7	0.3	1.1
Southern	57.7	18.4	23.0	1.0	—
Northern	75.0	5.5	19.5	—	—
Eastern	72.2	11.9	16.0	—	—
Northwestern	48.0	21.7	28.3	1.4	0.6
North Central	57.8	10.6	30.6	1.1	—
Uva	59.8	10.6	26.3	3.4	—
Sabaragamuwa	54.6	19.2	23.6	2.2	0.4
Grades 1–5	47.5	12.7	39.8	—	—
Grades 6–11	48.3	18.2	31.8	1.2	0.5
Ready for A level	57.2	22.4	19.1	1.3	—
Passed A level	62.3	22.7	11.6	3.3	—
BA or higher	72.2	21.5	5.1	1.3	—
No schooling	21.1	21.3	42.1	5.3	5.3

Source: Hettige 1999b.

Table 5.5. Ethnicity of Middle-Level Executive and Manager Respondents

	Public Sector	Private Sector
Sinhalese	27 (88.8)	106 (76.2)
Tamil	5 (3.4)	22 (15.8)
Muslim	3 (2.7)	6 (4.3)
Burger	4 (2.7)	2 (1.4)
Malay	3 (2.0)	3 (2.1)
Others	1 (0.6)	1 (0.6)
Total	143	139

Source: Hettige 2000.

Table 5.6. Factors That Public and Private Sector Employers Believe Should Affect Hiring

Factor	Public	Private
School	40 (27.9)	61 (43.8)
Sports	19 (3.2)	35 (25.1)
Political patronage	36 (25.1)	3 (2.1)
Informal social contacts	14 (9.7)	48 (34.5)
Religion	3 (2.0)	0
Ethnicity	4 (2.7)	0
Caste	1 (0.6)	0
Education	38 (26.5)	30 (21.5)
Professional qualifications	9 (6.2)	10 (7.1)
Experience	16 (11.1)	19 (13.6)
Family background	4 (2.7)	2 (1.4)
Aptitudes	5 (3.4)	4 (2.8)
Other	9 (6.2)	8 (5.7)
No response	10 (6.9)	16 (11.5)
Total	143	139

Source: Hettige 2000.
Note: These are the factors that were perceived to be helpful by the respondents. Multiple answers were allowed.

However, when the survey results are examined more closely, it becomes clear that the private sector recruits come from more privileged backgrounds, be they Sinhalese or Tamil. Interview data about higher executives' family backgrounds indicated that a majority of private sector recruits came from families in which the father had a high status occupation (i.e., professional or managerial). Moreover, these recruits come from more urbanized districts such as Colombo and Gampaha rather than more rural districts, either in the south or in the north. On the other hand, many public sector executives originate in less urban, southern districts such as Kalutara, Matara, and Galle. Finally, the private sector executives interviewed admitted that social factors mattered in getting both public and private sector employment, but more so in the private sector. School type, sports participation, and social contacts were indicated as important by one-third to almost half of the private employers, whereas political patronage and education were more important for one-third of the public employers. Ethnicity and religion figure almost not at all for both, particularly for the private sector (Table 5.6).

As the data in the tables indicate, the post-1977 increase in private sector jobs has not met the aspirations of upwardly mobile, educated rural youth. The public sector still is perceived by both youth and employers as being more egalitarian in terms of the social backgrounds of its recruits than the private sector. While the private sector is seen as being biased in favor of urban upper and middle classes, the public sector recruits employees from a much wider spectrum of social backgrounds and from different parts of the country.[14] However, this does not apply to ethnicity. In the private sector, ethnic representation approximates national proportions, although even the minority recruits come from privileged social backgrounds. This does not, however, mean that ethnic discrimination can be ruled out in the private sector altogether, particularly in less cosmopolitan, smaller business organizations that often tend to recruit managerial personnel on an informal basis from family and social circles. In fact, one private bank established in Sri Lanka after economic liberalization is well known for its Sinhala-Buddhist bias.

Conclusion

The radical shift in economic policy in 1977 had a major impact on the structure of the economy. The private sector, which was stagnant for many years after independence, emerged as the dominant player, providing income and employment opportunities to thousands of people, both urban and rural. Yet its impact on different segments of society has varied a great deal. The role that the public sector played in facilitating upward social mobility of thousands of educated rural youth has not been matched by the expanding private sector. In fact, the private sector has helped freeze the process of upward social mobility that had been under way for several decades after independence. Swabasha-educated, monolingual rural youth, in both the south and the north, do not see much opportunity in the private sector, which they perceive to be biased in favor of privileged, westernized social strata in urban areas.

The expansion of private and transnational educational institutions in and around Colombo, and in several regional urban centers, has resulted in a rapid increase in the number of potential recruits to middle and higher positions in the private corporate sector, leaving little chance for the products of rural schools throughout the country. So the transfer of decision-making power from a political elite to a business elite with respect to employment of educated youth has not made the situation any better for the underprivileged rural youth with educational qualifications whose main interest is to find white-collar employment with job security, social prestige, and old-age pensions.

The expanding private sector has provided income opportunities to social groups ranging from construction workers to retail traders. It also has opened up business opportunities to people with the necessary investment capital and entrepreneurial skills. There is no doubt that these opportunities are available to ethnic and regional groups.[15] Yet these are not necessarily the kinds of opportunities for which educated rural youth are searching. So they continue to believe that their future prospects depend on the political process, both in the south and in the north. However utopian this orientation may be, it is certainly in keeping with their past and present lived experience. Hence they remain preoccupied with state power, either at the national or regional level, which they believe is the primary source of redress for their grievances.

As mentioned earlier, the triumph of the private sector after economic liberalization led to a restructuring of the opportunity structures, but the new opportunities have not been made available to social groups equally. As for the members of ethnic groups, those belonging to privileged strata have benefited most from economic liberalization. In fact, those who have joined the new urban middle class[16] have mostly hailed from privileged urban families, irrespective of ethnicity. On the other hand, the less privileged youth belonging to all ethnic groups in general are unable to achieve upward social mobility within the expanding private sector, largely due to their Swabasha education. So, as far as Swabasha-educated Tamil youth are concerned, the shift from state domination to private sector domination has not improved their life chances. Like their Sinhalese counterparts in the south, underprivileged yet educated Tamil youth continue to seek state sector employment, which is perhaps as difficult to find today as ever. Yet, having been born and socialized in ethno-linguistically segregated communities and educated in similarly segregated schools, the disadvantaged Tamil as well as Sinhalese youth do not readily recognize the commonality of their predicament. Hence they identify with two divergent sociopolitical movements, one in the north (LTTE) and the other in the south (JVP). Their respective political projects tend to be antithetical to each other.[17]

Notes

1. As will be discussed later, social indicators of the Jaffna district compare favorably with more underdeveloped districts in the north as well as in the south (Gunatilleke 2000).
2. The National Youth Survey was carried out by the University of Colombo in 1999, with financial support from the United Nations Development Program. I was the principal researcher. The others in the team included Markus Mayer, Nishara Fernando, A. Robinson, Jinali Chandrika, and Anton Piyaratne. About 3,000 youths, both male and female, aged 16–29 years, from all parts of Sri Lanka were interviewed using a semistructured questionnaire. The purpose of the survey was to develop an up-to-date profile of Sri Lankan youth in terms of their socioeconomic background, sociocultural orientations, subjective assessments of economic, social, political, and cultural processes, and grievances and aspirations. This is the first islandwide survey of its kind, and it provides an excellent baseline for future research. Much of the data in this essay comes from that survey. Forty-six percent of respondents were female. The slight male bias of the sample was due to the exclusion of married persons from the sample. Age at marriage continues to be lower for females in Sri Lanka. Currently, age at marriage is about 26 for men and about 24 for women.
3. Citizenship rights were restored to most plantation workers in the 1980s, leading to increasing political representation and participation. Consequently, attention paid to their socioeconomic problems is greater today, and some significant improvements seem to be taking place in the plantation areas.
4. School enrollment ratio increased steadily after independence. By 1990, nearly 75 percent of the age cohort 5–19 years were attending school. The correspond-

ing figure was only 63 percent in 1981 (source: Sri Lanka Department of Census and Statistics 1981a).

5. Even after two decades of economic liberalization, educated rural youth, both northerners and southerners, continue to aspire to government jobs. The 1999 National Youth Survey showed that 75 percent of northern Tamil youths prefer government jobs (Hettige 1999b).

6. For detailed data, see Sri Lanka Department of Census and Statistics, 1944–79, 1996.

7. The domination of state institutions in many parts of the country by Sinhala-speaking people tended to alienate those who did not speak Sinhalese. This no doubt made life difficult for the latter. It is only very recently that this issue received some attention, but due to the absence of bilingual employees in many state institutions, it remains largely unresolved. Monolingual Tamil speakers even in the south continue to complain that they have difficulties in transacting official business in many situations.

8. It is interesting to note that, when English was the official language, many educated Tamils occupied white-collar jobs in the predominantly Sinhala south as railway station masters, postmasters, technical assistants, government clerks, etc. They are now retired, and many of them recall how they interacted with local people. Most of them are trilingual whereas most Tamil youths in the north and east today are monolingual.

9. The first major political murder in the north took place in 1974 when the suspected Tamil militants gunned down the mayor of Jaffna, Alfred Duraiappah, who was a member of the Sri Lanka Freedom Party, at the time headed by the prime minister, Mrs. Sirimavo Bandaranaike.

10. A majority of youth in the 1999 National Youth Survey expressed the view that the private sector tends to discriminate on the basis of social background.

11. See also Hettige 1999b.

12. This survey was conducted in 1998 with a research grant from the University of Colombo to determine the patterns of upward social mobility in public and private sector institutions. We interviewed middle-level executives/managers drawn from twelve institutions. The survey elicited information about the socioeconomic background of the respondents covering such areas as father's occupation, place of origin, type and place of schooling, social networks, educational attainment, and place of residence.

13. Approximately 16 percent of the private sector sample were Tamil, compared with only 3.4 percent in the public sector sample.

14. Recruitment to public sector institutions at middle and higher levels has usually been based on competitive examinations. This allowed both men and women to compete equally for public sector jobs. As a result, women have been represented in the public service to a considerable degree. This was revealed by the survey that I conducted. The same survey also pointed to the fact that the private sector is not as open to women as it is to men, particularly at higher levels of employment. The proverbial glass ceiling exists in the expanding private sector. On the other hand, the liberal economic policy led to the creation of many lower-level job opportunities for women such as those found in the Free Trade Zones and the Middle East. In the Middle East, they are mostly employed as housemaids.

15. The escalation of the ethnic conflict since the early 1980s inhibited free mobility

of youth from Tamil-dominated areas to the south due to security reasons. This no doubt prevented even less educated Tamil youth from moving into areas where low-status jobs became available.

16. For an account on the rise of the new urban middle class, see Hettige 1998.
17. While the LTTE is fighting to carve out a separate state in the north and east for the Tamil community, the JVP stands for an undivided state of Sri Lanka.

Part Three: *Articulations of
Civil War in
Everyday Life*

Introduction

Michael D. Woost

The authors in Part II helped to reinforce the argument that conflict and violence cannot simply be read off the prior interests of various categories of participants as they are positioned within an abstract overarching structure of opportunity. Participants in conflict and violence do not come into conflict and violence as ready-made subjects (in some respects, assuming that they did was a problem with Gunasinghe's analysis). Instead, subjects enter into that form of agency as people wrapped up in many scale-making projects (family, kin networks, party affiliations, different forms of employment, and so on). While some of these (class and party affiliation) are relatively discrete and can stand in opposition to each other, others (family and kin networks) may resonate more easily. Consequently, it is possible for multiple forms of identity, and hence agency, to emerge and be submerged in the course of everyday life and the extraordinary moments that punctuate its routines. Of course, this is why there has long been an understanding in the social science literature that identities should be seen as socially constructed and historically constituted. Even so, in many ways there is little ethnographic documentation as to how this social construction actually occurs. This, then, is the contribution of the authors in Part III. Francesca Bremner, Michele Gamburd, and Caitrin Lynch all attempt, in differing ways, to demonstrate just how people become articulated with violence and the war.

Previously, studies of the conflict often concentrated on how ideologies of national identity were disseminated to the public (see, for instance, Serena Tennekoon 1988, and the various articles in Spencer, ed. 1990). This was a useful endeavor, providing an outline of the many ways in which people of all walks of life become immersed in articulations of national identity, often without realizing it. More recently, other studies, such as Val Daniel

(1996; see also some of the essays in Gamage and Watson 1999; Das, Kleinman, Ramphele, and Reynolds 1998) have begun to provide more detailed studies of how conflict and violence are articulated in identity, consciousness, and practice. The effort involves looking not only at the experience of violence but also at its transformative effects on those people involved in its reproduction day to day.

To this end the essays in this final section bring us to the ground zero of articulation. Chapters by sociologist Francesca Bremner and anthropologists Michele Gamburd and Caitrin Lynch describe how three local groups—a lower-class community in Colombo, rural lower-class villagers in the southeast, and *juki* girls, women who work in Free Trade Zone garment factories— have engaged with the war through the material realities of their different lived experiences. Bremner's essay, based on 2001 fieldwork with people who participated in the 1983 riots, examines how lower-class ethnic identities were transformed in the process of that participation. She also makes it clear that ideologies of national identity were not always at the root of the emergent violence. Rather, it could be seen to emerge as many scale-making projects (employee/employer relations, community and temple relations, party politics) collided in the conjuncture of violence. Gamburd looks at military employment among poor rural men. For many of these young men, enlistment is not so much a matter of national patriotism; it may be their only source of employment. Or it may be the only source of employment that provides them with a sense of dignity. Being without a job or having a low-status job can undermine their sense of masculinity. Enlistment thus provides another avenue for alleviating their sense of lost dignity in their communities. Lynch explores the way moral panic about "good girls" exposed to western immorality (by sewing underwear for Victoria's Secret) resonates with concerns about the vulnerability of the Sinhalese Buddhist nation. Shortly after the Free Trade Zone factories were opened, there emerged considerable concern and then panic about the behavior of these factory women. Among the issues voiced were prostitution, rape, premarital sex, and abortion. As years went by, with more and more women working in factories, the moral panic grew louder. The issue of women in the factory became increasingly articulated with the scale-making projects of various politicians, taking the historically shifting forms of panic as an opportunity to raise their own stature in the public eye. What ensued was an argument about the loss of Sinhalese Buddhist tradition: as these women workers were making their lives, they were undermining the nation itself. Thus their identities were clearly transformed by their engagement with factory work. In their new day-to-day lives, making a living became a threat to the nation. This in turn further reinforced ideas of national tradition.

The technology of vision provided in these three essays demonstrate clearly how unpredictable the articulation of identity and agency can be. Policy changes are made, war is expanded, new "opportunities" arise, and others are lost. Yet reference to these raw facts alone cannot predict or explain the manner in which people articulate with such changes, nor can it explain the extent or form of the conflict or violence that could possibly ensue. For that we have to sharpen our vision, look at the space where lives are made and unmade. Even so, we contend that all these forms of vision are needed. Taken together, they give us a multidimensional view of conflict and violence as it emerges and is reproduced.

6   Fragments of Memory, Processes of State: Ethnic Violence through the Life Histories of Participants

Francesca Bremner

Sri Lanka in July 1983 again? The dust has settled on 1983, and the formations of violence appropriate to a civil war have bypassed that momentous turning point. To go back to 1983 in the light of these subsequent challenges seems doomed to be an intellectually jaded project. The reasons that I do so are twofold. One is that I do not view 1983 only as a moment that gave momentum to the civil war. On the contrary, I attempt to illustrate the way in which the structural and ideological effects of 1983 continue to emerge and shape everyday life. Thus, rather than move away from this moment, I examine the ways in which that conjuncture continues to be implicated in current social formations.

The other reason for this study is that my analysis of 1983 is built upon the life histories of a group of men who participated in the acts of violence. Identity is here conceptualized as a social production of state formation. In this study the men who participated, and who are treated as passive templates upon which the state drew its ideological formations, give "voice" to their own violence and their relationship to the state. The "I" that these men bring to the study is valuable in understanding the social constructions of identity, its continuities, ruptures, and limitations from the point of view of the participants in the violence as prior identities shift within the tight press of the unfolding context. The social construction of identity is not presupposed here, but is explored in the grit, blood, and sweat of its etchings as the participants move through the pathways of their everyday lives. People experience the impact of macro structures only within these pathways as they move through the micro politics of its spatial and conceptual realms in which history and context coalesce and sometimes collide. Thus the emphasis of this chapter is on these pathways, in which complex identities already emergent in social life are further transformed and reshaped within new practices that condition new contexts, new conceptual possibilities, and new ways of being.

The majority of the people who participated in this ethnic violence were from squatter settlements within Colombo. My study is set in a settlement that residents call Apee Gama, "our" (*apee*) "village" (*gama*), although it spans only the upper part of one little street. In 2001, I spent six months collecting life histories from about 25 men who participated in the violence against their middle-class Tamil neighbors.

I employ a web of life histories that move through approximately the same space and time to produce a matrix of interactions. This matrix takes this study beyond personal narratives into the heart of the community in which the actors are embedded. Along the way, the life histories are seen to intersect, forming the coordinates of the social matrix as well as the points where the social matrix unravels and separates.

The Setting: Apee Gama

Apee Gama forms the entryway into the street. It begins with a small grocery store that is also a hangout for the men. A whole world outside Apee Gama comes into view when one stands at this entry point, for it is situated at the confluence of four streets. It gives a clear line of vision to the Buddhist temple and to the margins of the police compound. Although only about a quarter-mile in length, it contains a public bathroom, little alleyways that open into rows of tenements, and a common tap that bounds the lower end of Apee Gama. Next to the bathroom is a trishaw stand. The trishaws are parked in the order of their arrival, and hires are taken in the order of arrival. After each hire the trishaw returns and takes its place at the end of the line once more. These young men, who are mostly in their twenties, have created a space for themselves at the side of the street where they sit reading newspapers while they wait for the next ride. The washing of the public bathroom rotates daily from family to family and, as in the trishaw stand, there is a strong sense of order and fairness.

Apee Gama seems to be characterized by a certain relative equality that is reflected in the absence of "strong men." The inhabitants of Apee Gama pointed out that the only "strongmen" were a few women who belonged to the same family. They were bigger in size than the men and had the power of rhetoric. They could "outswear" anyone anytime, and the others kept out of their way during fights. These women were verbally and sometimes physically violent during fights; otherwise, they did not attempt to dominate anyone.

Within this broad frame of equality was a landscape of hierarchy in which those few who had a steady income were given respect. Those who held government jobs (usually at its lowest end) with pensions and benefits fit into this category. The other men in Apee Gama were mostly fruit vendors (a seasonal job), trishaw drivers, and masons. These men were mostly Sinhala Buddhists and were related through kinship or marriage.

Many residents, especially those who live in the tenements, lack water and electricity because their dwellings are classified as "illegal," and so they use the public bathroom and tap. The street is an explosion of life, color, and interaction as vendors pass by calling to the residents; women wash themselves, children, and dishes at the public tap; men "hang out" to chat and watch the girls; and friends drift in to join the action. Arguments break out intermittently, adding to the excitement as some residents calm and other residents rush to take sides. Thus this little spatial area teems with life. To the middle classes, the street is merely the connection between destinations. It is a surface of entry and departure points. The innermost realm of a middle-class home, the bathroom and tap, are here set within the street for the people who live in Apee Gama. The small tenements become the domain of the women as the men spill out into the street. Relations that are built into practices unfurl in these spatial locations, drawing the various sites of the street into the nooks and crevices of everyday life, thus contouring the street as a place of pulsating interaction.

The class composition as well as the texture of the rest of the street is markedly different. The houses here range from middle to upper middle class. This area was once one of the elite residential areas of Sri Lanka and was characterized by old-style mansions. One of the few remaining mansions was owned by the family of the first head of state of Sri Lanka. The second head of state of independent Sri Lanka was born in this residence. Another elite residence that comprised guest homes, servants' quarters, and stables is now one of the schools for the children of Apee Gama. Most of these elite residents sold their mansions to middle- and upper-middle-class residents and moved to more prestigious locations. Today the ethnic makeup of this part of the street was mostly Tamil with a generous sprinkling of other ethnic groups. This part of the street is striking by the absence of life and textures of movement that characterize the upper part. Walls and gates hide inside spaces within which a very different life unfolds. The street thus is used by the middle class only as an entryway to and from the home when going out beyond the walls. Few cars travel the street, since cars cost as much as a house in Sri Lanka. Those who passed by in their cars in 1983 were perceived as arrogant if they had not had any prior contact with the residents of Apee Gama.

Lives produce spatial realms through interaction, and these realms entangle and shape intimately the world of everyday life. The macro structures of state and nation, by being part of the relational and ideational pathways of daily life, move through these spatial realms. Thus these spatial realms seethe with social bonds and entangled conceptual possibilities which are crucial to the shaping of action. An understanding of the sociospatial world of the participants of the violence before the actual moment of violence is important if we are to understand prior identities of the participants.

The sites at which the men of Apee Gama met the middle class were at the walls, gates, and backdoors of the middle class as they performed the tasks of domestics. The relations that the middle class had with the poor revolved around the axis of keeping their distance socially so that the hierarchy of respect and authority could be upheld. Thus the tradition of the backdoors for the poor. The tap was a transition point for the middle class who journeyed through the street to various enduring destinations such as work. The sight of women bathing at the tap caused the men of the middle class to hurry by with averted eyes. The only middle-class Burgher man who gazed at the women from the vantage point of his house directly opposite the tap was a source of hilarity to the middle class and the poor alike, who considered him to be deviant.[1] Beyond the tap was a profusion of noise and activity to the women in the middle class who walked by quickly to avoid the crowd of men who hung out. This was also a site of unpredictability, for the men could "cast remarks" about the women if they did not conform to certain expected norms of behavior. Usually the men did not make remarks about the middle-class women, but there was the fear among the middle-class women that they would, and any remarks could bring shame on the family. This was one way of the poor denting the class hierarchy if the middle class did not conform to their expectations. Thus, relations did not hinge on a straight model of domination and subordination between the classes but was negotiated, although the axis of class was its organizing core. The bathroom came next, and this was a source of olfactory repugnance to the middle class. Thus those of the middle class who walked hurried by through the poor section as quickly as they could. Everyday practices spooled into these spatial structures, and the lived relations within this street were that of class. My descriptions attempted to capture the different ways in which these different classes used the same space.

Yet the mere act of living on one street brought the middle class and the poor into contact. Thus the middle class and the poor were implicated in a web of relations that began when the middle class walked through Apee Gama seeking people to work in their homes, or when the poor went to the middle class to request donations for a community *daansala* or personal need.[2]

In the ethnic violence of 1983, however, these residents of Apee Gama moved into the rest of the street to break into and burn the Tamil homes and sometimes to commit acts of violence against the Tamils who lived in the other half of the street. These acts were committed in the name of a Sinhala Buddhist state and nation. Yet these protagonists seemed to have many ambiguities in their intersection with state and nation.

The Nation

The residents of Apee Gama categorize themselves as Sinhalese Buddhists, yet they move with fluidity between and within other religions. A resident from Apee Gama paid me a visit at my family home. The family dog, a Doberman Pinscher, broke away from his moorings and charged at us (I was a stranger to this dog, too). The resident from Apee Gama repeatedly made the sign of the cross on himself as the dog drew closer. After the dog was intercepted in mid-pounce by apologetic relatives and led away, I asked this young man if he was a Catholic. He replied that he was a Buddhist. Hindu gods and Catholic saints were constantly evoked to cure the sick, seek revenge for injustice, and bring prosperity. There was a mutual understanding that all gods were equal, and this led to an acceptance of and respect for Buddhism, Hinduism, and Catholicism, religions with which the residents were familiar. Yet Buddhism as a rigid category with unyielding boundaries seemed to exist only within the abstract sphere of the nation. The lived relations with the monk and temple were deeply problematic.

The ancient temple at the top of Apee Gama had figured prominently in the fight for Buddhism over Christianity during independence and had been declared a historical monument by the state. The residents of Apee Gama claimed this temple as their own and were proud of its history as well as its connection to them. In the far past the temple has had close ties with the mansions, as well as with the people of Apee Gama. In the 1960s, this era came to an end with the advent of a young chief monk who carried a pistol in his robe, bred dogs for sale on sacred ground, openly nurtured an all-consuming passion for pretty women, and attempted to "civilize" the inhabitants of Apee Gama through physical force.

The residents resisted the monk by withholding symbolic legitimacy. They routinely called him a *pina*, a derisive term for a person who lives off others. It is considered a duty and an honor to give to a monk, and the meaning of this word brings into focus the unworthiness the residents attributed to this monk. On April Fools' Day, residents joked that the monk had died (*pina apawathvuna*). The structure of the sentence was innovated upon to produce an incongruity between the noun and the verb. Although the noun *pina* denoted a lowly man, the verb *apawathvuna* indicated the death of a noble man. This juxtaposition threw into relief "what was" with "what should be" and produced much hilarity in its wake. The residents rejected the monk and covertly and overtly resisted any symbolic power due to him. One young man recalled:

> I was ten and flying a kite on the temple/school grounds. It was difficult to get my kite off the ground. I struggled with the rope, not noticing the monk walking along. I looked up just in time to see the kite smash into the side of his head. He put his hand up by his ear and crushed my kite in one fist. I reached down and picked up a handful of red clay and threw it at the monk. I can still remember the clay breaking against his head into a cloud of dust, like red smoke. I then raced to the wall, climbed over, and ran home. I never went back.

The temple became a site of struggle rather than an affirmation of Buddhism and a testament to the nation.

The State

Almost every man in Apee Gama has suffered some form of police brutality. The police are seen as corrupt and unjust, building up their lives on bribes. Some of the most vicious cases of police brutality seem to be within a feud between two closely related families in which one family had the resources to bribe the police to terrorize the other family. The residents who are marginal in the social order and powerless are very vulnerable to the power of the police. To go against the police is perceived as exceeding one's limitations of power. "Like hitting your head against a rock. It is only your head which will break," explained one man. The powers which the residents evoke are the weapons of the weak.

> Once my brother was taken to the police station because of some complaint. We think the other party bribed the police. The policeman beat him so much and dragged him all along the street to the police station. He almost died. The people in this village gathered around and cursed and cried. The women gathered up dust from the earth

and cursed the policeman in the name of God. Later this policeman married a police-woman from the same station and had two children, both of whom were born handicapped. They cannot walk. Curses made with such pain have power.

Although these residents understand their vulnerability and limitations in the face of certain powers, they are also able to create spaces that buffer the mental vulnerability of this structural power in some way.

The state also enters the lives of the inhabitants of Apee Gama through the office of the local government minister for the district. This is an elected office. Political party affiliations fracture the inhabitants. There are two parties, and those who choose wisely and end up with the winning party are amply rewarded by the politician with government jobs at the lowest rungs. These jobs carry a pension and some benefits, and they create a certain hierarchy in the social landscape of Apee Gama.

Therefore, the minister's office becomes a resource, albeit an unpredictable and arbitrary one. One young man told me of how he had waited for hours to meet the minister, who was invited to a festival at the temple. When the minister arrived, this young man stepped forward and said, "Sir, I worked very hard for you during your campaign." His cousin, with whom he had very close ties, stepped forward and said, "Sir, his family belongs to the other party." Thus, although he worked for the party putting up posters, he lost his chance of a government job and felt terribly betrayed by his cousin, someone he cared for and trusted.

As he put it, "It is hard to have any long-term collective action because people who live side by side with you inform on you to the minister." For example, one group planned to build a bathroom with the help of an independent candidate who ran for office. The people who came together began to split as different people turned informants to the existing minister and people perceived a drop in the minister's willingness to help them in the future. The minister helps out with funeral expenses, writing letters of recommendation for jobs, and assists in emergencies, although only if one is in his good books. It is vital that one be on the right side.

People in Apee Gama help each other out constantly, and open rifts are papered over quickly. However, no one knows who will become an informant. The enemy is invisible and could be someone close to you. Alliances between the inhabitants shift constantly, creating rippling movements of conflict and solidarity, and the state sometimes silently moves these tracks as it sifts into the closest spaces between people who are so physically close that one cannot even sigh without being heard.

The ties between residents and the state are conflictual, ambiguous, and problematic. They were part of the Sinhala Buddhists for whom the nation had been built and looked to the state to provide them with viable strategies for living, but the links that the agents of the state built with them fractured their unity and were sometimes brutal and unpredictable. They lived marginal lives economically, socially, and politically; thus, although they were part of the "chosen" people of the Sinhala Buddhist nation, everyday life exposed this as irony, and yet it was in the name of the Sinhalese Buddhist nation that they rose up.

Moments of Collective Violence

There is a disquiet at the anticipation of violence. I have experienced it many times as a Tamil before and after 1983. Normal talk dwindles into hushed whispers in a space of waiting that seems to have multiple incomprehensible possibilities. The Tamils slowly melt into private places, leaving the public spaces for the Sinhalese. These public spaces provide the most unpredictable points of rupture and violence.

On this particular day, gruesome scenes of violence emerged on the streets as crowds beat and burned Tamils who had the misfortune of being out in the streets. Studies of this particular day have shown the presence of an "institutional riot system" in which violent specialists played a vital role. In my study I move from anonymous violence by skilled specialists of violence to ask how people who are usually not violent could be moved to violence against their neighbors in the name of state and nation.

Theories of state formation have illustrated the ability of the state to shape and "fix" identities in the process of nation building that bursts into violence (Bastian 1990; Kakar 1996). Although some of the men of Apee Gama had followed the nationalist discourses in the newspapers and felt for the nation, it was not enough to move them into violence. The nation did not entangle with the minute texture of everyday life. They defined their feelings of "before 1983" as respect and not love. Yet, after their participation in the violence, they felt deeply about the nation and their place in it. Their feelings had changed from respect to that of moral entitlement to the nation. What were the elements of this shift, and how was the state implicated in it? It is possible to explore answers to all the questions above only through a journey into the tangle of events and emotions of that fateful day.

A group of men at Apee Gama had been up all night building a little shop for a friend who wanted to open a business in tailoring. Toward dawn, fragments of information on the impending ethnic violence began to sift in. The junction at the top of the street seemed devoid of movement as people stayed away from work. There was no movement from the Tamils in Apee Gama, either. Other men in Apee Gama joined the group at the newly built tailor shop. A few decided to go to what they considered to be the center of the action, an open street that was the heart of the business area, a half-hour fast walk from their little street. To the men this area seemed to represent the heart of the nation. Here they joined a group of men who pried open the locks of Tamil shops and surged inside to take what they could before setting the shops on fire. The Apee Gama men hung around the fringes of this crowd, stole a few long steel rods from a burning warehouse, and then ran away.

They made their way home, self-conscious because the rods were so long and because they had never stolen before. They encountered three policemen with guns and almost dropped their rods and ran in fear, but the policemen did not say anything to anyone. They just watched the groups. Relieved, the men kept walking, only to run into a few "strong men" from the area who stopped them, took their steel rods, and ordered them to get lost. Thus neighborhood territorial boundaries came to rest upon the monolithic idea of the nation. The nation began to revolve around the lived relations and networks embedded between and within each neighborhood. These networks also encompassed state actors.

The mob boss arrived formally with his retinue to ask the men of Apee Gama to avenge the nation. He had given them money when they were in need, and thus they felt that reciprocation of his favors was in order. So a few men from Apee Gama set off with the mob boss to avenge the nation. This took the form of burning some shops this mob boss wanted back from his Tamil tenants. The men were forming the core, but they still felt like outsiders because this was not their neighborhood, although it was only a few blocks from where they lived. Neighborhood is more than spatial proximity; it is the dense relations that harbor a sense of belonging. The violence perceived as ethnic was also deeply embedded in the relations within each neighborhood.

Meanwhile the police, the army, and the local politician came to Apee Gama to incite its inhabitants to go on a rampage. They were assured by state actors that this was low-risk collective action, so they could only gain by such linkages. It was a momentary opportunity structure that would afford them a better bargaining position with these tangible sites of power. Yet they waited, not knowing what to do.

According to Swarna, who was about 15 years old in 1983:

> The riot came to this street around two thirty in the afternoon. Gamini had gone to the tap to wash his face. It was as if he suddenly became possessed with some feeling. He yelled, "Everyone else is burning out the Tamils, and we are sitting here, doing nothing." He then rushed to no. 46 or the house next to it and brought out a chair, which he set on fire in the street.

No. 46 lies just beyond the tap, which the residents of Apee Gama perceive as their boundary line. It would be reductive here to place the moment of violence either on structure or on agency. These structural conditions were activated only within the emotion-filled performance of an unfolding context. The men were emphatic that they would not have participated without some belief in state protection. The police and the minister came by to ask the men to "protect the nation." When the violence began, there was a specific pattern to the violence. Not all Tamil homes were attacked, and this pattern entangled the dense web of relations between the men of Apee Gama and the Tamils. Although a "safe space" for violence opened up for these men through the activation of certain existing state ties, they waited and evaluated the situation until they were propelled into the violence by the unfolding *context* (Latour 1988; Suchman 1987). Action thus is a product of conditions and context, background and foreground factors.

Once drawn in, however, the nation, which revolved around the monolithic axis of Sinhalese Buddhism, began to acquire multiple meanings as the participants sketched violence into different formations at the local level of lived relations.

Vajira, who was 20 years old in 1983, told me:

> My dove flew onto the roof of the doctor's house. [The doctor is Tamil, but he was out of the country.] I climbed onto the roof to get my dove back, and the Tamil caretaker

called the police. The police slapped me and made me apologize to this man. A month later, the riot began. This was the first house we attacked in this street. We dragged the old man out and kicked him. Then I found a piece of metal with a raw edge and drew it down this man's back. We ran away because we heard the police. Later the police gave me petrol to set that house on fire. I didn't want to, but I did because they asked me to.

The violence seemed to be the worst at the points where the antagonisms of the nation intersected with those of the local. The now sharpened boundaries of the nation articulated lived experience with ease. But this Durkheimian moment of collective euphoria had its ruptures as the ongoing struggle for power broke through.

"Jolly Boys" is the name of the Apee Gama cricket team. Jolly Boys and their supporters encompassed almost all the men of Apee Gama. Each generation of Jolly Boys included a few young men from the wealthy Tamil homes down the street, such as Rajan, who was a member of the team in 1983. He had formed a deep bond with Sugath, a man who lived in Apee Gama. Sugath ran all the way from work to Rajan's home where he was entrusted with three milk cans of gold, which he kept safe for Rajan. Sugath slept in Rajan's home on the night of the riots, but he could not prevent the house from being broken into by the older men from Apee Gama. Sugath belonged to Apee Gama and yet was on its margins because he was pursuing higher education at a prestigious high school. This struggle for power yielded a compromise that kept the house from being razed. Since different Tamil households had had different modes of relations with the many households in Apee Gama, this protection was dependent on the structural, rhetorical, and physical power that the protectors had over the other residents of Apee Gama.

Although the violence lay on the basis of a unified nation of the Sinhalese, territorial claims and fractures among the Sinhalese played a vital role in it. The residents of Apee Gama had to protect their territory against invasions from groups who came in from other areas. This did not happen very often, as groups usually respected the territory of others. When it did happen, the men and some of the women of Apee Gama arrayed themselves on the sides of the street to frighten the invaders off. At times this did not work, and they formed momentary alliances with these groups.

A big, two-storied house on the edge of Apee Gama, which also bordered a squatter settlement, became a violent site of struggle. The Tamil inhabitant of the house was well liked and held in high esteem by the residents of Apee Gama, and they rushed to his defense as the men of the squatter settlement entered his home and began beating him with iron rods. The men of the other settlement had pistols with which they warded off the men of Apee Gama and claimed this house as their own.

The participants thus groped within the realm of lived experience for the abstract sphere of the nation. The categories of identity here were not linear. Thus the same young men who burned some homes and cars protected others at great risk to themselves. In most cases they took that risk out of personal choice, though others protected Tamil homes and lives for a payment. Violence emerged through the emotions and meanings of lived experience, territorial claims, and ongoing struggles for power.

The easiest thresholds to cross symbolically and physically were those of new migrants who had just moved into the neighborhood. The social templates remained a blank without a past, and these interactions were characterized by the absence of anger or trepidation on the part of the men of Apee Gama. The narration of these interactions was playful and lighthearted:

> There was some soft clay which one of my brothers had mixed with water to make something. We, the girls and boys, dipped our hands in this clay and ran through this house putting our hand prints all over their walls. We would then go into their bathroom and wash our hands in the water tank. The boys would try to hold the hands of the girls under the water. The girls just giggled. We then went out again and dipped our hands in the clay again and continued. That house was our plaything.

This house was one of the last to be invaded, mostly because it lay on the borderland of class. None of the Tamils who lived within Apee Gama was attacked. Even the new arrivals were protected. This particular home was well within the spatial territory of Apee Gama, and yet the Tamil daughter of the house was a chemist, placing the family on the margins of Apee Gama with regards to class. Many of the men expressed their apprehension at attacking the house, and so they left it until the end. Yet the crossing of the threshold made it into a "Tamil" home that they could spatially imprint with their presence.

As many symbolic and physical thresholds were crossed, the crossing became easier and was justified through feelings of inequity which brought forth contours of a new sense of entitlement that was being articulated in the name of the nation. Honda, who was 25 years old in 1983, spoke of the violence to the property of a new migrant:

> There was the crackling of things burning all around us. It was our doing. We went into the house of that jeweler and pulled out his car and set it on fire. It was fun for a group of young boys to do. In that crackling sound and smell there was a freedom, an enjoyment. It was our kingdom.

It was not "our nation" but "our kingdom" which evoked an even stronger right, that of a monarch over his monarchy. This was one of the same young men who had been so self-conscious about stealing as they carried the steel rods away from the burning warehouse. The moral narratives he held then placed the action firmly as stealing; however, as he was drawn into the collective press of emotion, choice, and relational discourses and ties, this narrative of morality began to change to one of entitlement.

Immediate Aftermath

The state through the national media justified the violence of the actors and reaffirmed its link to the Sinhala people. Thus the violence became "fixed" as a riot of Sinhalese against the Tamils. Structural forces at the local level strained this link. The breakdown in the transport systems produced a severe shortage of food in the city in the immediate aftermath of the violence. Inhabitants of Apee Gama who only earned enough for their daily bread had no stocks of food to tide them over. They now turned on the Sinhalese food markets, which were closed due to the curfews. Breaking the windows with crowbars, they stole everything. "The police, who were friendly until then, began to glare at us," said one inhabitant. Thus this sense of entitlement had begun to spill into other arenas, and rumors began to circulate that the Sinhalese Christians would be next. The Sinhalese Christians were perceived as belonging to the middle classes. These visions of the nation were different from the ones that the state had structured through the national media. Soon the state began to crack down on "disorder."

The army was called in, and they set up camp on the grounds of the temple with its direct visibility of Apee Gama. The police and the army rampaged through Apee Gama relentlessly, searching every little tenement and sweeping the inhabitants away to the police station and army camp, which was the school on the temple grounds. The monk opened parts of the temple as a refuge for the now homeless Tamils whose homes had been razed. The army made a public spectacle of punishing the men. They were dressed as women and paraded on the streets with stolen goods on their heads and made to shout, "I was the keeper and protector of the nation" and whipped as they were thus paraded. These rituals of humiliation unfolded on the very street that these men had possessed as their own. Their masculinity and sense of entitlement through nationhood were parodied as state actors attempted to invert the meanings and entitlements these men claimed.

One man had 100,000 rupees buried in his one-room tenement, and it was stolen by the next morning. The rough equality of Apee Gama was placed under a strain as rumors circulated about the money, jewelry, and other such items others had the good fortune to find.

The momentary unity and context through which meanings of entitlement and nationhood had been forged were splintered. Yet the meanings produced within these darkly relational webs emerged stark and untouched. The subjectivity of nationhood that had emerged from the experience of collective action had shifted from respect to a deep feeling of entitlement. The state then attempted to reverse these new entitlements by negating their effects through violence inscribed on the bodies of these participants. This violence of negation, however, became the site through which the participants imagined the state, the nation, and the other groups in relation to it. The state was now viewed as separate from the nation to which these participants belonged. The police, the rich Sinhalese, and the state officials were all in league with the Tamils. They had sold out the country by supporting the Tamils. "It is only us, the poor Sinhalese, who have a love for the nation," said one man. "It is because we can cry for another. It is only the poor who can cry. The rich man only whizzes by in his car. The ability to cry is the foundation for *jaatika alaya.*" The phrase *jaatika alaya* means love of the nation and is also synonymous with love of the race, here the Sinhala race.

The nation, imagined from the site of state betrayal, was thus drawn from the depth of lived emotions and physical experience. Its members, however, were an excluded group, separate from the state actors who attempted to link themselves to the poor through the violence on the Tamils. It was a nation of the poor Sinhalese disconnected from the rich Sinhalese as well as the Tamils. Thus was articulated another vision of Sri Lanka.

Continuities

The riots of 1983 had consequences that involved the national and international levels through the escalating war and different patterns of migration. Many Western countries opened their borders to the Tamils. Middle-class Tamil families left. The second wave of migration happened after the international borders were closed. Those who attempted the dangerous journey to the West through illegal means were young people, mostly from Jaffna, who were fleeing the war. These young people left their families behind and sent foreign exchange to these families to get out of the war zone and into Colombo. Soon the houses in Apee Gama were bought by Tamils from Jaffna, and the residents of Apee Gama were confronted with the "real enemy." The men suddenly began to feel in the minority and collectively pored over the loss of the Sinhalese nation while lamenting the absence of "Sinhala faces" in the neighborhood.

"If only we knew . . . that they were not from Jaffna, then we would not have attacked them," said some of the men rather shamefacedly of the Colombo and Indian Tamils they had attacked. They thus extricated one category of Tamils from the others. However, they felt that they had to watch all Tamils every second. All Tamils were all supporters of the LTTE. This conceptual boundary began to bleed into the relations and solidarity of the men themselves, as one man told me of his interaction with his friend, a Tamil man who participated in the violence with his Sinhalese friends from childhood: "We scold him for the bombs the Tigers set off and joke that he is a Tiger. He says that he is not and then we tell him that he is a Tamil and so a Tiger. I really want that to cut into him."

A Tamil man from the same squatter settlement spoke of the fear his family felt as new entrants into this Sinhalese enclave. They had only been there for a year when the violence began. Although they did not know their Sinhalese neighbors well, these neighbors did not bother them in any way. They closed their doors and stayed inside. Yet, after 1983, the boundaries of ethnicity were so sharpened that at the perception of any slight neighborly transgression he was called *Demala* (Tamil) by the neighbors. This stopped him from forming any close relationships with the participants.

Although this milieu could be assumed to create clear polarization and boundaries, this was not so. There were sites at which the Tamils from Jaffna and the men in Apee Gama interacted with each other; this created new ties, even though these men did view the people from Jaffna as the enemy. Some of the men from Apee Gama were trishaw drivers, and in this category they interfaced between communities. Tamils were their regular customers, and they ferried Tamil children and young women back and forth and took pride in the fact that the Tamil parents trusted them. The most generous donor to the *daansala* was a Tamil man who was thought to contribute to the Tigers. Stories abounded of the visits of the Tigers to this man. Although the honor of "opening" the *daansala* was always given to a Sinhalese Buddhist man, the organizers of the *daansala* felt obliged to award the honor to this particular man from Jaffna, since he had made a significant contribution. This event caused rifts in Apee Gama. As these new ties were formed between the Jaffna Tamils and the men, some of the old ties with the long-standing Tamil residents of the street were losing their density.

A common custom of reciprocity is for the organizers to send portions of the food from the *daansala* to the donors. The mansion was overlooked this year, and the inhabitants of the mansion were sure that all of their share of food as a reciprocal gesture for their contribution had been sent to a Jaffna Tamil home in the street because they used the trishaw of the organizer often. Thus even while the structure of ethnicity underpinned everyday practice, the categories and boundaries sutured for this formation were crystallized or blurred within the tangle of different contexts. The escalation of the war in the north was articulated in the south through sporadic bomb attacks by suicide bombers. The police invited the residents of Apee Gama to be part of the vigilante force against the Tamils. The spatial structure was ideal for this purpose, since Apee Gama formed the entryway to the street, and the police station was a few feet away. The people at Apee Gama took the task of vigilante duty very seriously. They watched the movements of any new Tamil carefully and made immediate reports to the police. On the first two days of my research, I was unaware that I was being watched by a group of women who then reported to the police that I was a suicide bomber. A home guard from the police station at the top of Apee Gama threw me against a wall, attempting to defuse the bomb I was supposedly carrying. I was rescued before he could take me away. Once picked up, the antiterrorist laws give open license for anything, including torture. Thus this net of surveillance is also one of terror for the Tamils, as one could easily get lost within the myriad custodial mazes. (Aside from the police, there are other cadres out in full force, such as the army, the special operations people, the dreaded special task force, and the central intelligence department, to name a few, and any one of these could be contacted by the public to report "suspicious" activities.) The power of surveillance given to the residents of Apee Gama was a potent one indeed.

This power of surveillance was given under the structure of the Arakshaka Samithiya (protection committee), which was started by a high-ranking police officer who invited volunteers to protect their communities from terrorism. The middle class of the street, including the Tamils, were invited. The structure of hierarchy within this society began to closely resemble the everyday world of the inhabitants of Apee Gama. "The police and the rich Sinhalese and Tamils talk in English knowing we cannot understand the language. We sit there saying nothing," said one man bitterly. There was a sense of betrayal and the solidarity of being poor together. Their alternate vision of the imagined nation was reaffirmed once more.

Conclusion

The rioting of 1983 had consequences at the national and international levels through the escalating war and different patterns of migration. These shaped a new geography of ethnic interactions at the local level. The social construction of identity at the "ground zero" of lived practice is the site (see introduction to this volume) at which ethnicity is reproduced and blurred. Historically specific meanings tangle with contexts to create new collages of conceptually possible interactions and ways of being, both violent and nonviolent.

Notes

1. A Burgher is a person of mixed Sri Lankan and Western heritage. Burghers are perceived as not belonging to either the Sinhalese or Tamil ethnic categories.
2. *Daansala* means "hall of alms," a booth built on the roadways to distribute food and drink. The men host them during Buddhist festivals. The middle class funds the *daansala,* organized by the men of Apee Gama; it feeds hundreds of people a day and remains open for two or three days. The organizers invite an important guest to "open" it, and the closing is accompanied by rituals performed by a Buddhist monk.

7　The Economics of Enlisting:
A Village View of Armed Service

Michele Ruth Gamburd

"The war is like nothing for Prabhakaran and the government. Young lives are over like smoking a cigarette, with no result." Thus lamented Timon, a 48-year-old maintenance man from Naeaegama,[1] during one of the most intense periods in Sri Lanka's civil war. In 2000, many people from this Sinhala village on the south coast of Sri Lanka shared Timon's opinion that the national government saw human lives as cheap and consumable. At the same time, many men enlisted in the military to fight against Velupillai Prabhakaran's Liberation Tigers of Tamil Eelam (LTTE), a rebel group seeking an independent homeland in the North and East.[2]

Although scholars and journalists have written extensively about Sri Lanka's ethnic conflict, most have focused on constitutional issues such as the devolution of power, humanitarian issues such as human rights and refugees, and identity-related issues of ethnicity and nationalism. This essay, based mainly on data gathered in the village of Naeaegama between April and July 2000, provides a snapshot of locally situated knowledge about the war. Naeaegama residents raised issues of political corruption, unenlightened self-interest, censorship, and loss of faith in national leaders. In the process, villagers also voiced powerful and provocative accounts of poverty, patriotism, masculinity, risk, fate, and death.

Anthropological research in Naeaegama reveals local motives for enlisting that are significantly at odds with the national context for pursuing the conflict. The stories that people tell themselves about themselves, such as patriotic narratives about the nation and its enemies, reflect the political context in which the representation takes place, particularly the wishes, fancies, fears, and objectives of the storytellers. The official gloss of the war as a "terrorist problem," not an "ethnic conflict," portrays brave patriots defending the country from unreasonable and intransigent insurgents. In contrast, village tales of the war pay scant attention to the national enemy under any designation, and instead reflect deep helplessness and frustration over the dearth of local economic opportunities. From this perspective, men enlist more for economic incentives than for chauvinistic patriotism.

Stories from the village suggest that in 2000, the war, well into its second decade, had spawned a self-sustaining, self-justifying nexus of cultural rationales, social structures, and economic patterns. Both villagers and city dwellers saw the ethnic conflict as a moneymaking business venture for decisionmakers and leaders who received numerous perks and benefits from the war economy. Numerous Naeaegama residents felt that the strict government censorship attributed to the necessities of military confrontation actually concealed illegal economic activities of highly placed people within the state apparatus. Villagers voiced a growing disillusionment with the state and its agents, a general distrust of people in positions of power, and a prevalent perception of widespread corruption in politics and the war effort. Despite their skepticism, young men from the village turned to armed service as a dangerous but dependable job in a time of employment scarcity. Both soldiers and politicians had a financial stake in the perpetuation of the conflict, but the overwhelming nationalist discourse of war repressed open discussion of such economic factors.

Did Sri Lanka evolve a self-perpetuating economy based on internal warfare expressed as ethnic conflict? Writing about economic dynamics during the six years immediately prior to the onset of the civil war, Newton Gunasinghe (this volume) insightfully suggests that liberal policies adversely affected certain sections of the majority Sinhala population. He argues that while economic situations may not directly cause ethnic tensions, they can intensify and exacerbate them, and that the open economic policy initiated in 1977 led to the deterioration of ethnic relations in Sri Lanka. Following this line of reasoning, I ask whether the economic realities of 2000 sustained and promoted the ethnic conflict, while the ethnic patriotism and censorship that the war generated deflected discussion about economic matters. This essay approaches the economics of enlisting from the village perspective and lays out the practical and ideological grounds on which local people made decisions about involvement in the war, in the hope of adding a new ethnographic dimension to the study of Sri Lanka's civil conflict.

Economic Contexts: Sri Lanka and the Village of Naeaegama

Despite the war, Sri Lanka has for many years stood head and shoulders above other countries in the region in general quality of life indicators. This island nation of 18 million ranks highest in South Asia in terms of literacy, life expectancy, and sanitation, and lowest in terms of infant mortality and population growth (Shah 1995; Central Intelligence Agency 1998). Sri Lanka has been integrated into the global economy for many years through the export of spices, coconut products, rubber, tea, and, more recently, the migration of labor to the Middle East. Although burdened with less international debt than many other countries, Sri Lanka has undergone structural adjustments that devalue its currency, reduce its social welfare programs, and open its economy to foreign investment (Shastri, this volume). Many women produce garments and other items for export in factories in rural areas as well as in the large Free Trade Zone near the international airport (Lynch 1999, this volume). The government's liberal economic policies since 1977 have stimulated trade and investment, and despite nearly two decades of civil strife, Sri Lanka has sustained a creditable rate of economic growth (Arunatilake, Jayasuriya, and Kelegama 2000: 5). At the same time the gap between the rich and the poor has widened dramatically (Richardson, this volume), and many well educated youth lack suitable employment (Hettige, this volume).

Circumstances in Naeaegama reflect the national situation. This Graama Niladhari division (village administrative area), located near the ocean on the fertile southwest coast of Sri Lanka between the towns of Kalutara and Ambalangoda, consists of five small villages, including Naeaegama proper, and covers a little over one square mile. During the past 30 years, the population of the area has doubled, from about 500 people in 1969 (G. Gamburd 1972: 68) to roughly 1,100 in 2000.[3] A small number of proprietors own paddy fields, coconut gardens, and cinnamon estates. The majority of people own only the small plots of land where they live, and few have enough acreage to farm either for subsistence or for profit. Available jobs have not kept pace with population growth, and underemployment and unemployment are major factors of concern in the village, especially for well educated young men and women. Main occupations for women include coconut ropemaking, factory work, teaching, assisting their families in cinnamon peeling and broommaking, and domestic service in the Middle East. Main occupations for men include cinnamon peeling, broom peddling, security work, day labor, tourism, and military service (M. Gamburd 2000: 17–18). In 2000, rampant inflation associated with an ongoing economic crisis had pinched many Naeaegama families, challenged their ingenuity, narrowed their choices, and added a tone of urgency and desperation to their search for viable financial strategies.

Village Views of the Conflict

When I began interviewing Naeaegama residents about their views of the ethnic conflict, I expected to hear many local stories closely correlated with the prominent nationalist rhetoric about Sinhala Buddhist identity. I expected to find a patriotic discourse about preserving the unity of the nation against attacks from the enemies of the state. I expected to hear vibrant arguments about federalism and constitutional reform. Discussions did occasionally touch on such themes. Villagers sporadically mentioned the cultural heroes in the *Mahavamsa* chronicles, Buddhism and the ethics of killing in defense of the country, the government's proposed devolution package, and the ferocity of the intractable Tigers. But the most frequently and passionately expressed local views about the war concerned political corruption and illicit profit-making of government leaders.

When asked about the history of the conflict, a number of villagers mentioned opportunities lost due to short-sighted leadership. One man, a cook at a tourist hotel, said that instead of dealing directly with Tamil grievances, a series of Sinhala regimes had caved in to opposition pressures and had failed to negotiate settlements. A peace activist in Colombo attributed the continued conflict to the lack of bipartisan cooperation in politics in the past 40 years.[4] Anura, a 27-year-old working with the police Special Task Force, quoted a Sinhala proverb, "The sprout that could have been broken with a fingernail now can't be cut even with an ax,"[5] and suggested that the country's problems had grown very large. He felt that various Sinhala politicians had struggled to gain political influence by destroying ethnic harmony and scuttling negotiated settlements. Village discourse about the history of the conflict identified its origin in imprudent leadership rather than in an inherent incompatibility between ethnic groups, and some villagers even suggested that the people in power had deliberately exacerbated the ethnic conflict in order to enhance their political influence. These historical assumptions and presuppositions colored people's analysis and interpretation of the war and the state.

Villagers suggested that the past pattern of seeking political power at the cost of public institutions continued into the present. Comments on the status of Sri Lankan politics almost invariably included discussions of corruption, nepotism, election violence, and the disintegration of democratic practices. Villagers and city dwellers alike voiced the opinion that people in positions of power had regularly taken bribes, told lies, and sold out the country. A source in the police department and a prominent politician independently mentioned that government representatives sought and obtained sway over the police, using it to protect their followers and persecute their enemies. Secure in their impunity, politicians and businessmen entered into legal, semilegal, and extralegal activities, often in cahoots with local gangs and thugs who silenced protests and overpowered resistance (Perera 1998).[6] Such behaviors undermined the legitimacy of the state in the eyes of Naeaegama citizens.

When asked why the ethnic conflict had gone on for so long, many people independently brought up issues of corruption and dishonesty, suggesting that these pervasive practices extended to the army and the war effort as well. To describe the relationship between those in power and the war, and to explain the long duration of the conflict, people used the phrase "The big people cultivate and eat."[7] Unpacked, this phrase suggests that like farmers, people in power grow and harvest the ethnic conflict, perpetuating it for their own benefit. Informants suggested that some politicians kept their political power by using the war to get themselves reelected. Because of the war, some politicians and military officials received privileges and perks, such as bullet-proof cars, nice houses, high salaries, and trips abroad. Some people got commissions and kickbacks from arms deals and supply contracts. All of these people had a financial and political stake in keeping the war going. In villagers' views, economic and political dynamics created a situation where the unenlightened self-interest of a small but influential elite led to the perpetuation of the ethnic conflict, and where leaders and decisionmakers valued private gain over peace for the country.

Naeaegama villagers are not alone in pointing fingers at shady dealing. Allegations of corruption concerning a variety of activities came from many angles. For example, Iqbal Athas, the defense correspondent for a widely circulating English newspaper, the *Sunday Times*, repeatedly blew the whistle on irregular government procedures. For his audacity, he was allegedly intimidated by two air force officers who were charged with entering Athas's residence and threatening him and his family (*Sunday Times* 2000c). In the *Sunday Times* of 25 June 2000, Athas published a piece on irregularities in the purchasing of military equipment, from which the government censor deleted two-thirds of the text. The next week, during a brief window of opportunity when the Supreme Court declared the censorship system unconstitutional,[8] the *Sunday Times* published the full version of the same article (Athas 2000a, 2000b). Commenting on this and other incidents, Naeaegama residents suggested that censorship relieved the government of its responsibility to account for its use of public funds, and intimidation suppressed critical voices in the press and in other contexts.

After hearing from a number of villagers how "big" people made money from the war, I began to ask if "small" people could do the same. The replies I received suggested that while small people could not grow and eat the war, they could at least glean something from its killing fields. Villagers suggested that some soldiers smuggled grenades and guns out of the operation zone, which they could use to intimidate their neighbors, or sell to the LTTE or to gangs and thugs in Colombo. While the soldiers might not have a say in cultivating the war, they too could profit individually from materials that passed through their hands. As Winslow and Woost suggest (this volume: 8), for this war, "An explanation of origins no longer serves as an explanation of persistence." The cultivation of the war benefited many individuals at all levels of the decisionmaking structure and may have influenced them against taking actions to end the conflict.

Corruption emerged as a theme not only in the past and present of the ethnic conflict but also in discussions of its likely future. Commenting on how prospective war efforts might unfold, a number of Naeaegama residents independently compared the war to a beggar's wound.[9] Such a wound will never heal. My first reaction upon hearing this metaphor was to think, "Oh, the poor beggar, he has a chronic medical condition!" But in village use the phrase has a more cynical twist. Some beggars are quite fond of their wounds, since such wounds provide their livelihood. Several informants told me that some beggars even make fake wounds, binding a piece of dried fish in a bandage. The arm or leg then smells bad and attracts flies, and people give the beggar money. I heard that one legendary local beggar even wrapped marijuana in all his little "bandages," which he peeled off and sold to passersby who gave him money. When I listened to these stories about the beggar's wound, I went through a mental transition from thinking "poor beggar" to "deceptive beggar" to "beggar doing illegal things under the cover of bandaged 'wounds.'" The phrase suggests that a discerning physician might question the cause of such a wound, the methods and motives for its elaborate dressing, the reasons for its continuous exhibition, or even if that which is so profitably displayed actually exists at all.

To distract attention from corruption, people in positions of power need to silence criticism and disseminate a persuasive rationale for war not grounded on individual self-interest. Sri Lankans from various backgrounds suggested that the twin techniques of censorship and propaganda furthered this cause. In response to devastating military defeats in late April 2000, new emergency regulations banned printing of information that jeopardized "national security" or "the preservation of public order" (Kumaratunga 2000), phrases that local journalists said translated into a ban on any information critical of the government or any information about military activities, especially losses (*Island* 2000b; Chengappa 2000). People in Naeaegama, and probably most ordinary citizens in the country, had little access to solid information. Lack of access to news created a climate ripe for the circulation of rumors and corrosive to any sense of trust in "facts." Most people interviewed in Naeaegama felt that the media failed to report events as they actually happened. A number of local soldiers remarked that the government figures for war deaths held very little relationship to reality, speculating that the actual figures would discourage both soldiers and citizens. Others said that the reporters came up with false information that the government had to correct, that the reporters deliberately altered information to make the government look good or bad depending on the reporters' political persuasion, that the reporters tried to tell the truth but the government deleted everything that would give away military strategies, or that the correct details about casualties and losses might spark ethnic riots. Villagers held differing perspectives and opinions about media coverage, but all showed a nuanced awareness of its persuasive powers.

Censorship and the resulting epidemic of possible truths led to a general skepticism about the use and abuse of information. A local politician felt that the British Broadcasting Corporation (BBC) showed its favoritism for the Tigers by reporting incorrect and censored information to the international community.[10] In addition, three local men independently accused the International Committee of the Red Cross (ICRC) of interfering in events in favor of the Tigers by supervising police and army interrogations and prohibiting the use of powerful and effective weaponry by claiming that it could endanger civilians. People worried that a bad report from these "biased" organizations could jeopardize Sri Lanka's international connections, particularly supplies of foreign aid. Villagers clearly recognized the connection between the politics of representation and international economic relations, and considered images of events equally or more important than the events themselves. Both fact and fiction bowed to political necessity. Government and citizens alike adopted the view that media coverage created an image advantageous for accomplishing the goal of the moment.

Who Are the Soldiers?

Military service as a profession grew dramatically in Sri Lanka as the conflict progressed. Early in the war, casualties remained minimal, especially for people in nonfighting units and for people not stationed in the war areas.[11] With the gradual escalation of conflict, greater numbers of soldiers joined the services. Despite high unemployment levels, the army had trouble recruiting sufficient soldiers due to skepticism about the causes of the war and the corrupt behavior of political leaders. Entry standards relaxed, danger levels increased, and the job lost some of its former prestige.

How many soldiers fought in the civil war, and what areas of the country did they come from? In 2000, estimates of LTTE cadres ranged from 2,000 to 10,000. Estimates of men and women in the government forces and police totaled 225,000, with about 75,000 in the army, 25,000 each in the navy and air force, and another

100,000 in the police (Arunatilake, Jayasuriya, and Kelegama 2000: 4). Although women did serve in the forces, the majority of soldiers were men.

The composition of the Sri Lankan military services did not mirror the percentages of ethnic groups in the general population. The armed forces were overwhelmingly Sinhala, with a very small percentage of Muslims and almost no Tamils.[12] Regional distinctions also appeared in enlistment data. Dayaratna, the head of the Association for Disabled Ex-servicemen (ADEP), headquartered in Colombo, said that the members of his organization were mainly from north-central Sri Lanka. He felt that the more difficult the local employment and education situation, the more men from an area went into the forces. Further research is needed into regional variations in enlistment patterns.

The armed services provided a range of possible careers. Naeaegama villagers distinguished between jobs in fighting units and other sorts of military employment, such as jobs in supply or engineering units, which did not take men to the front. Until shortly before 2000, jobs in the air force and navy were deemed much less dangerous than those in the army. Many enlisted men also suggested that officers, particularly higher officers, stayed well back from the action. Those on the front lines received higher wages and got more promotions than those serving in other areas, which led some soldiers to prefer working in hardship areas (*dushkara palat*) despite the danger. Differences in skills, wages, and risks affected who enlisted for which job.

Data from the national context sheds light on enlistment patterns in Naeaegama, where, in 2000, there were 41 men with some sort of association with the army, navy, air force, and police, including 2 World War II veterans, 4 more recently retired veterans, 28 active soldiers, and 7 deserters. These 41 men made up 14 percent of the male villagers over 18 years of age. Given the increasingly dangerous circumstances, why do men (and some women, though none from Naeaegama) continue to sign up and serve in the army? What role do economics, patriotism, and politics play in their decisions?

Motives for Enlisting: Poverty

Although exacerbated by war-related events, the difficult economic circumstances prevailing in Naeaegama in mid-2000 were not a new situation. Poverty and underemployment for both men and women provided one of the main push factors that sent women to work as housemaids in the Middle East (M. Gamburd 2000). The same economic situation led men to enroll in the army.[13] Kumari, whose son was nearly killed in the war, said, "Some people go to the army because they like the idea of fighting, and they want to save the country. Buddhism says that you shouldn't kill, but these men go for the sake of the country, to save the country. Also, they go because there aren't any jobs in the village. There are no jobs even if you study. It is easy to go to the army. People go even if they might die." Although some villagers occasionally mentioned patriotism as a motive for joining the army, economic explanations predominated.

Lack of other job opportunities topped the list of reasons for joining the service.

Anura, the 27-year-old mentioned above, signed up with the Special Task Force, a branch of the police, in 1993. When I asked why he joined, he said, "My parents couldn't help me for my future because they had no property and no savings. As I grew up, I realized that even people with university degrees can't find jobs. My parents couldn't offer me anything else. If there had been another job, I would have gone to that instead." Although his education did secure Anura a career in a relatively prestigious branch of the police, Anura's family lacked the social and economic capital to provide him with alternative employment.[14]

Even those who had other jobs often turned to armed service because of the attractive salaries. I asked Samantha, whose husband was killed in action in 1992, why her husband had joined the army. "He joined mostly for the job. He was working as a bar bender (welder) at Tangerine Beach Hotel in Kalutara. I was in the Middle East then, and I didn't understand the danger. I said that he should go because working in the army would be a better job than the other one he was doing. We had two kids then, and we needed the money." When asked if she would let her son join the army, she answered, "Yes. It would be better to go to the army than to get involved with drugs and alcohol in this neighborhood. He says he would like to join." Samantha's husband held another job before joining the army, but the family felt his salary was not sufficient. Despite their intimate losses, both son and mother continued to see armed service as a viable career path, preferable to the one perceived alternative of sliding into the idle delinquency of unemployment.

Local class distinctions between Naeaegama families affected the positions young men obtained in the armed services. In 2000, two village boys had recently joined officer training programs. Their perspective on enlisting showed a wider range of choice and opportunity. Kapila, from one of the richest and most respected families in the village, joined what he called the "cream of the cream" officer's training section in the navy. He could have become a teacher or pursued a college degree in engineering, but he wanted to go into the navy instead. Another village youth from a prestigious family also passed up the chance to go to university, choosing to enlist in the air force instead. Although his parents said that they were "without blood" with fear when he traveled alone at night back and forth to Trincomalee (a city in eastern Sri Lanka), his father and mother approved of his choice. His father noted with approval that his son would become "an officer and a gentleman." Past and future social capital and educational prospects clearly played a stronger role than economic necessity and lack of other job opportunities in the career choices of these middle-class, well-educated young men.

Most of the soldiers with whom I spoke had signed up for the standard 12-year or 22-year contracts. If the peace process initiated in 2002 unfolds successfully, the government will need to honor its contracts with these men. In 2000, the army offered salaries considered generous by local standards. Soldiers earned about Sri Lankan Rupees (SL Rs.) 9,000 ($120) a month, for a take-home pay between SL Rs. 6,500 and 8,000.[15] Soldiers working in operation areas made an extra allotment of about SL Rs. 2,500. Kavinda, a Naeaegama soldier, told me that after the military defeats in late April, the government gave soldiers on the front a raise of SL Rs. 80 a day (2,400 a month). With that bonus, his salary came to SL Rs. 12,000/month

($160). Higher officers and those who had served for 10 or 15 years could earn as much as SL Rs. 20,000–25,000 a month. In comparison, a schoolteacher with 20 years of service might earn SL Rs. 6,000 a month, and a housemaid working in the Middle East might earn SL Rs. 7,500 ($100). Military salaries clearly surpassed most other local earning opportunities.

In addition to their salary, soldiers received perks and benefits. Separate queues moved servicemen to the head of the line when boarding public buses. Servicemen and their families had access to military hospitals, which, at least in theory, had better facilities and more medicine than ordinary hospitals.[16] For their injuries, wounded soldiers received insurance compensation.[17] Families of soldiers missing in action received their salary for a year, after which the man was declared dead. After a soldier's death, his family received quite a bit of aid from the government. For example, at the time of Samantha's husband's death in 1992, the army paid for his funeral. Samantha, her mother-in-law, and her three children received a total of SL Rs. 129,000, and Samantha got SL Rs. 150,000 for improving her house (M. Gamburd 1999). Each month she received between SL Rs. 12,500 and SL Rs. 13,000 as her husband's salary and pension. Her two older children had also received various scholarships of SL Rs. 250 or 300 a month. The family lived in an unfinished but spacious house and had enough money to live well by local standards.

The sums of money related to injury and death gave rise to a certain wry humor in the village that reflected the inappropriateness of putting a price on a human life. My research assistant, Siri, reported that a drunkard at the illicit liquor bar had loudly announced that he had two sons in the army, and if they died he would be a millionaire. The other drinkers disapprovingly decided that the man had "army fever" because he so easily valued death in monetary terms. On the other end of the scale, the father of Punya, a village soldier, rejected the commodification of human life. He said, "I told my son Punya not to go back to the army. He wants to go back, but I say that receiving a SL Rs. 100,000 death compensation is pointless without him. I worked hard to raise my son, and I don't want to auction him off this way." Although people clearly felt ambivalent about the exchange of danger undergone for money received, this articulation had worked its way into public perceptions of the war.

Motives for Enlisting: Patriotism

When discussing the war, people often compared the motivations of the government soldiers and the Tiger cadres. Timon, the older Naeaegama man quoted earlier, remarked, "Prabhakaran's boys are fighting for their *jaati* (nation or race.) Our boys are fighting for a salary. A certain percentage of them, maybe 10 to 12 percent, are fighting to save the country." Many villagers cited the Tigers' suicide bombers as examples of intense Tamil dedication to the goal of Tamil Eelam. At the same time, the Sri Lankan press often emphasized the idea that Tiger cadres were forced to join the LTTE. In May 2000, the government media reported that the LTTE had conscripted high school students to replenish its ranks (Jabbar 2000), implicitly suggesting that the Tamil soldiers felt ambivalent about fighting for their cause.

Naeaegama discussions of forced conscription voiced contradictory ideas; while no one wanted his or her child to be drafted, many parents wryly remarked that if military service were mandatory for politicians' children, the war might end a great deal sooner. The lack of local economic opportunities created a de facto conscription for lower-class men from the poorer, less-educated parts of the population and from communities with few other job opportunities. Although the Sri Lankan army remained a voluntary force, pragmatic necessity overdetermined many men's choice of military employment.

In Naeaegama, patriotism ebbed and flowed. It played an important role in drawing boys into the army to begin with, but after they enlisted, other factors kept them working, such as the lack of other jobs, a sense of duty, and the fear of arrest. A nationalist mentality idealized wearing a uniform. Ten-year-olds made palm fronds into bunkers and peeled cinnamon sticks into guns. Eighteen-year-olds watched ubiquitous military recruitment programs that glorified training and battle. A skilled 22-year-old tailor desperately wanted to go into the military instead of spending his life sewing. His parents repeatedly tore up the army application papers he sent for. The tailor prized the poster of an armed commando in camouflage gear that he had placed in a prominent spot on the living room wall. As Kusuma, a local high school teacher, said about her three younger brothers and the students she taught, a sentiment of *"Yamu!"* ("Let's go!") often carried young patriots away.

Patriotism and the glorification of battle tie in to a bigger question of gender and masculinity. Elsewhere I discuss at length a crisis of masculinity in the village of Naeaegama, where many migrant women have taken over the breadwinner role for their families (M. Gamburd 2000). Men find it shameful to do "women's work" and have a hard time accepting their inability to provide adequately for their families without the income that their wives earn abroad. It is much more manly to be a commando than to be a tailor, a three-wheeler driver, a coconut plucker, or an underemployed laborer. Braving danger is a quintessentially masculine activity (Risseeuw 1991; Katz 1995), as is drinking alcohol (M. Gamburd 2000). Weerasinghe, an officer with 17 years of service, talked about drinking and peer pressure in the army: "Women don't drink, and if you don't drink, you're a girl." A hard-drinking soldier is as manly as they come. In addition, many younger men liked to have what Anura describes as "a butterfly life," with enough money to do fun things, have nice clothing, and support a family. In 2000, the army offered such men money and fundamentally masculine employment, both in short supply in the village.

Issues of patriotism and masculinity affected how men talked about their motivations for joining the army. In 1995, when he was 35 years old, Nimal joined a support unit made up of men with government jobs who were willing to work for five years for the army. When I asked Nimal why he took a leave of absence from the Ceylon General Railway (CGR) to work for the army, he gave a very patriotic answer about defending the country. In a separate interview, Nimal's wife talked at length about a large housing loan that the couple had taken from the government through the CGR. By joining the army, Nimal received a net salary increase, and the family could pay the money back faster. Nimal made no mention whatsoever of the loan. Although love of country and financial considerations doubtless influenced the decision, Nimal chose to present his motives solely as patriotic. In the politics of self-representation, patriotism seems to outrank financial gain, although both reflect prestige and masculinity.

Podi Mahattaya, a 19-year-old soldier with whom I spoke on his first visit home after going to the front, said that he had deliberately signed up for a fighting unit. "Why?" my research associates and I asked in surprise, having grown accustomed to hearing men say they had done all they could to avoid the battlefield. Podi Mahattaya smiled and said that he wanted to go and *do* something, otherwise "*vaeDak naeae*" (there's no work or it's no use). "There's no use going to the army if you're not going to fight." Weerasinghe also expressed dedication to his job, saying that he wanted to be able to show his children what the army had accomplished for the country (presumably referring to maintaining its unity). Both the newly enlisted fighter and the seasoned veteran clearly valued not only their paychecks but also the purposes of their jobs.

Although the patriotic sentiments in the statements above find echoes in other voices, many experienced soldiers felt that new and potential recruits did not understand much about war. A number of village soldiers told me that they would not have gone into the service if they had known what it would really be like. I asked Kavinda, "If you were advising an 18-year-old about whether to go into the army, what would you say?" He replied, "I would say, 'If you're going into supplies, okay, otherwise don't go!'" I asked Prasanna, "If you were 21 again and knew then what you know now, would you go into the army?" "No," he answered. "I went because I wanted to go, but now I am continuing to go back just because I have to. I am fed up with the army. I am only staying with the job out of respect for the uniform. And if I stopped going, I couldn't find another job. If I stay in for another six years, then I can finish my 12-year contract and quit if the war conditions are still this bad. Then I would be able to stop legally, without forfeiting my retirement money." Although many soldiers said they would not have enlisted in retrospect, others said that despite the difficulties they had encountered, unless their economic circumstances were different, they would still have to join and remain in the army. For many, patriotism wore thin, but economic necessity endured.

Despite love of country and the need for a paycheck, many soldiers deserted the armed services. Television coverage reported that in June 2000 there were approximately 8,000 deserters in the country. The government alternatively offered amnesty periods in which deserters could return to their units free of punishment and sent the military police out to catch soldiers absent without leave. On July 5, 2000, the *Island* reported that nearly 1,000 deserters had been rounded up and taken back to the army (Island 2000a). My research associate, Siri, told me that the previous afternoon he had seen Punya, the soldier whose father asked him not to return to the front, on the back of a military police truck with about 40 other young men.

I asked numerous villagers, including deserters and men still serving in the army, why some soldiers failed to return to duty. Villagers reported that men deserted because (1) they were afraid, (2) their families were afraid and asked them not to return, (3) they did not like the life in the army (particularly, one soldier reported, the sexual harassment), (4) they preferred the freedom at home, or (5) they had saved enough money to live for a while and planned to go back to the army during some future amnesty period if they needed the job. Quite a number of men I interviewed had been absent from service without leave at some point.

Deserters encountered a number of problems. First, they found it difficult to get another job, especially a government job, since the government officially forbade public organizations and private companies to hire deserters. Firms that did hire deserters often paid them less than the standard salary and withheld retirement benefits if the men were forced to return to the army. Second, deserters lived in fear that their enemies might report them to the military police, especially if they quarreled with a neighbor or caused trouble in the village. Villagers found no easy way to escape the omnipresent socioeconomic formation of war once they became involved in it. Lack of security and a dearth of employment options led one mother to say of her son who had deserted the navy, "He has no future." Weighing risks at the front and at home formed part of the village calculus for making decisions to enlist, continue service, or desert.

Risk, Fate, and Fortune: Different Ways to Die

Issues such as the strength, determination, training, and weaponry of the enemy, the equipment and leadership of the army, and the ferocity of the conflict affected village assessments of the risks of battle. In 2000, many local families blamed the army's recent stunning defeats on treachery and the lack of competent leadership. Over the course of the war, both sides acquired increasingly more sophisticated and deadly weaponry. In a major confrontation in late April 2000, the Tigers captured several rocket launchers from the government forces and turned them against government strongholds in the north. The Sri Lankan government then hastened to purchase new weapons from various foreign countries (Athas 2000a, 2000b; Island 2000c; Chengappa 2000). Although by July the war seemed to have returned to a lower level of engagement (Defense Correspondent 2000), a clear escalation in armaments characterized the progression of the war. The change in technology made many of the Sinhala soldiers reluctant to stay at the front.

Although many families risked sending a man to the army, few families sent their only sons to the war. Nevertheless, several families had two or three members in the army. I asked one soldier if he was afraid to die in the war. He replied, "If it's your time to die, it's your time to die, and you can die falling from your bike at home. So it's better to go and fight as a soldier instead!" Many army men and their families voiced similar views of fate and death, suggesting that individual choices and actions cannot change a death-date determined by prior ethical behavior (*karma*) or planetary influences. This view undercuts the causal association between armed service, danger, and death, and weakens a class-based critique of the unequal burdens of the war.

Local perceptions of the danger and risk inherent in village life also reduce the clear connection between death and the army. The three Naeaegama army fatalities that occurred between 1983 and 2000 were not the only violent or untimely demises in the local area. Suicide, fights, accidents, and illnesses also caused a number of deaths. Unpredictable village violence took place quite frequently. For example, two fights occurred in April 2000; one led to a murder in a nearby village, and the second, a land dispute, so incensed one man that he cracked his neighbor's skull with the rice pounder. Informants half-jokingly told me (in what I hope was narrative hyperbole), "That sort of things happens about once a week in that part of the village!" Many villagers shared the perception that village life could be violent and dangerous, especially in the poorer areas.

My ethnographic data suggest that men did indeed die fairly frequently of unnatural causes.[18] Of the five such deaths between October 1992 and May 1993, only one man, Samantha's husband, died in the war. His family received political recognition and a financial settlement, unlike the families of the other dead men. Two young men died after being beaten up and stabbed for trying to take alcohol by force from an illicit distillery; two poisoned themselves experimenting with cheap alcoholic drinks. Of the 11 men over 18 who died between 1997 and mid-2000, only the two youngest died in the war. Two died in vehicle accidents, two died of causes related to alcoholism, and the rest (all over 60 years old) died of natural causes. The numbers in this sample are too small to provide any sort of significant statistical data, but they do suggest that army fatalities are not the only unexpected way that village men die. These events reveal the normalization of violence both in and away from the war zone.

Several other village stories blur the distinction between private and military deaths and injuries. Although military deaths merit compensation, injury in the army does not necessarily lead to security or care. Kumari's oldest son was wounded in combat, shot three times in the chest and once each in the neck, back, and right arm. He only narrowly escaped death. Terrified that he would be forced to go back to the front, he came home as soon as he was released from the hospital and never returned to the army camp, even to collect his back pay and compensation money. In July 2000 he still had not regained full movement in his injured arm. He lived with his wife and infant son in a tiny two-room clay hut and earned money peddling brooms by bicycle. Kumari's second son was seriously injured in a work-related lorry accident with two other village men. Doctors removed part of his kneecap, and he had still not regained full use of his right leg and right hand. Both of Kumari's sons had work-related physical handicaps, neither got help from the government, but only the deserted army man worried about visits from the military police.

Rumors circulated in the village about how private grudges could affect men's experiences in the military. One Naeaegama grandmother, Caroline, said that sometimes the Sinhalese killed each other over personal disputes under the cover of war. She related a story, saying that one payday someone asked a soldier from a nearby town for SL Rs. 5,000. He refused to give the money, saying his family needed it to live. His enemy said, "Just wait. I'll kill you on the battlefield." Several weeks later, the man was shot in the head. Asanka, a deserted soldier, related a story about soldiers taking revenge on corrupt or cruel officers, killing them at the front and blaming the death on the LTTE. The lack of detail and degree of removal in both of these narratives gives them the tone of "urban legends." Although they probably reveal little about specific past events, they do suggestively illustrate collective fears and hatred.

As a group, these stories reinforce the ideas that the military is not the only source of violent death and injury, that not all military injuries receive compensation, and that not all military deaths are due to the LTTE. Villagers believe that life is uncertain, insecure, and treacherous both in the armed forces and at home. A death in the army, however, receives ample compensation, while a death in the village receives none. When jobs are scarce and staying home does not necessarily guarantee safety, a career in the military may become an attractive option.

Conclusion

Ethnographic perspectives reveal the practical and ideological grounds on which local people experienced Sri Lanka's ethnic conflict, particularly the role that economics has played in perpetuating the civil war. As even the most cursory of literature reviews reveals, serious issues divide the Sinhala and Tamil communities. Escalating ethnic hostilities based on years of grievances have polarized the confrontation, making reconciliation an uphill battle. By focusing on economics, I in no way wish to deny or minimize the realities of identity politics. Rather, the data presented in this chapter and volume suggest that economic analysis might shed at least a small amount of light on why communal hostilities arose in the first place and why they have festered for so long.

Sri Lankans from all walks of life had come, in 2000, to accept the ethnic conflict as the background against which they contemplated economic and political action. These actors preserved and perpetuated the system by accepting the situation and by working within the structures it created. Although patriotism played a part, most Naeaegama soldiers said that they joined the armed services because they could find no other jobs; many youth experienced a de facto class-based conscription into armed service. After nearly two decades of warfare, Naeaegama villagers had come to rely on armed service as a dangerous but ever-present job option. The transition to a lasting peace must offer alternatives that reshape this mental landscape and provide viable economic opportunities for rural youth.

For years, politicians and businessmen also worked within the war's social horizon. Politicians engaged in daily activities under circumstances not wholly of their own choosing and acted within a cultural context replete with established norms and values. In 2000, these standards seemed to encourage (even require) greed, thuggery, and the pursuit of personal gain. Cynicism about politics (or, as Siri calls it, "poli-tricks") indexed a local understanding that those who played the game successfully played it corruptly. Naeaegama residents held politicians and businessmen responsible for creating and perpetuating the violent system in which they operated. This system included, in local estimation, the "growing and eating" of the war. Local insights into the articulation of economics and the ethnic conflict suggest that scholars should indeed question whether the business of war arose solely from issues of identity and nationalism or whether the causal arrow runs both ways.

Transformations such as those now unfolding in the peace process initiated in 2002 emerge from preexisting social formations. Years of conflict have normalized violence—not only the physical and psychological trauma of the battlefield but also perceived injustice and inequality in the rest of the country. In Naeaegama in 2000, residents expressed loss of faith in state narratives, frustration over employment opportunities, and cynicism about government corruption. Despite the relief and enthusiasm generated by the cease-fire, these attitudes, as well as the social, political, and economic situations that they reflect, persist into the present.

Having explored the links between economics and conflict, one might next ask about the articulations between economics and peace. What economic contexts preceded and perhaps prompted the cease-fire? And how might emerging economic considerations affect the unfolding of the peace process? The distribution of financial incentive packages and the allocation of foreign aid may become the new fields on which politicians cultivate their careers, the nation's youth scramble to make a living, and future identities sprout and grow. Understanding the preexisting toxic logic of distrust, frustration, and ethnic antagonism may help planners on the slippery steps into a peaceful future.

Notes

This essay is based on research supported in part by National Science Foundation grant SBR-9903314. Sharon Carstens, Veronica Dujon, Alan Keenan, Trish Rainey, Shawn Smallman, Deborah Winslow, and Michael Woost provided very helpful comments and suggestions on earlier drafts of this essay. The remaining flaws are solely the author's responsibility.

1. In this essay I use pseudonyms for most people and places to protect the privacy of my informants.
2. Velupillai Prabhakaran is the leader of the Liberation Tigers of Tamil Eelam (LTTE). At the time of my interview with Timon, the LTTE had fought for an independent homeland on the island of Sri Lanka since the beginning of the civil war in 1983. For more information on the history of the conflict, see Abeyesekera and Gunasinghe 1985, 1987; Bastin 1990; Eller 1999; Kapferer 1988; Obeyesekere 1988; Ram 1989; Spencer, ed. 1990; Tambiah 1986, 1992.
3. Exact population figures for Naeaegama are difficult to obtain for a number of reasons: people constantly move in and out of the village, and at any point in time many migrants are away in the Middle East. The 1999 election list for the Naeaegama area named 582 registered voters over the age of 18. I have roughly doubled this number to obtain an estimate of the local population. Although Sri Lanka's growth rate is lower than that of other countries in the region, national population has increased dramatically over the past four decades, from

just under 11 million in 1963 (Yalman 1967: 13) to over 18 million in 2000 (Sri Lanka, Department of Census and Statistics 1996).

4. Many scholars agree that in the current political climate, even if a leader genuinely wants to stop the war, she or he will be thwarted by the opposition, who can gain political ground from criticizing any compromise with the enemy (see Eller 1999; Spencer, ed. 1990; Tambiah 1992).

5. *Niyapotten kapunDa tibunu paelee daen poravenvat kapunDa baeae.*

6. Many people identified this pattern of influence peddling as a cause for the Marxist-nationalist Janatha Vimukthi Peramuna (JVP, People's Liberation Front) rebellion, an internal insurgency led by disgruntled Sinhala youth that paralyzed the country in 1988–90. These voices cautioned that short-sighted political opportunism had fueled the JVP rebellion, and warned that a continuation of such practices could very easily spark another rebellion, engulfing the country in violence once again.

7. *Loku minissu wawaagena kanawaa.*

8. A brief but bitter court battle between government and the publishers of the banned *Sunday Leader* publication brought the censorship issue to national attention, winning a short but welcomed window of press freedom in early July (*Island* 2000d; *Sunday Times* 2000b; Weerarathne 2000), after which the government quickly reestablished strict censorship.

9. *Hingannage tuwaale.*

10. Lack of space curtails exploration of the fascinating debate between the BBC and the Sri Lankan government concerning whether and to what extent the Sri Lankan emergency regulations affected international news reported abroad and broadcasted locally.

11. Estimates of casualties in the war vary greatly. Newspaper articles often put the figure at around 50,000–60,000 people (Jayasinghe 2000). Defense Ministry statistics suggest that 10,014 government soldiers had been killed and 13,545 had been injured between the start of the war and 1 January 1997. The government estimated LTTE casualties at 22,116, while the LTTE claims to have lost 9,301. An additional 20,000–30,000 civilian casualties are also reported (Arunatilake, Jayasuriya, and Kelegama 2000: 24–25). These figures do not reflect the high casualties reported on both sides during the Tiger offensive in early 2000 (Island 2000e, 2000f, etc.) In June 2000, Dayaratna, the head of ADEP, estimated 15,000 government soldiers dead, another 10,000 missing in action, and between 10,000 and 15,000 disabled. An NGO source suggested a figure of 16,000 disabled in the army alone. Punya, a Naeaegama soldier, wryly noted that one could probably get the most accurate count of the war dead from the Jayaratne florist shop in Colombo, which handles the military funeral contract.

12. People in Sri Lanka refer to the Tamil-speaking Muslim population as "Muslims" and the Tamil-speaking Hindu population as "Tamils." The Tamil population is further subdivided into Ceylon Tamils, whose ancestors have long inhabited the island, and Estate Tamils, whose ancestors were brought by the British to work on tea plantations in the central highlands. The Estate Tamils have remained largely marginal to the ongoing ethnic conflict, and they make up about one-third of the Tamil population. The Sinhalese make up 74.0 percent of the population, the Tamils 18.2 percent, and the Muslims 7.4 percent (Eller 1999: 96; Tambiah 1986: 4).

13. I am not the only one to see the correlation between poverty, migration, and

military service, and Naeaegama is not the only village where it appears. A newspaper article about Amunichchiya, a village in north-central Sri Lanka, noted that many of the women were in the Middle East and the men were in the army. "Where are the parents?" the paper asks. The reporter found only children and grandparents at home (Samath and Hettiarachchi 2000). The Naeaegama situation, though not so extreme, reflects a similar pattern of adult employment.

14. See Hettige (this volume) for a discussion of youth aspirations and employment prospects.

15. Between April and July 2000, the exchange rate averaged around US$1 = SL Rs. 75. By February 2001, the rupee had devalued to US$1 = SL Rs. 95.

16. Injured soldiers receive treatment in military hospitals. Although many people believe these hospitals are well run, and they may indeed be better than other local hospitals, Dayaratna suggested that after a week or two on a bed, patients are moved to the floor. When a member of Parliament comes to visit, the hospital sets up one neat and tidy ward where all the soldiers rest on beds, and television crews film the event. With this sort of publicity, everyone thinks that all the wards have good facilities. The cameras never show the rest of the hospital.

17. The following list of compensation figures was compiled using estimates from various soldiers, including several who work at ADEP and had received such compensation in the past. They noted that their figures pertained to the early 1990s and that the amounts might have changed. One eye: SL Rs. 40,000 (other sources said SL Rs. 25,000); two eyes: SL Rs. 90,000; an arm or leg: SL Rs. 60,000 (other sources said SL Rs. 25,000); normal shot wound: SL Rs. 20,000 (other sources said SL Rs. 3,000); paralysis: SL Rs. 90,000; death: SL Rs. 100,000.

18. Women also died of unnatural causes, but at a much lower rate.

8 Economic Liberalization, Nationalism, and Women's Morality in Sri Lanka

Caitrin Lynch

In 1977, Sri Lanka's United National Party (UNP) government introduced an economic liberalization package. The centerpiece of the "Open Economy" was the establishment one year later of the Katunayake Free Trade Zone (FTZ) in an urban area on the outskirts of the capital city, Colombo. From the start, the workforce consisted primarily of women from villages who were employed in various export industries, particularly the garment industry. Since shortly after the FTZ was established, there has been considerable moral panic about "good girls" going bad in Katunayake. Moral panic about these women has focused on reports of the following issues in association with FTZ and other urban women factory workers: prostitution, premarital sex, rape, sexually transmitted disease, abortion, and sexual harassment. Since the early 1980s, Sri Lanka also has been the site of an increasingly violent civil war. The government, which is associated with the majority Sinhala Buddhist ethnic group, has been fighting the Liberation Tigers of Tamil Eelam (LTTE), who are waging a war for independence in the north and east of the country where Tamils form the majority.[1] Newton Gunasinghe argued persuasively in a 1984 essay that the rise in ethnic hostilities in Sri Lanka since 1977 can be connected to economic liberalization (Gunasinghe, this volume). If Gunasinghe was correct, given the visible role of women in this new economy, one may then pose the following questions: How has the moral panic about the behavior of female factory workers been associated with the ethnic hostilities? What kinds of connections have been made between factory women's morality and concerns about the dissolution of the Sinhala Buddhist nation in the face of the LTTE's separatist campaign?

In this essay I address these questions to demonstrate how Sri Lankan economic liberalization policies have been argued out socially in terms of women's behavior. I consider the social position of Free Trade Zone women workers in relationship to women workers in a later UNP economic development scheme: President Ranasinghe Premadasa's 200 Garment Factories Program (200 GFP), which was begun in 1992. I demonstrate that a shift in the primary focus of the 200 GFP from youth unrest to women's morality was related to moral panic about "Juki girls" (a derogatory nickname for urban garment factory workers) and societal concern about a potentially crumbling rural/urban divide. I argue that the public visibility of Juki girls indicates to many Sri Lankans that these women who have crossed the rural/urban divide by leaving their villages for employment symbolize the dissolution of Sinhala Buddhist traditions. These concerns about Sinhala Buddhist national culture have led to Juki girls being cast as key symbols of the problems of modernization since the 1977 introduction of economic liberalization. Although it has historical precedents (Lynch 2002), this intense concern with women's morality seems to have taken on renewed importance during the post-1977 period of ethnic conflict.

Ethnic conflict certainly has economic roots (among others) and economic tolls, and several recent publications provide a glimpse of the compelling and tragic accounts of the economics of the Sri Lankan conflict (Arunatilake et al. 2000; Edirisinghe 2000; World Bank 2000b; cf. Shastri and Richardson, this volume). Here, I analyze a seemingly purely economic strategy of the Premadasa government to think about how economy and culture are intertwined and are best conceptualized in interrelationship. Although Premadasa's 200 GFP was certainly motivated by economic concerns,[2] Premadasa's implementation of the program and the changes made in it over time raise important *cultural* questions about what it means to be Sinhala Buddhist in this era of ethnic conflict. The 200 GFP story reveals that economic and cultural interests are tightly interwoven and mutually constitutive, and as such they must be addressed in interrelationship. Mine is a cultural angle on the 200 GFP, in which I examine the cultural significance and place of the program's transformations and of Premadasa's rhetoric about the program— in particular, in this essay I focus on his use of Sinhala Buddhist gender ideologies. The 200 GFP raises questions about how to conceptualize the relationship between cultures and economies, and I argue that these very questions belong at the center of theorizing the relationship between the economy and ethnic conflict.

Youth Unrest and Women's Employment

In 1992, Premadasa began his 200 GFP, an ambitious rural industrialization program in which 200 export-oriented factories were to be established in villages throughout the country. The program continued the state's economic liberalization agenda and yet, significantly, moved industry out of urban areas and into villages. It was a program clearly aimed at earning foreign exchange and increasing the country's GNP (Shastri 1997). But rather than highlighting such materialist concerns, Premadasa argued in numerous forums—from the moment he introduced the program to investors[3]—that the program would bring discipline to the nation's rural heartland, which recently had been the source of revolutionaries for a violent youth revolt by the Janatha Vimukthi Peramuna (JVP, People's Liberation Front).[4] Premadasa and his supporters explained to investors and the public that, by bringing jobs to villages, the 200 GFP aimed to address the perception that recent political instability in the country—especially the JVP revolt, but also marginally the LTTE separatist movement—was caused by rural, vernacular-educated, and unemployed (or underemployed) youth who felt that the benefits of economic liberalization policies reached only the urban, English-educated elite.

These notions were described in the findings of the Presidential Commission on Youth, which was established at the height of the JVP revolt in October 1989 to determine the causes of and possible solutions to youth unrest (Sri Lanka 1990; cf. Hettige, this volume). Premadasa implemented the 200 GFP in direct response to the commission's report. With the establishment of 200 factories outside the usual industrial zones, the 200 GFP was to address youth "frustration" by generating rural industrial jobs. The program was to provide both direct employment in factories for 100,000 youth and indirect employment (in related jobs in transportation, shops, and food service) for many others. There was to be one factory in each of the 200 Assistant Government Agent (AGA) divisions in the country. Investors were Sri Lankans and foreigners, with some factories financed jointly.[5]

Comments by Premadasa and his supporters reveal the following utilitarian rationale for the program: If rural youth have money, they will have a stake in the stability of the state and there will not be another youth revolt. Here development and welfare are offered as a solution to unrest (or as "insurance" against it, as Premadasa said on several occasions [e.g., *Observer* 1992]), all the while preserving the discursive importance in Sri Lanka of the nation's villages as the locus of Sinhala Buddhist tradition. Furthermore, by learning capitalist discipline and associating it with what is configured as good, "village-y" behavior, there would be less inclination toward the JVP in the long run. Premadasa often insisted that the program was pluralistic and nondiscriminatory in terms of who was to be employed, and there were factories established in primarily Tamil or Muslim areas. Yet its focus on the JVP, which consisted primarily of Sinhala Buddhist youth, is one of many aspects of the 200 GFP that situate the program as a Sinhala Buddhist nationalist development program. In particular—as I demonstrate elsewhere (Lynch 2000)—in order to make this discursive connection between capitalist discipline and a disciplined citizenry, Premadasa and his supporters mobilized in a complicated and contradictory manner a tradition of discipline associated with "Protestant Buddhism," a term used by Gananath Obeyesekere (1970) to describe Sinhala Buddhism as configured by the anticolonial nationalist Anagarika Dharmapala at the turn of the twentieth century.

Although analysts note that the JVP was composed primarily of men,[6] a 90 percent female workforce was intended from the start when Premadasa mandated that each factory must employ 450 women and 50 men. Thus, the program rested on an apparent contradiction: The state enlisted female workers in a program that was being touted in the media and in the president's 200 GFP speeches as a means to prevent male unrest. I received one suggestion for how to overcome this contradiction from some state representatives and factory owners and managers—but only when I solicited it. They explained that the factories employ women because women are better suited than men to factory labor.[7] Nevertheless, they contended, the goal of providing jobs to prevent unrest would be attained because, in the case of brothers or husbands of female workers, at least they would have access to money even though they would not be earning it themselves. Moreover, many added, jobs for men would be available in support sectors due to the increased need for buses, bakeries, shops, and so forth near factories.

Yet this after-the-fact reasoning does not explain how Premadasa could have spoken forcefully and eloquently at factory opening ceremonies about preventing youth unrest—which was generally considered a male problem—while always mandating a primarily female workforce. Employing women makes practical sense. Premadasa must have known that it has become the norm for Sri Lankan garment factories to employ mostly women; he probably always thought women would form the bulk of the 200 GFP workforce. Additionally, while women are naturalized as factory workers, Sri Lankan men are naturalized as soldiers.[8] Given the need for men to fight in the army's campaign against the LTTE, Premadasa would have joined with the many people in all strata of Sri Lankan society who told me that "women work in garment factories, men work in the army."[9] (I also heard of a saying in Sinhala to the same effect, which went something like *geni juki, pirimi thuwakku*—Juki for women, guns for men.)[10]

Of course, there does not need to be a logic or rationality to any of the ideological claims made about the 200 GFP. In fact, rather than an explanation for this apparent contradiction, I offer an analysis that begins with this as the framing contradiction of a state development program that was conceived by the state and experienced by the state, its supporters, factory owners, managers, workers, and their families in terms that were fundamentally contradictory, ambivalent, and uncertain. Significantly, however, several months after the 200 GFP began, the fact that it employed mostly women would not have seemed like a contradiction to many people anyway. By then the 200 GFP had become redefined as a program for protecting women's morality; youth unrest had dropped out of the picture.

This shift from youth to women is significant for what it reveals about the manner in which ideologies of gender, nationalism, and economic liberalization came together in this influential state program of economic development and rural employment. Understanding this shift necessitates an analysis of the interrelation between gender, nationalism, and economic liberalization. Only then will it be possible to understand why a program that was first touted as a means to prevent youth unrest evolved into a program whose primary claim was that it would prevent women's improper behavior. Keeping women in their villages began to be promoted as the means to restore the nation's moral and political order after the JVP revolt (and during the LTTE separatist campaign). In time, women's behavior rather than youth unrest became the official focus of the 200 GFP. This shift illuminates how involvement in economic liberalization altered the way ideologies of nationalism and gender were configured by the state, its supporters, and the people involved in this rural industrialization program on an everyday basis.

From Youth to Women

A widely publicized critique of the 200 GFP raised by the political opposition was the catalyst for this shift from youth to women. Opposition politicians argued that in garment factories "our innocent village girls are sewing panties for white women" (in Sinhala, *apee ahinsaka kello suddiyanta jangi mahanawa*).[11] I heard about this critique from numerous people of various social positions, from garment workers themselves to government officials. This was a critique of the perpetuation of Sri Lankan subservience to the West, through a contrast between the morally pure Eastern woman and the depraved Western woman centered on the figure of white women outfitted in suggestive underwear.[12] In effect, the opposition was contesting Premadasa's nationalist justification for involvement in global capitalism by arguing that the nation should not be proud of putting its women (and the nation) in this morally compromised and subservient position. This critique appealed to the fact that, regardless of political or ethnic affiliation, an East-West binary and women's behavior are central issues that accompany the Sri Lankan experience of development. Although this is the case for people in the Sinhala, Muslim, and Tamil communities alike, the specifics of this concern vary in each community. Because the 200 GFP was cast as centrally concerned with the JVP and the Sinhala Buddhist nation, it is by extension Sinhala Buddhist women's behavior that would have been in question here.

This underwear critique, first raised in October 1992, was politically and socially potent, and its impact could be felt as late as mid-1996, when I was completing my research. For instance, 200 GFP women workers would tell me with much sadness that men who know they work in a garment factory tease them by asking if they are going to sew underwear. As I demonstrate below, Premadasa responded with his own angle on protecting women's morality, arguing that it is precisely by keeping women in villages that the program protects women's morality. From this point on, the government touted the program as being concerned primarily with women's behavior. It became a program for preventing women from migrating to Colombo and its outskirts, where they are widely rumored to become involved in prostitution or at least in premarital sexual practices (neither of which are socially acceptable). The underwear critique and the government's response reveal that economic liberalization raises anxieties for everyone—politicians and factory owners, women workers and men who tease them. Here the anxieties are cast in terms of whiteness, sexuality, and intimacy.

The 200 GFP shift from youth unrest to women's morality can be tracked by examining changes in Premadasa's rhetoric. The 200 GFP began in February 1992, and in the early months it was cast as a program for preventing youth unrest. My analysis of newspaper and parliamentary Hansard reports on the program shows that criticism of the 200 GFP intensified in October 1992, when the frequency of factory openings peaked and factories were opening almost daily. The first published reference to the underwear critique that I found comes from this period. Premadasa responded to the underwear critique in two ways: He dismissed it as a political ploy by the opposition, and countered by initiating a discussion about morality and social class. For instance, the president argued in one factory speech that their interest in the panties of foreign women reveals that it was the opposition politicians who were morally compromised, not the factory workers. He said:

The garment sector is expanding rapidly, though the opposition is criticising this. They say rural women are sewing panties for foreign women. This is how they humiliate the rural masses. We also go abroad, but during our visits we gather something useful and fruitful. They go overseas to look at panties of foreign women! (Mohamed 1992b)

With this shift in argument, Premadasa turned the tables on the opposition by latching on to the fact that the critique was not just about the actual articles that were made but about the moral status of the women workers.

This argument about morality and class had an enduring social effect and resulted in the long-term transformation of the 200 GFP from a program for youth unrest to a program for women's morality. Premadasa's supporters (such as newspaper reporters, politicians, garment factory investors, and villagers) began to take up this line of argument as the dominant item of importance about the program. These people began to emphasize how the program protected women's morality. This is what was remembered during my research period; it was only when pressed that most people recalled a vague JVP connection. So in the end the opposition and the government were agreed on the importance of women's behavior to national development.

This class and morality response was also seen in a theme that Premadasa raised

Although it was not only underwear that was produced in the 200 GFP factories, the opposition party's "underwear critique" was extremely politically and socially potent. The critique highlighted the concerns about women's behavior that have been central to Sri Lankan responses to economic liberalization. Photograph by Seamus Walsh, used by permission.

in a number of speeches starting that October. He argued that the opposition's criticism of the 200 GFP was an attempt to discredit a program that was providing good jobs for the rural poor. He claimed that the opposition was critical because their party consisted of the aristocracy, who wanted to maintain a poor class of servants for their homes (P. de Silva 1992a, 1992b, 1993). In some speeches Premadasa accused the opposition of simply wanting to keep down the poor. Although I have not found a written reference to this, numerous people told me that on several occasions Premadasa made the morality connection here as well by adding that when poor women become servants, "all they come home with is something in their stomachs from the rich man." In other words, they come home pregnant. Perhaps this was just a bit too unsavory to report in the newspapers, and perhaps this was what one reporter meant when he wrote that Premadasa "recalled how poor rural children and youths were employed as servants in aristocratic homes and subjected to untold hardships" (P. de Silva 1993).

Also alluding to this issue of servants and morality was a 200 GFP television advertisement. In this advertisement—which I never saw but heard about from various people—a couple in a fancy car arrive at a poor villager's house and tell the mother that they will hire the daughter as a servant in their home. The mother refuses the offer by responding with pride that her daughter works in a garment factory. Later the girl is shown after she receives her first paycheck, bringing home a sari for her mother and a sarong for her father. Numerous people I spoke to said that the fact that the girl brings these gifts for her parents was another reference to Premadasa's claim that if she were a servant, rather than clothing she would have brought her parents an illegitimate grandchild.

In my research I found only one instance prior to the underwear critique in which the president linked the 200 GFP and women's morality—in marked contrast to the frequency of the linkages in the period following the critique. In a June 1992 opening ceremony speech, he referred to the "nefarious activities" into which some Free Trade Zone (FTZ) girls had been forced because very little of their salaries remained for their families back home once they paid for room and board. Readers would have understood this to be a clear reference to rumors that urban FTZ women engage in prostitution in order to supplement their meager factory incomes. The president pledged that with jobs in villages, these nefarious activities would be avoided (Mohamed 1992a).

But even before the moral accusations became common, press coverage of the 200 GFP in the government-controlled newspapers often pointed out the moral benefits of the program. An unabashedly pro-200 GFP newspaper reporter wrote that, under the 200 GFP, "The factory workers, many of whom are young women, will continue to live in their homes and contribute to family welfare, thus preventing the breakdown of traditional values and family life which often occurs when workers move to the cities in search of employment" (A Special Correspondent 1992).[13] This quotation is just one of many examples of how journalists emphasized issues of gender, morality, and changing social values to argue that the program would solve many of the nation's modern problems with a modern solution: global economic development. Subsequent to the underwear critique, the argument that the program prevents immorality by preventing women's migration to Colombo became even more widespread and was voiced by the president himself. In short, the claim was that keeping women in their villages would keep women—and the nation—from going bad.

Innocent Girls and the Rural/Urban Divide

Why, and for whom, is it a problem if village women sew panties for white women? The underwear critique was about "our innocent [*ahinsaka*] girls." The concept of "innocence" is important for understanding the articulation between lingerie as an immoral product and the production of lingerie as bad for the nation. We know from context that these innocent girls are villagers, and it would have in some ways been redundant for the critics to say "our innocent village girls." The Sinhala word *ahinsaka* is translated into Sri Lankan English as "innocent" or "harmless," and it is also the Pali word for nonviolence. *Ahinsaka* connotes purity, including sexual purity, and it implies being innocent of all foreign and "modern" corrupting influences. It always suggested to me a positively valued naiveté, so that part of being innocent has to do with lacking knowledge of and being protected from foreignness.[14] It is often used to describe village women and is another way of saying they are "good girls," a term used for women who act properly in terms of moral norms.[15] In the same way that they would describe each other as good girls, women at Shirtex and Serendib—the 200 GFP factories where I did ethnographic research—would often use the term *innocent* (she is very innocent, *eyaa hari ahinsakay*). So, by employing the term *innocent,* the opposition was raising issues of sexuality but also of cultural purity. The implication was that innocent girls, who should just be associated with local traditions, are now working in global capitalist industry and, even worse, sewing immoral products for white women.

This concept of "innocence" is an important component of a widespread spatialization of authentic Sinhalaness in terms of a rural/urban divide. The rural/urban divide serves as a key metaphor for the social transformations and conflicts of postcolonial Sri Lanka, and it consists of a pervasive conceptual linkage between villages, discipline, tradition, and morality that is ascribed to by many Sinhala Buddhists. Sinhala villages are often considered the locus of tradition and impervious to moral degradation—in stark contrast to the capital city Colombo and its surrounding urban areas. Thus, underlying the 200 GFP there was a narrative, familiar in other times and places,[16] that associates the city with the modern and corrupt and the countryside with tradition, culture, and moral order. And in this case, the gendered dimension of this romantic idea of villages is that village women are considered to be innocent and to naturally adhere to codes of morality and respectability that in turn preserve the distinctive characteristics of Sinhala tradition that many Sinhalas fear are disappearing in post-liberalization Sri Lankan society.[17] Hence we can begin to understand the power of the opposition's underwear critique.

We know from context that "our innocent girls" are villagers. The implication is that if good village girls become involved in activities associated with white women, their sexual purity will be questioned. The reference to white women (*suddi*) was a familiar ploy.[18] There is a pervasive racial "othering" of white women as sexually immoral in contemporary Sri Lanka. To name just a few of the ways in which this assumption is evident today, pornographic films available in Sri Lanka feature white women, and white women who frequent the country's southern beaches in skimpy bathing suits are the object of much criticism. Often pornography and tourism are the only sources of contact that Sri Lankans have with white women.

Ready-made underwear is the symbol of foreignness and sexual impurity in the opposition's critique. Sri Lankans generally consider underwear (*jangi*) both sexual and dirty.[19] This dual association is seen in everyday social practices, such as the following: Although most Sri Lankans dry their laundry outdoors on rocks, grass, bushes, or clotheslines, it is common to dry underwear in a private location. As one Shirtex worker put it, underwear is not a topic Sri Lankans speak about (she referred to underwear in Sinhala as "unmentionables" in an interview), and they tend to sew underwear at home rather than purchase it ready-made. And so, in the same way that hearing this taboo subject in a political argument made people uneasy, the mere fact of women sewing underwear in export-oriented garment factories would also make people uneasy. By sparking feelings of discomfort about this inappropriate work, the opposition suggested that if they were in power, their party would continue its tradition of paying attention to the economy *and* morality—it would not provide such morally suspect jobs.[20]

The underwear critique was unsettling not just because village girls would be sewing these items which should not be discussed. It was also unsettling because white women would be wearing this underwear. White women, already sexualized figures in Sri Lanka, were linked to innocent village girls in an inappropriate way. Of course, everyone knew that it was not only underwear that was sewn in these factories. That did not matter. Involvement with foreignness at this level was itself problematic. With the underwear critique, the opposition fed already extant nationalist concerns that associate foreignness with immorality, cultural decay, and the disintegration of village traditions. As is the case elsewhere in the world, in Sri Lanka these concerns often target women's behavior. Since Colombo often symbolizes negative foreign influence, there is concern about village women who are associated with Colombo or foreign people, things, and behaviors. The concern arises because this association raises the prospect of disintegrating village traditions. Thus, the underwear critique was asking: If good village girls are going to start behaving in new ways by working in garment factories, what will happen to the rest of Sinhala society that is reproduced through women's normative behavior? But note that this was not just a question about women's behavior. It was also a question about what village women's presence in garment factories—and the presence of garment factories in villages—implies about the feminization of the nation as a whole under global capital. This critique about village girls sewing underwear came down to important cultural questions—normally cast in rural/urban terms— about the relationship between women, nation, and moral purity.

Because the disciplined behavior of women is central to the rural/urban divide, the opposition lambasted Premadasa for subjecting the nation's moral core to this immoral type of work. Below, through the analytical concept of "moral panic," I argue that the public visibility of Juki girls as women who have crossed the rural/urban divide has led to these women being the key site of the anxieties of modernization since the 1977 introduction of economic liberalization. But before turning to Juki girls, I focus on one prominent village woman who has been a target of censure. One can gain insight into this woman's experiences by bringing to her story these questions of women, nation, and moral purity in the context of the rural/urban divide. The parallels to the experiences of Juki girls are instructive.

The Perils of Crossing the Divide

In September 2000, Susanthika Jayasinghe won a bronze medal in the 200-meter sprint at the Olympics in Sydney, Australia, thus becoming Sri Lanka's second Olympic medalist ever.[21] At the news conference following the win, in the presence of the gold and silver medalists, Susanthika (as she is known in the Sri Lankan press) pleaded to the numerous reporters in attendance to "find me another country." This comment came soon after the following, delivered in hesitant English and quoted in newspapers throughout the world: "It was trouble for me, including doping and sexual harassment. After I won the world championships in 1997, the minister (she identified him). . . . . .the big guy. . . . He wants sex with me. But I refused. I have a husband. . . . " (*Sunday Times* 2000a: 1; unconventional ellipsis points in original).

These pleas and accusations were the latest episode in a long and complicated story that demonstrates the problems that can face village women who try to cross the rural/urban divide and lead lives that diverge from conventional gender roles. When I first took note of her in 1996, Susanthika was celebrated in the national media as a Sri Lankan sprinting sensation from a village.[22] Media coverage of Susanthika increased that same year when she was accused of taking performance-enhancing drugs. Her response was that she is a village girl and would never have done such a thing. The implication, which Sri Lankans would understand when reading her response in the newspaper, was that being from a village she is inherently a good girl and thus would not have and could not possibly have cheated by taking drugs. Her fans largely agreed, and she pulled through this scandal, still "our sprint queen" in the national media.

But in April 1997 Susanthika's reputation suffered as a result of her involvement in another scandal. It was widely reported in the Sinhala and English press that she had been drinking alcohol at a party in Colombo. She was subject to disciplinary action by the minister of sports, and her fan club was outraged at her behavior. The feminist Cat's Eye column in the *Island* newspaper described the response:

When Susanthika, the much-lauded "village lass," was accused of drinking beer and partying, the vultures swept down; Susanthika has "betrayed village values," she has eaten "forbidden fruit." "Who does she think she is?" they cried. She was even punished with a 6 months ban on sporting activity, but the ban was lifted after women's groups and many others protested. (Cat's Eye 1997)

In an open letter to Susanthika, Janaka Biyanwala, a Sri Lankan Olympic athlete and political scientist, read the controversy as an urban versus rural morality play, in which the good village girl has gone bad by tasting the forbidden fruit (in this case, drink) of the city.[23] Biyanwala wrote, "The bitterness of the city and the eternal sweetness of the village, you know the usual, village is pristine, and our women are only corrupted by the city or foreigners" (Biyanwala 1997: 25). Biyanwala argued that the outrage arose because drinking is not considered appropriate for respectable women who should fit into the restrictive models of women as only wives, mothers, or good girls.

In August 1997, when she was only 20 years old, Susanthika won the silver medal in the 200-meter sprint at the World Athletics Championships in Greece. The first Sri Lankan international medalist since the 1948 silver Olympic medal, she was welcomed back to the country by thousands of fans, and she met with the president, who presented her with a gift of 1 million rupees (Reuters, SLNet newsgroup posting, August 12, 1997). Despite this grand welcome, at this same moment her reputation took another dive, and she went unequivocally beyond being a good village girl. She did this by cutting her hair short and wearing a revealing runner's outfit in the competition. "Colombo Calling," a left-oriented media watchdog, critiqued the general media coverage:

> Susanthika Jayasinghe, a rural peasant woman from Kegalle, recently cut her hair short, and dispelled any attempts at myth-making about herself as a symbol of traditional Sinhalese womanhood. Wearing a skimpy swimsuit-like athletics costume, she won the silver medal in the 200-meter run at the world athletics meet in Athens. But no Sunday newspaper in Colombo found her picture or story worthy of front page coverage. So, glory in winning a global medal in athletics by a woman, wearing modern sports attire, is not news enough—or nationalist enough—for the print media. (Colombo Calling, SLNet newsgroup posting, August 14, 1997)

This report then contrasted Susanthika's situation to that of the village men of the nation's cricket team who had also recently attained a historic win and whose faces were all over the newspapers and television.

Up until she drank alcohol, cut her hair, and wore an objectionable outfit, Susanthika had been a worthy national symbol of a traditional Sinhala Buddhist woman. Even during the 1996 drugs scandal, her picture was on newspaper front pages. But now she had finally exceeded the limits of acceptable appearance and behavior for an innocent (*ahinsaka*) woman or a good girl, that is, a respectable Sinhala Buddhist woman. Many Sri Lankans associate short hair, skimpy clothes, and alcohol with Westernized Sri Lankan women who, they say, have betrayed their cultural heritage. Even at the turn of the twentieth century there were intense accusations that Westernized and Burgher women had betrayed their culture. It was in this context that Dharmapala introduced the sari as modest clothing for Sinhala Buddhist women in contrast to Western dresses. Clothing, hairstyle, and alcohol use have been indices of women's cultural authenticity since the time of the Buddhist revival (Jayawardena 1994; de Alwis 1998: 110–112). Manisha Gunasekera has written about the importance of such "physical markers of cultural purity" to the late 1980s Jathika Chintanaya (JC, the National Ideology), an indigenist middle-class intellectual movement followed by Sinhala-speaking members of the professional classes who opposed aspects of the economic and social changes related to the open economy (Moore 1993: 627; cf. Chandraprema 1991: chap. 17; Goonewardena 1996). JC ideologue Gunadasa Amarasekera lamented that long hair and the sari were vanishing, and the group prohibited women from wearing miniskirts on university campuses during this time (Gunasekera 1996: 10).

In the Sinhala Buddhist tradition, at least since the Buddhist revival, such markers of cultural purity have been undergirded by controls on women's sexuality. In fact, the strictures regarding short hair, skimpy clothing, and alcohol are all read as relating to women's sexuality: Women who behave in these ways are assumed to be sexually loose. This is an attempt at ensuring cultural purity through policing genetic purity. Kumari Jayawardena has argued that gender roles under Sinhala Buddhist revivalism were consistent with many Asian countries where an interest in women's sexual purity is designed to ensure that women "reproduce the ethnic group and socialize children into their ethnic roles" (Jayawardena 1994: 113). Indeed, the more general notion of women as the carriers of tradition is a common trope in societies throughout the world.

Predictably, Susanthika's sexuality became an issue after her appearance and behavior were read to signal that she was not a respectable woman. In October 1997, Susanthika accused members of the Sports Ministry of sexual harassment. The next year she accused a Ministry official of "spiking her urine with banned steroids after she refused his sexual advances" (hence her comments at the 2000 Olympic news conference) (Xinhua, SLNet newsgroup posting, September 2, 1998). The response in Parliament was to refer to her as looking like a "black American man" (Cat's Eye 1997). Since black skin is associated with Tamils and is considered ugly for its racial impurity, this was a deep double insult: Susanthika was stripped of her femininity and of her authentic Sinhala ethnic purity.[24] Being neither a woman nor a pure Sinhala, she was not worthy of respect. Clearly she was being treated as something other than an innocent village girl at this point.

Susanthika had previously been able to inhabit a compromise between being too modern and urban, on one hand, and solidly traditional and rural, on the other. But cutting her hair, wearing an immodest costume, and drinking alcohol pushed her too far on the side of the city and foreignness. The story of Susanthika's rise and fall is familiar in Sri Lanka. Like actresses and female athletes and politicians in the United States, Susanthika's public social role created space for the possibility of moral criticism.

But the Sri Lankan story is different because it was not just due to her public visibility that she risked social censure. The problem arose also because Susanthika was a village girl who attempted to cross the rural/urban divide by becoming a modern, cosmopolitan athlete. Had she been from Colombo, it's likely there would not have been any (or at least not as much) concern about her appearance and behavior—she wouldn't have had any chance of being a national symbol of purity in the first place. Juki girls are similarly situated in Sri Lanka. Susanthika and Juki girls face criticism both because they circulate in public and also because they are innocent village women who are now associated with the city and the moral degradation that the city connotes.

Juki Girls and the Dangers of Urban Public Mobility

"Juki girls" (*jukiyo* or *juki kello*) is a nickname for women who work in garment factories in the Katunayake FTZ or in non-FTZ factories in and around Colombo.[25] Consistent with the rural/urban divide I have discussed earlier, Colombo is perceived by many Sri Lankans to be a corrupt, morally degrading space, and this perception is symbolized by the position of Juki girls. Most of the thousands of factory workers in Colombo work in the garment industry, and they are especially stigmatized as sexually promiscuous women who behave in a manner antithetical to cultural traditions. These women, most of whom migrated from villages for employment, live in boarding houses away from their parents and are frequently seen walking in the streets, going to movie theaters, and socializing with men. In May 1997, a federation of trade unions launched a campaign called "New Dawn" (Arunodhaya) that "aims at uplifting the morale of the working women and promoting respect for these important workers in their communities and the nation as a whole" (*Sunday Observer* 1997). The campaign was aimed at women in the FTZs, and one of the central campaign posters read: "Juki—that's not my name. We have an identity of our own" (Thaheer 1997).

The nickname "Juki" unequivocally connotes sexual promiscuity, and it is derived from a Japanese industrial sewing machine brand commonly used in Sri Lankan garment factories. Juki identifies women not only with machines (which would be significant enough) but with a foreign machine brand. As far as I know, there is no Sri Lankan industrial sewing machine brand, but if there were, a nickname based on an indigenous product would not have been as effective as the Juki moniker. By highlighting the foreignness of the machine and the foreignness of the production process, the name symbolizes the prostitution of the Sri Lankan state to foreign investors through the metaphor of the prostitution of Sri Lankan women. As such it is a key metaphor for anxieties connected with the country's post-1977 social and economic transformations.

The Katunayake FTZ (officially called the Katunayake Investment Promotion Zone), situated near the international airport on the outskirts of Colombo, is the oldest and largest of eight FTZs. It was established in 1978, and it employs nearly 60,000 workers, the majority of whom are women working in the garment industry.[26] These are the classic Juki girls, as are the thousands of garment workers in and around Colombo who work in urban factories outside of the FTZs. In Katunayake, the overabundance of women in one area and the reputation for sexual behavior among these women are symbolized by several nicknames for the town and the FTZ: *isthiripura*, literally "women's city," but with "the subtle undertone of a city of easy women or easy virtue"; *vesakalaapaya* (the zone of prostitutes, a play

Named for the Japanese industrial sewing machines commonly used in Sri Lankan factories, the derogatory "Juki girl" nickname is a key metaphor for the anxieties many Sri Lankans feel about the social and economic transformations that have accompanied economic liberalization. Photograph by Seamus Walsh, used by permission.

on the real name *nidahas velenda kalaapaya*, literally the zone of free trade); and *premakalaapaya,* the "zone of love."[27]

Why are female urban garment factory workers considered only in reference to sexuality, and why are they regarded as sexually immoral? Other researchers have argued that the attitudes of the people who live in the town of Katunayake have been largely responsible for perpetuating the negative Juki girl stereotype (Voice of Women 1983; Weerasinghe 1989). But while I will concede that there may be a role played by jealousy (the meaning of which needs to be examined) of un-employed men or parents of local girls who are eclipsed for jobs by out-of-towners, the stereotype is not simply a local problem.

I argue that the Juki stereotype emerged at least in part because the women's public visibility indicated their lack of adherence to the mother and wife roles pre-scribed for rural women. These women are crossing a firm rural/urban divide that relies on rural women to be the carriers of Sri Lankan (and, in the case of most FTZ workers, Sinhala Buddhist) tradition, an especially important social role in this time of national crisis. Asoka Bandarage argues that these women, like Sri Lankan women who work as domestic servants in the Middle East, are condemned because they are away from the patriarchal control of husbands or fathers (1988: 72), and their economic and social independence threatens male authority (69). Because most of these women live in boarding houses away from their parents, they enjoy more freedom in their social lives than other single women of their age. For instance, they walk home from work in groups or with boyfriends, and they go with men to films or to watch airplanes at the nearby airport. In response to reports by human rights advocates that Sinhala newspaper proposals sometimes disqualify FTZ workers, Yasmine Tambiah argues,

> The clear message is that women who work outside the home are sexually available to men and sexually promiscuous, and this possibility of being sexually impure by virtue of their bid for economic freedom puts them outside the ranks of possible candidates for institutionalized heterosexuality and (ironically) the material dependence on men that it connotes. (Y. Tambiah 1997: 29)

Clearly, the widespread visibility of these women combined with reports about their sexuality leads to general censure of their behavior.

Moral Panic

There seems to be a connection between the public visibility of Juki girls, their class position, their attempt at crossing the rural/urban divide, and the con-siderable moral panic surrounding their place in contemporary Sri Lankan society. Similar linkages seem to have been made in reference to the position of Susanthika, about whom there is also moral panic. Societal alarm about the bad character of Juki girls resembles Stanley Cohen's formulation of moral panic: "A condition, epi-sode, person or group of persons emerges to become defined as a threat to societal values and interests" (Cohen 1972: 9; cf. Carby 1997; Goode and Ben-Yehuda 1994;

Thompson 1998). Juki girls and Susanthika pose such a threat in contemporary Sri Lanka: To people in various social positions, there is something about these women that signals the disintegration of revered cultural traditions.

If we consider Juki girls as yet another social context for the potency of the underwear critique, Cohen's notion of "moral panic" and Erving Goffman's notion of "stigma" further illuminate the social context for the underwear critique and the state's subsequent refocusing of the 200 GFP on the issue of women's morality. Cohen analyzes the moral panic through which Mods and Rockers in 1960s Britain were positioned as "folk devils" whose deviance from normative social roles was constructed as a material threat to society and a threat to the social order. He describes how a group who is "highly visible and structurally weak" can become an easy object of attack for moral panics orchestrated by more powerful members of society because of conflicts of interests and power differentials (1972: 198). When Mods and Rockers began to blur class lines by "passing" as members of the middle class through new consumption practices (manifested especially in style of dress), they were met with hostility from the more powerful members of society who wanted to maintain the status quo (195). Cohen argues that the mass media created the moral panic by reporting on deviant behavior in order to delineate behavior that is "right" or "wrong." Furthermore, the media and the public created the panic by using emotive symbols (such as the terms *hooligans, thugs,* and *wild ones*) and creating "composite stigmas" (55–57).

Cohen helps us understand that moral panics are a form of social control that creates and reinforces a moral dichotomy of right and wrong. While I find Cohen's framework useful because of its attention to the role of moral panic in the maintenance of values and interests, I should note that the situation I am describing is more pervasive than the top-down sense implied by Cohen. It is not simply people in power who desire to maintain certain values—these desires are more hegemonic and self-disciplining.[28]

Goffman focuses on the "management of stigma" by stigmatized people and demonstrates that even people on the deviant end of a moral panic may have quite complicated identities since, as members of society, they have internalized the normative categories. Goffman's study is primarily about individuals stigmatized because of physical deformities, but he also discusses the stigma resulting from "blemishes of individual character" (1963: 4), such as that of prostitutes and alcoholics. These morally stigmatized people are like Cohen's folk devils in that they too are perceived as collectively denying the social order (144).

For both Cohen and Goffman, "passing" as a person of a different social class or as a nonstigmatized person is a significant moment in the construction of normativity. And when they see members of their stigmatized group acting in stereotypical ways, stigmatized people who pass as "normals" can be both repelled and ashamed. Susan Seizer (1997, 2000) has examined the "stigma of public mobility" experienced by dramatic actresses in Tamil Nadu, India—women whose occupation puts them in a stigmatized position, and who love their jobs yet won't admit it because they are embarrassed. Seizer beautifully describes the negotiations women make to overcome this stigma of public mobility when they move between different public spaces and the kinds of femininity they deploy in these different spaces.

Juki girls are likewise positioned as stigmatized objects of moral panic, and their unusual extent of public mobility certainly plays a role in their stigmatization. But the moral panic about Susanthika and Juki girls is only in part attributable to this stigma of public mobility. It should also be understood in the context of nationalist constructions of gender identity where their attempt to cross the rural/urban divide becomes problematic. The main "emotive symbol" that is used to describe garment workers is the term *Juki girl,* and many garment workers inside and outside FTZs are at pains to pass as non–Juki girls. Many of the women I knew at Shirtex and Serendib tried to "pass" by enacting certain sartorial and social practices. For instance, most would be sure to brush cotton dust and thread out of their clothes and hair before leaving the factory gates, and many would choose to commute alone rather than among packs of women who could be clearly marked as garment workers.

Elsewhere I argue that many of the Shirtex and Serendib women tried to manage the Juki stigma by deploying new kinds of good girl identities, and yet they also participated in some ways in the moral panic through which they were stigmatized (Lynch 1999, 2000, 2002). Many women at Shirtex and Serendib frequently drew stark contrasts between urban and rural garment factory workers, and some even used the term *Juki girls* in a negative manner to refer to the urban workers. In so doing they perpetuated certain repressive gender constructions. Their attitudes resemble those of the Malaysian electronics workers observed by Aihwa Ong whose "positive attempts at constructing their own gender identity depended on a cult of purity and self-sacrifice" (Ong 1987: 191). In numerous conversations, women who worked in Shirtex and Serendib indicated to me that they understood job scarcity, productivity, and competition, and that they knew that investors and buyers would make choices between their factories and those in the logistically more accessible FTZs. By forging identities as good girls, these women justified their employment over the urban women who they believe lack the self-control to be good workers and good girls. And in doing so they also created a space for their own new social practices (inside and outside of work) within the safety of the villages. They were clearly ambivalent in their feelings about their experiences as factory workers, and they tried desperately to evade this moral censure and panic by inhabiting a world that has some elements of a new, urban, and modern life but also important elements of their traditional village lives.

Susanthika's story and the Juki stigma are both aspects of moral panic about the prospect of a crumbling rural/urban divide during this era of ethnic conflict in Sri Lanka. The underwear critique also should be understood in these terms. Because women's behavior is seen as central to the maintenance of a rural/urban divide, with their underwear critique the opposition was arguing that if our last holdout ("our innocent girls") would be corrupted, the nation would be doomed. Furthermore, because the 200 GFP was presented as a post-JVP program for reintroducing discipline to rural citizens, by raising the issue of women's sexuality, the opposition made a predictable shift to a more gendered discipline.

Conclusion: Sexuality, Morality, and Sinhala Buddhist Nationalism

The underwear critique and the government's response are best understood in the context of the widespread concern in Sri Lanka about women's morality, especially the morality of rural women who leave their villages for employment in Colombo and are rumored to engage in premarital sexual relations.[29] The intense concern with women's moral behavior has a complex history but today forms half of the ideologies of male heroism and female moral purity that pervade war-torn Sri Lanka. While men are encouraged to be aggressive and fight for the country, women are valorized both as mothers who heroically sacrifice their sons for the nation without complaint and as traditional women who maintain ethnic purity through their heightened morality.[30] Consider, for example, the following image:

> A poster promoting breastfeeding . . . was issued by the Ministry of Women's Affairs. The poster, which was displayed during the height of one of the first major government offensives against the Tamil militants in the north, in 1986–87, depicted a woman dressed in cloth and jacket—a marker of Sinhalaness—breastfeeding her baby while dreaming of a man in army fatigues. The Sinhala caption below exhorted: "Give your [breast milk] (*le kiri*) to nourish our future soldiers." (de Alwis 1998: 206)

In the case of Juki girls, the notion seems to be that if so-called traditional village girls are not behaving properly, the nation that is being threatened by the LTTE's separatist movement is doomed. And so an implicit question behind the underwear critique may have been: If the nation's women cannot be counted on to reproduce disciplined Sinhala soldiers because they are busy producing naughty garments, what kind of undisciplined army will protect our Sinhala Buddhist nation? Once again, through this line of argument the opposition would have suggested that attention to morality is important to the nation's future.

There is a long history of spatially imagining and socially constructing Sinhala Buddhist identity in terms of a divide between villages and the city. Such a divide connotes differential access to wealth, power, and knowledge, as well as varying degrees of tradition and pure Sinhala Buddhist identity in a politically charged landscape in which village Sri Lanka is claimed for Sinhala Buddhists (and, to a certain extent, other Sinhalas) and not minorities (particularly Tamils). The 200 GFP was first presented to the public as a means to prevent youth unrest. By providing rural industrial jobs, the 200 GFP promised the restoration of the nation's moral and political order when the LTTE was threatening secession and when the country was recovering from the JVP revolt. It may seem contradictory that placing nontraditional, global capitalist industry in villages could be considered a solution for preventing the disintegration of tradition. In fact, the underwear critique addressed this apparent contradiction, but in explicitly sexualized terms (by bringing in the specter of white women). In response, the government played up the fact that, within the terms of a socially produced rural/urban divide, villages were considered pure and pristine locales. Thus it follows that villages would purify factories, the consumer practices that come with factories, and even the male managers who in an urban setting might be inclined to abuse female workers. Keeping women and factories in villages would protect the nation's moral order. So did this, in fact, occur? Factories such as Shirtex and Serendib were certainly modern industrial workplaces that employed scientific management techniques. But were they—and the women workers—also somehow pure and traditional due to their location in villages? Perhaps not surprisingly, I demonstrate elsewhere that this heroic picture of the purifying power of villages is much more complicated when we look at how the women at Shirtex and Serendib experienced this work and their new lives and attempted to forge ways of living as good girls, despite being garment workers (Lynch 1999, 2000, 2002).

A more recent example also provides a nuanced picture of the lived effects of the 200 GFP. In the 1997 Sinhala film *Pura Handa Kaluwara* (Death on a Full Moon Day), the boyfriend of a garment factory worker in Anuradhapura suspects that his girlfriend is involved in prostitution. When he goes to the factory to see if she really works there as she claims, he finds soldiers "looking for girls." After describing this part of the story line in this way in a March 2000 interview, director Prasanna Vithanage then discussed its social context. He mentioned Premadasa's 200 GFP and continued:

> When I made the film in July 1997, prostitution was just beginning in Anuradhapura. Now, after Colombo, the highest prostitution rate in Sri Lanka is in Anuradhapura, the sacred city. Soldiers who come from the north spend two days in this city, and a whole prostitution industry has developed. The wages in the garment factories are very low, and so some of the girls go to massage clinics, and from there they are pushed into prostitution. I heard of one incident involving a young soldier who went to a brothel and was shown all the girls available. He saw his sister amongst these girls and became so angry that he attempted to kill the brothel-keeper and his sister. The brothel-keeper took him to another room, calmed him down, and got him another girl. You see how the war has eroded basic human values and the conception of Sri Lanka as some great Buddhist civilisation. (Phillips 2000)

This Sinhala film vignette gives me pause on several counts. The story disrupts the easy dichotomies of rural/urban and pure/impure that pervade Sri Lanka and underlay the underwear critique. And, if it is true (as it is throughout the world with towns located near army bases) that Anuradhapura is providing prostitutes for the nation's soldiers, the story demonstrates through the conjuncture of these two socioeconomic factors—the presence in the area of soldiers on leave from the nearby warfront and the presence of underpaid garment workers in rural 200 GFP factories—yet another connection between the war, economy, morality, and gender that is worth considering in more detail. Finally, one must consider the possibility that connections such as those I am making may be important for people in positions of power. Shortly before its scheduled first screening in Sri Lanka in July 2000, the Sri Lankan government banned this film, citing a fear that the film might adversely affect the morale of the armed forces. However, one year later, the Sri Lankan Supreme Court lifted the ban. The court argued in terms of freedom of expression and ordered the government to compensate the filmmaker for damages (Sturgess 2000; BBC 2001).

This vignette brings to the fore the questions of economy, sexuality, morality, and Sinhala Buddhist nationalism in a time of ethnic conflict with which I began this essay. It also returns me to Gunasinghe, who famously drew a connection between the shift to a free market and a rise in ethnic hostilities in Sri Lanka since 1977. One might argue that the nationalist concerns about women's behavior that became so evident in the political conversations around the 200 GFP had nothing to do with the ethnic conflict that was then and continues to be waged in Sri Lanka.[31] But I would argue that—in addition to showing how nationalism is struggled over in the process of engaging in the world economy—the story of the 200 GFP sheds considerable light on the interconnectedness of nationalism, gender, globalization, and the ethnic conflict in today's Sri Lanka. Anthropologist Michael Woost told me about a conversation he once had with Gunasinghe about whether it would be possible for Sri Lankan political activists to recapture nationalism, or Buddhism itself, for a more progressive cause. As Woost described it to me, the question was whether the meaning of nationalism could be uncoupled from chauvinism and put to other uses (personal communication, September 2000). Of course, there are numerous examples from throughout the world of nationalism without ethnic conflict, but given the current configuration of nationalism and chauvinism in Sri Lanka, the violent and protracted civil war must figure into any discussion of contemporary nationalism. The 200 GFP story that I have only begun to tell in this essay is relevant to the ethnic conflict in this respect: When a state is fighting an ethnonationalist war, ethnonationalist political rhetoric will likely be interpreted by the citizenry in terms of the war. Meaning is made in the context of historical and social contests for power.

Notes

The research for this essay was conducted from 1994 to 1996 in Sri Lanka. Factory-based and village-based ethnographic research (interviews, surveys, participant observation) was complemented with archival work on the garment industry and President Premadasa's social policies. I also conducted interviews with government and industry officials as well as investors, and visited numerous factories in Colombo, the Katunayake Free Trade Zone, and villages throughout the country. The factory names in this essay are pseudonyms. I am grateful for critical comments on this essay from Deborah Winslow and Michael Woost. Thanks also to participants at the American Institute of Sri Lankan Studies (AISLS) workshop on "The Economy and Ethnic Conflict in Sri Lanka," August 25–27, 2000, Durham, N.H., where I first presented this essay. Finally, I am grateful to the numerous people in Sri Lanka who helped me with this project, especially the women at Shirtex and Serendib.

1. The majority of Sri Lankans (74 percent) are Sinhala, and most of them are Buddhist (with a small minority of Christians). The minority ethnic groups in-

clude Tamils (18 percent, mostly Hindu, some Christian), Muslims (7 percent), and very small populations of other groups. Following the postcolonial election in 1956 of the government of S. W. R. D. Bandaranaike on a platform of Sinhala Buddhist ethnic revivalism, and subsequent legislation that made Sinhala the national language to the exclusion of Tamil and English, the contemporary Sri Lankan state has increasingly become Sinhala Buddhist. Ethnic minorities have become alienated by state policies on language, government hiring, and university admissions and by the Buddhist symbolism and linguistic references that pervade electoral politics (Rogers et al. 1998; see also Hettige, this volume). The term *Sinhala Buddhist* was first used by the anticolonial nationalist Anagarika Dharmapala in the early twentieth century (Gunawardana 1990: 76), and although not all Sinhalas are Buddhist, Dharmapala's Buddhist revivalism produced a naturalized equation of Sinhalas with Buddhism. Central to this so-called revivalism, Sinhala Buddhists have claimed a right to political domination of the island by arguing that the Buddha designated Sri Lanka to be the *dhammadipa*, the island that exemplifies and preserves the Buddha's teachings.

2. As I have been reminded by political scientist Amita Shastri (personal communication, July 2000). See Shastri 1997 where she clearly delineates the economic pressures Premadasa was under at this time.

3. Excerpts from Premadasa's inaugural 200 GFP speech can be found in Fernando 1992 and Observer 1992.

4. The UNP government under Premadasa faced a strong challenge in the late 1980s with the violent uprising of the JVP, an armed youth group composed primarily of Sinhalas whose ideology combined a critique of foreign economic forces with Sinhala chauvinism. An estimated 40,000–50,000 deaths and disappearances occurred at the hands of the JVP and as a result of the brutal government crackdown. Estimates vary as to how many of these deaths and disappearances were the responsibility of which group, although there seems to be agreement that the government was responsible for the bulk. For instance, Amnesty International (1990) quotes some observers who hold the government responsible for 30,000 and quotes the government holding the JVP responsible for 6,517. Chandraprema (1991) breaks it down as 23,000 killed by the government and 17,000 by the JVP. On the JVP, see Alles 1990, Chandraprema 1991, J. de Silva 1998, Gunaratna 1990, and Moore 1993.

   It is conceivable that Premadasa simply used the JVP line of argument to sell the program to the nation and that it had little to do with Premadasa's true motivations. However, the late president's true motivations (which we cannot know) are of less interest to me than his actual actions and rhetoric.

5. The full 200 factories were never built. In April 1996, when I was completing my research, 161 were in operation, 5 were under construction, and 12 had been closed. As of September 1995, 77,000 people were employed. These figures were compiled for me in April 1996 by the Board of Investment (BOI), the government office that administers the program. Investors received tax breaks and other financial incentives from the state, such as duty-free vehicles and priority on quotas for exporting to the United States. Sri Lankan investors were Sinhala Buddhists, and many were members of minority groups such as Tamils, Muslims, Sindhis, and Gujaratis. Foreign investors included American, German, and Hong Kong firms.

6. There is little written on women in the JVP, but see Gunaratna 1990 and

de Mel 1998. Hettige (ed. 1992: 65) writes, "Only a small minority of female youth have taken part in militant youth politics."

7. In interviews and conversations with me, state representatives and factory owners and managers described a preference for female rather than male garment workers through the familiar depiction of women's nimble fingers (when I asked one factory owner why he employed women, he simply wiggled his fingers in my face and said, "You know, these"), women's proclivity for sewing, and the ease of controlling a female workforce. There is a vast literature on the preference for cheap and docile female labor in capitalist industry throughout the world, but a basic formulation is found in Elson and Pearson 1981. See also Fuentes and Ehrenreich 1983, Nash and Fernandez-Kelly 1983, Ong 1991, Sassen 1998, and Standing 1989.

8. See Gamburd, this volume, on why men enlist in the army.

9. Gamburd notes the same formulation in her essay in this volume when she quotes a Naeaegama man named Timon making this very point.

10. The situation has changed slightly. In 1997, the government began a drive to recruit women for the armed forces, since they were increasingly unable to recruit enough men in the fight against the LTTE. During my research, many workers understood that because garment revenues are a major source of foreign exchange for the state, and because the war is a major expense, garment revenues are used by the state to fight the war. On this reasoning, many garment workers claimed that they were doing a service to the country by working in the 200 GFP factories. Explaining the importance of earning foreign exchange, they proudly paralleled their national service to that of their boyfriends, husbands, and brothers who were in the army. Some even told me that, given the chance, they would have joined the army. I must note, though, that the Sinhala Buddhists among whom I did research made these claims; how Tamil women experience this involvement in the state's plan remains an important question.

11. See Lynch 2002 for an extended analysis of this critique.

12. Sri Lanka is a top producer of lingerie for companies such as Victoria's Secret and Marks and Spencer. Other foreign clothing manufacturers whose garments are produced under contract at the 200 GFP factories include Liz Claiborne, Warner Brothers, Helly-Hansen, and Gap.

13. This article has the byline "By a Special Correspondent." It is likely that the author is Anthony Fernando, the government official responsible for promoting the program through the media, who wrote numerous articles with this same moral tone in the government-controlled *Daily News*.

14. The concept of *ahinsaka* has been critiqued by the Sri Lankan feminist journal *Options*. In early 2001, *Options* commented on "Ahinsa," a new insurance policy for women. *Options* noted how the insurance policy plays on expectations for women to be innocent and harmless such that the insurance policy is "for those who possess the essentially female qualities of innocence, harmlessness, and 'weepiness'" (Options 2001).

15. Sinhala speakers used the English term interchangeably with the Sinhala, *honda lamay*. Nationalist and capitalist gender ideals came together in this figure of the "good girl." A good girl both embodied Sinhala Buddhist traditions and was an efficient and productive factory worker. Good girl for the nation or good girl for the factory—in general, the importance of these nationalist and capitalist

gender ideals seemed to be conceived of as conjunctural, although this was not completely clear-cut (as I demonstrate in Lynch 2000).

16. For instance, Raymond Williams (1973) has famously examined the role of the country and city dichotomy in the English moral imagination. Likewise, Herman Lebovics (1992) has written about the role of the pastoral in the French tradition. Unlike the situations described by Williams and Lebovics, though, it is not only urban Sri Lankans who think about these dichotomies: Rural people are equally invested in thinking about their world in rural/urban contrasts—contrasts that nevertheless are continually complicated in everyday social practices.

17. Briefly I will note that because of the romantic place of the village in the moral imagination of Sinhala Buddhists today, the village is imbued with deep social and moral significance for Sinhala villagers and urbanites alike. Deteriorating family values and rising individualism are thought of as important elements of the general disintegration of community that has been feared for at least 100 years, even since well before a number of "disintegrating village" studies, such as the 1951 state-appointed Kandyan Peasantry Commission, which portended the imminent disintegration of Kandyan villages, as did later sociological studies in 1957 and 1979 (both entitled *The Disintegrating Village*) (Sri Lanka 1951; Sarkar and Tambiah 1957; Morrison, Moore, and Ishak Lebbe 1979). The Presidential Commission on Youth even named "unbridled individualism" as one cause of the late 1980s JVP revolt (Sri Lanka 1990: 94). Women's behavior is once again invested with meaning: To be a traditional village woman means adhering to codes of morality and respectability in order to maintain community standing but also to preserve the distinctive characteristics of Sinhala tradition that Sinhalas believe to be disappearing in modern society. In this context, it has become particularly meaningful if a woman acts in a manner perceived to be antithetical to community norms in terms of sexuality and marriage choice. A woman's disregard for the ideal of virginity at marriage and for marrying a man of the appropriate caste is often interpreted as indifference to both her family's social standing and the perpetuation of the Sinhala ethnic group.

18. The term *suddi* could refer to *foreign women*, although it usually refers to white women. In this case the sexual connotations of the critique clearly recommend its translation as *white*.

19. Unlike the English *underwear, jangi* refers to underpants only, not to brassieres as well.

20. The opposition at that time was the Sri Lanka Freedom Party (SLFP). When the People's Alliance (PA), a coalition of parties led by the SLFP, came into power in 1994, it portrayed its policies with the slogan "open economy with a human face," in contrast with the UNP's policies (Stokke 1995: 124). I have also seen this motto called "capitalism with a human face" (Goonewardena 1996). In his essay in this volume, Richardson refers to this same set of concerns as "capitalism with a Buddhist face," but he is referring to UNP policies. Thus we can see that each party has asserted its moral superiority over the other in these same moral terms. See Richardson's essay for how these questions of Sri Lanka's "traditional values" became important political issues when the liberal economic reforms were first implemented.

21. A Sri Lankan man won a silver medal in the 1948 Olympics.

22. Her village origins remained important and were often connected to class-

based analyses in the media even as late as September 2000, when Susan-thika was preparing to compete in the Sydney Olympics. One article noted, "Jayasinghe, who is from a poor family, practiced running barefoot among rubber trees in central Sri Lanka where her father worked as a laborer" (*Times of India* 2000).

23. One Sinhala-language newspaper article was entitled "Susanthika tastes the forbidden fruit."

24. See Trautmann 1997 for a discussion of skin color and the Aryan construction and for a history of the Aryan and Dravidian linguistic and racial categories in general. Briefly, although the terms *Aryan* and *Dravidian* were originally Orientalist linguistic and racial constructions, they have a strong place in the popular imagination in Sri Lanka. The term *Aryan* was developed to refer to people and languages spanning from North India to Europe, while *Dravidian* referred to South Indian languages and people. In Sri Lanka currently, Sinhalas are considered Aryan (and fair-skinned, after their European Aryan relatives), and Tamils are considered dark-skinned Dravidians.

25. For studies of Sri Lankan FTZ workers, see Fine 1995, Hettiarachchy 1991, Rosa 1991, *Slaves of "Free" Trade: Camp Sri Lanka* 2001, Voice of Women 1983, Weerasinghe 1989, and *Women of the Zone: Garment Workers of Sri Lanka* 1994. The earliest study of Colombo factory workers I have located is based on research in the late 1940s, and it, too, refers to moral concerns about such employment (Ryan and Fernando 1951).

26. Employment statistics are as of November 2000, as provided on the website of Sri Lanka's Board of Investment (http://www.boisrilanka.org/about/freetradezones.htm, available as recently as October 20, 2001, but no longer on-line).

27. The quote about *isthiripura* is from Voice of Women 1983: 69. The usage of the term *vesakalaapaya* is noted in Weerasinghe 1989: 319, and *premakalaapaya* is a term I frequently heard.

28. This relates to my comments earlier that rural people are equally invested as urban people in thinking about their world in stark and value-laden rural/urban contrasts.

29. There are similar concerns articulated about the migration of women to the Middle East for employment as domestic servants or as factory workers. For an analysis of gender transformations related to Middle East migration, see M. R. Gamburd 1995 and 2000. In her discussion of "horror stories" about migrant workers, Gamburd (2000: chap. 9) follows Heng and Devan (1992) in using the term *narratives of crisis* in a manner similar to my use of the concept of moral panic.

30. Among other writings that have explored this issue, see de Alwis 1998, de Mel 1998, Jayawardena 1994, Perera 1996, and Tennekoon 1986.

31. A discussant made this argument at the AISLS conference in August 2000, where I first presented this essay.

Epilogue, or Prelude to Peace?

Michael D. Woost and Deborah Winslow

LTTE Declares Monthlong Cease-Fire

> —*TamilNet News*, Wednesday, December 19, 2001

Gov't Welcomes LTTE Cease-Fire

> —*Sri Lanka News*, U.S. Department of Information,
> Thursday, December 20, 2001

Cessation of Hostilities Begins Today

> —*Sri Lanka News*, Department of Information,
> Monday, December 24, 2001

Over the summer of 2003, as this book was being prepared for publication, the Sri Lankan government and the LTTE were struggling to break a two-month deadlock in peace negotiations. The talks had begun officially in September 2002, although the first monthlong cease-fire was unilaterally declared by the LTTE to begin at midnight on December 24, 2001, to which the government had reciprocated by having its forces also cease hostilities. Even before the first cease-fire, there had been enough "rumblings" of peace on the horizon that roadblocks throughout the city of Colombo had been removed, allowing traffic to flow unhindered by military checkpoints and barriers.

After a month of backstage negotiating, the cease-fire was extended for another month. Then on February 22, 2002, as the second monthlong cease-fire was drawing to an end, a Memorandum of Understanding was signed by the government and by the LTTE, paving the way for official talks to begin. Since the beginning, the peace talks have been brokered by the royal government of Norway through its ambassador and special envoys. Six sessions were held in a number of venues outside Sri Lanka: September 16–18, 2002, in Sattahip, Thailand; October 31 to November 11, 2002, in Nakhorn Pathom, Thailand; December 2–5, 2002, in Oslo; January 6–9, 2003, in Nakhorn Pathom; February 7–10, 2003, in Berlin; and March 18–21, 2003, in Hakone, Japan. Official negotiations were suspended on April 21, 2003.

The talks began cautiously by reinforcing the commitment to the cease-fire and continuing with the peace process. Practically, they concentrated on issues where agreement was most likely: the need for emergency humanitarian aid in the north and east, including accelerated resettlement and rehabilitation of "internally displaced persons." Part of the second session was also devoted to preparing for an international donor conference to be held in Oslo on November 25, 2002.

The third session, held after the donor conference, witnessed a major political breakthrough. The government of Sri Lanka and the LTTE issued a statement through the Norwegian government agreeing to the "principle of internal self-determination in areas of historical habitation of the Tamil-speaking peoples, based in a federal structure within a united Sri Lanka" (Royal Norwegian Government 2002). This meant that not only had the LTTE abandoned the demand for a separate state but that the Sri Lankan government was now willing to change its constitution to create some form of a federal system. The fourth session again focused on urgent humanitarian needs and set up an Accelerated Resettlement Program for the Jaffna District and a North East Reconstruction Fund, creating structures through which funds from international donors could be channeled. The fourth session also set up a new Subcommittee on Gender Issues and a human rights agenda. However, the process faltered. Around the time of the fifth session, held February 7–10, 2003, in Berlin, it became clear that the situation on the ground continued to be militarily on edge. On February 7, near Delft, an island off the northwestern coast of Sri Lanka, the Sri Lanka navy fired on an LTTE vessel and killed three members of the Sea Tigers, the navy wing of the LTTE. The talks were shortened, but not before an agreement had been reached to keep working on immediate humanitarian aid to support the ongoing resettlement in Jaffna, which at that point was ahead of schedule. The need to engage Muslims in planning was recognized as well with the creation of three committees whose membership would be half Muslim and half LTTE. With one committee for each of the three districts of the Eastern Province, their brief was to consider "land issues and other issues of mutual concern" (Royal Norwegian Government 2003).

By the sixth session, held March 18–21 in Japan, incidents of violence were increasing; there was another naval conflict on March 10 in which 11 Tigers were killed. Nevertheless, the talks went on. They agreed to expand the mandate of the Sri Lanka Monitoring Mission, so that they could do more to keep the cease-fire intact. They also continued working on humanitarian measures and began work on a plan for power sharing and fiscal devolution within a federal structure.

Talks Suspended

Tigers Call Off Rehabilitation Talks Pending "Tangible Action on the Ground"
—*TamilNet News*, Sunday, April 24, 2003

Sri Lankan Tigers Make Fresh Demands before Reentering Talks
—*Yahoo Asia News*, Wednesday, May 21, 2003

The peace talks had begun amid widespread optimism in Sri Lanka and abroad. As more sessions took place and more were scheduled, and as more of Sri

Lanka began to look demilitarized, many people were euphoric about the apparent end to two decades of civil war. Although there continued to be small skirmishes between rebels and government forces here and there, the cease-fire seemed to be holding. Then in March 2003, right before the talks in Japan, an LTTE ship was fired upon and sunk by a Sri Lankan gunboat, the worst breech of the cease-fire to that date. Everyone held their breath, but the LTTE announced that this would not deter them from pursuing a peaceful agreement, and the talks went ahead as scheduled. However, not long afterward, the LTTE announced that they were regrettably suspending talks "temporarily" from April 21, 2003. They felt justified in this stance because of the government's slow progress on the normalization of security, administrative, and welfare issues in the north and east.

The Deadlock Remains

LTTE Insists on Draft Framework for Interim Administration to Resume Talks
— *TamilNet News*, Wednesday, June 11, 2003

Sri Lanka's Rebels Reject Latest Government Attempt to End Standoff
—Associated Press, Wednesday, June 11, 2003

LTTE Flays Lankan Gov't for Internationalising Conflict
—P. K. Balachanddran, Wednesday, June 11, 2003

June 2003 saw the deadlock continuing and signs of uncertainty mounting day by day. Despite widespread international appeals for their participation, the LTTE refused an invitation by the Japanese to join in the international donor meetings held in Tokyo, June 9–10, 2003. Efforts continued on many fronts to get the talks back on track; fortunately, the cease-fire held. On June 9, 2003, during the Tokyo donors meeting, the prime minister of Sri Lanka, Ranil Wickremasinghe, offered to alter the constitution in order to allow the LTTE to assume control of the north as an interim regional authority. The offer was quickly rejected by LTTE officials, dimming hopes that talks would resume anytime soon. In rejecting the government proposal, the LTTE said they also would not give in to the international pressure very much in evidence at the Tokyo conference. They castigated the government for "internationalizing" the conflict by allowing donor nations to interfere. A new proposal for an interim administration was put forward by the government in July 2003. The LTTE leadership hinted in late August that they might be willing to accept the new proposal for administration in the northeast but that the offer was still too ambiguous. In Paris, upper-level leaders of the LTTE met to discuss the proposal and how it might be revised. Meanwhile, pressure continued to mount.

Pressure from All Sides

Sri Lanka: Gov't Gets 4.5 Billion Dollars in Pledges, Tied to Peace
—*Lacnet*, Tuesday, June 10, 2003

World Bank Stresses Link between Peace and Development at Sri Lanka Donor Conference
—World Bank press release, Tuesday, June 10, 2003

Sri Lanka's President Warns PM against Accepting Aid
—ABC News, Tuesday, June 10, 2003

U.S. Tells Tigers to Restart Talks: The United States Says It Expects the Tamil Tiger Rebels and Sri Lankan Government to Resume Peace Talks Immediately
—BBC World News, Friday, June 13, 2003

Violence against Muslims Adds to Sri Lanka Peace Bid Worries
—Agence France-Presse via ClariNet, Tuesday, August 19, 2003

Sri Lankan Muslims Up in Arms about Proposed Tamil Power-Sharing Road Map
—Taiwannews.com, Friday, August 22, 2003

No doubt about it, international pressure has been very real. As one might expect, some of it comes from diplomatic sources who want to keep the negotiations on track. But the most public international pressure has come attached to offers of international aid. During the June meeting in Tokyo, donor nations, seemingly in an effort to get the talks going again, offered as much as $4.5 billion in aid, contingent on peace. The World Bank, too, pledged support, stating that peace and development necessarily go hand in hand. The United States, also deeply involved in the donor conference, additionally demanded that talks resume immediately. Despite pressure right up to the last minute, the LTTE did not attend.

Meanwhile, pressure also mounted from the political opposition, headed by President Chandrika Kumaratunga of the People's Alliance (PA). Because the Sri Lankan constitution provides for the separate election of the president, Kumaratunga continues in office until 2005 despite the fact that the United National Front (UNF) won a narrow parliamentary majority in the 2001 elections. Prime Minister Ranil Wickremasinghe leads the majority alliance, but under the Sri Lanka constitution he has less executive power than does the president. Therefore, Kumaratunga's demands variously to halt or to strongly modify the peace process have practical as well as symbolic significance: Her support is necessary for a peace agreement to be signed. In general, Kumaratunga, the PA, and other opposition parties (particularly the JVP) claim that the prime minister's UNF government is giving too much of the country away just to be able to sign a peace agreement. Kumaratunga, who sometimes says she supports the peace process and at other times voices opposition, even refused to send a message to be read at the donor conference on her behalf. She threatened to renegotiate the aid package, and she scoffed at the Japanese offer to help. Earlier, in statements to the press, she had called the Norwegian intermediators a bunch of "salmon-eating busybodies" (BBC World News 2003a).The president's comments and general opposition to the peace process also strike a chord among some sectors of the Sinhala population.

While it is difficult to know the extent of this apparently anti-peace sentiment, the opposition is both strident and vociferous. In addition to nationalist rallies, marches, and other protests, some Sinhala and English newspapers have daily caustic commentary about the LTTE, the government of Sri Lanka, and those who support the peace process. A sampling of translations of editorials from Sinhala dailies posted on one newsgroup, the *Daily Resume*, attest to this barrage of often enraged criticism. For instance, an editorial in the *Divaina* remarked that the intellectuals, journalists, and other vocal supporters of the peace process were ultimately "waiting to be awarded a medal" by the leader of the LTTE once a separate state is attained (*Daily Resume* June 18, 2003). In the *Deshaya* newspaper, a commentator against the peace process called for a boycott against products from Japan for meddling in Sri Lanka's internal affairs by supporting Eelam (*Daily Resume* June 18, 2003). An even more extreme example of this opposition appeared in *Divaina*. The editorial claimed the government was simply supplying blood to a bloodthirsty beast by entering into peace talks with the LTTE. The author concluded by saying that "The animal thirsty for blood cannot be satisfied with vegetables. Every single opportunity he gets, he would taste blood, and those who deal with it should decide whether or not they should permit him to do that. You must either keep on supplying him with blood, or kill him once and for all" (*Daily Resume* June 17, 2003).

There is also pressure coming from Sri Lanka's Muslim minority. In the districts claimed by the LTTE for a Tamil homeland, Muslim concentrations, according the 1981 census, vary from less than 2 percent (compared to the Tamils' 97 percent) in northern Jaffna District to much higher levels in the eastern region, where tensions between Muslims and Tamils are especially high. Muslims comprise 24 percent of the population (compared to Tamils' 72 percent) in Batticaloa District, 29 percent (compared to Tamils' 36 percent) in Trincomalee District, and 42 percent (compared to Tamils' 20 percent) in Ampara District, where Muslims actually outnumber Tamils (Census of Sri Lanka 2003).

Over the summer of 2003, Muslims in the eastern districts were subject to a new wave of selective violence as a number of Muslims were abducted and dozens of prominent Muslim leaders were murdered. Both the government and the Muslim community have tended to blame the LTTE, while the LTTE denies responsibility and claims that the attacks are being carried out by parties opposed to the peace process in general. Muslim leaders assert that this is another effort on the part of the LTTE to ethnically cleanse the region of Muslims and thereby gain a majority in the east as well as the north. They compare it to the early 1990s, when over 60,000 Muslims were expelled from Jaffna by the LTTE (an episode for which the LTTE later apologized). As of late August 2003, the government police and security forces continued on high alert in the east while people there often were subject to curfews.

Before this most recent wave of violence in the east, the plan had been to merge the north and east of the island into a single semiautonomous northeastern unit, presumably to be administered by primarily Tamil leadership once a peace pact is signed. However, the recent violence has given greater strength to calls to "de-merge" the north and east, so that Muslim and Sinhala populations would be proportionally larger in some districts and thereby able to claim more political power. Indeed, late in the summer of 2003, the nationalist Buddhist clergy was relentlessly pressuring President Kumaratunga to do just that in light of the escalating violence.

By August, the attacks on Muslims have resulted in increasing calls by a few Muslim leaders for the Muslim people to be ready to take up arms to defend themselves and their right to self-government. As Ferial Ashraff, chief of the National Unity alliance, said in August 2003, "A situation may come where there will be no other options left for the Muslims but to pick up arms and fight" (Taiwannews.com 2003). Further complicating the situation for Sri Lanka's Muslims is that there are still disagreements about how it is possible to represent the diverse interests of the highly segmented Muslim population when the talks are so focused on the Tamils and the government. Muslim refugees settled (after the 1990s expulsion) in Puttlam among Sinhalese have different concerns than Muslims who live in ethnically diverse urban areas, such as Colombo and Kandy, or Muslims who farm in the eastern region; and different Muslim communities in the east and west of the island have long had different religious and cultural practices. One can only wonder if, under these circumstances, Muslims might not ultimately play the scapegoat for both sides in an eventual peace (see, e.g., *Island Online* 2003).

In short, the struggle for peace is being waged on various interconnected fronts. The manner in which they articulate will affect the order that will emerge should a peace pact be signed. In this sense, peace is not simply a cessation of hostilities. It is the construction of new articulations of cultural, economic, and political hegemony on global, national, and local levels. The form that peace will take, should an agreement ever be signed, will be inscribed by all of these struggles. Peace is never generic.

Hope for "Reconstruction" and Peace?

As we go to press, there is much uncertainty about the prospect for peace in Sri Lanka. Clearly, whether or not a permanent end to war happens will depend on many factors. But what kind of peace will it bring? The nature of domestic politics hinted at in the confrontation between the prime minister and the president over the peace process makes it certain that even once a pact is signed and the guns supposedly go quiet forever, there are still many political battles ahead. Sharing power across regions is going to be a difficult structural arrangement to put into place. Obtaining widespread support for the arrangement is likely to be even more difficult. However it is done, it will undoubtedly not appease all ideological positions on state, nation, and ethnicity in Sri Lanka or in the Sri Lankan Sinhala and Tamil diasporas that have been so important in the persistence of war.

Unofficial talks continue over what form an "interim administration" in the north and east should take and who should control it. Should there be a single administrative unit—"the northeast"—that would empower Tamils? Or should the north and the east be "de-merged," which would give the greater concentrations of Muslims and Sinhalese in the east more political clout? As these issues are debated in public and private venues, political assassinations continue and each side struggles for both internal and external control (*Daily Resume* June 17–18, 2003). For example, in May 2003, the LTTE were accused by the University Teachers for Human Rights (Jaffna) of carrying out revenge killings of opponents in the north and east (University Teachers for Human Rights 2003). Most recently, a council member for the Western Province and member of the PA was allegedly killed by an opponent from the ruling coalition, the UNF (*Daily Resume* June 17, 2003). So power struggles within the combatants' respective communities are already underway.

Development and Peace?

The notion that peace and development go hand in hand also may be cause for concern. Such pieties from the press releases of the World Bank and other international institutions and leaders might be a way of getting the peace talks moving again, but there is much that is contradictory in the coupling of peace and development. There is no doubt that Sri Lanka is going to need enormous amounts of capital to rebuild the war-ravaged areas. Earlier chapters in this book have documented the war's costs, the destruction of roads and transport facilities, the thousands of displaced people, and the lost jobs. Furthermore, the war has provided economic opportunities for some, and its end will mean more people without ways of supporting themselves and their families.

Nevertheless, it should be remembered that development programs can be a source of conflict, in both obvious and subtle ways, as has been demonstrated repeatedly in Sri Lanka (see, e.g., Brow 1996; Pebbles 1990; Woost 1990) and elsewhere (e.g., Esman and Herring 2001; Walton and Seddon 1994). There is no reason to think that increased money toward development will not also bring about conflict in new ways after the war has ceased. Development resources are notoriously mixed up in systems of political patronage and party nepotism, not just in Sri Lanka but everywhere. How will these same sources of conflict and struggle be avoided once aid starts flooding the ministerial and NGO coffers? The spring 2003 stalemate suggests early signs of this problem. The LTTE wants to administer development in the north and east, and the government wants somehow to have its own strings remain attached to that portion of the promised aid. And once aid comes in and is distributed, will the perception or reality of unequal allocation of aid again be seen through the lens of ethnicity? Or will it be channeled through some new articulation of identities, as Hettige (this volume) implies is a real possibility? This is not idle talk. The World Bank estimates that the war-ravaged areas will require at least US$1.5 billion for reconstruction. That is, over a third of what donors promised in June 2003 will go into just a few districts. Is it unreasonable to think that nationalist Sinhalese elements in the south (where the World Bank notes poverty is still widespread) will see that as favoring the "other" ethnic group (World Bank 2003b)? This is not meant to be simple doom-saying, but rather a plea that the overly simplified discourse of development not go unexamined.

Whose Development?

Even more worrisome than the potential for massive influxes of development monies to exacerbate ethnic tensions is the way in which development is being defined. Besides the focus on resettlement and rehabilitation of refugees and the rebuilding of the regions that experienced the most destruction, the other major emphasis is on "growth." The two core planning documents put together and made public by the government of Sri Lanka are entitled "Regaining Sri Lanka" (RSL) and the World Bank's Country Assistance Strategy (CAS) document for Sri Lanka, made available on the World Bank website in April 2003, just prior to the donor conference in Tokyo in June 2003 (Sri Lankan Government 2003; World Bank 2003a).

In the introduction to RSL, the authors state that Sri Lanka is in an economic crisis due to deep indebtedness. According to the government, public debt in 2000 was larger than the country's GDP and was likely to increase (Sri Lankan Government 2003: pt. 2, p. 31; pt. 1, annex 1, p. 16). Where that debt crisis came from, particularly the role of post-1977 open economy liberalism, is not explained, and so it remains a mysterious subject, with a will of its own and a hunger for capital. Predictably, Prime Minister Wickremasinghe, in his preface to RSL, blames the current fiscal crisis on the war and on a history of economic mismanagement, presumably by the other political party. Yet as Shastri (this volume) indicates, the PA under Kumaratunga ran a tighter ship, with less debt and higher growth, than did the UNP. The solution proposed to the crisis is to increase the rate of growth *and* indebtedness dramatically. As the authors of the introduction to RSL put it: "There is only one way ahead. That is achieving a substantially higher economic growth. We are not talking of 4 or 5 percent growth levels, internationally respected levels which were sustained by the previous government in spite of the war. We are talking of a much higher growth rate such as 8 to 10 percent" (Sri Lankan Government 2003: 1). To accomplish this goal, they argue, Sri Lanka must be aggressive in acquiring foreign investment and improving productivity. The privatization of all commercial activities must be accelerated and the legal foundations of the economy reformed. Measures also will have to be taken to allow for greater flexibility in the movement of people between jobs, and any barriers preventing this movement must be removed.

The World Bank's Country Assistance Strategy for Sri Lanka basically builds on the RSL document and assesses what needs to be done to make it operational. The CAS commends the authors of the RSL for the ambitious nature of the proposals, which, taken together, they claim, will yield a macroeconomic environment that will support privatization, empower the poor, and help rebuild the conflict-affected regions. According to the CAS, the poverty reduction strategy that they see in the RSL, which they support, rests on three central themes: peace, growth, and equity. Of these three, growth is the most important, since it is cited as the "main instrument for achieving prosperity and creating more resources for distribution" (World Bank Document 2003a: i; see 7–9). Peace will make it possible to pursue a "pro-poor" economic strategy for the future of development equity in Sri Lanka (World Bank Document 2003a: i–iii and 7–20).

The World Bank, too, recommends that laws protecting employment be streamlined or removed because they are disincentives to investment. Land regulations need to be relaxed so that land given to farmers by the government can be freely mortgaged and sold in a competitive land market. Furthermore, this "pro-poor strategy" will include key improvements to transport and communications: construction of highways, enhancing the bus system, linking rural areas to the Internet, and upgrading rural communication systems. They call for "investing in" the people through education and health care, both of which will also promote private sector activity and hence growth. The poor will be empowered by making the state a facilitator of private sector activity rather than a provider of goods and services. The promotion of decentralization also will empower the poor by allowing local governance to propose and manage locally defined projects for poverty alleviation (World Bank Document 2003a: 10).

And so on. Such assessments sound a little too familiar, even though the overall strategy is described as new. These proposals are fully in tune with the growth and deregulation policies promoted in Sri Lanka (and elsewhere) since the late 1970s. Yet there are many ironies here. As Shastri aptly shows (this volume), growth has been fairly consistent at around 5 percent even through the war years. Furthermore, she notes that unemployment has actually gone down significantly during the war! Also ironic is the fact that the changes proposed in labor regulations, land markets, and business practice generally have all been heard before, especially in World Bank recommendations and reports. Trade union leaders already have protested many of the proposals, which have been developed without any trade union representatives present in the discussions (Shahul 2002). Flexibility in labor markets translates into changing laws that ease restrictions on a firm's ability to hire and fire in ways it sees fit, making these measures a means through which anyone involved in a union can be declared an obstacle to efficiency and fired. Other changes already enacted make it unnecessary to get the consent of women to have them work overtime. Rural farmers who mortgage their lands may now legally lose them to bigger farms and agricultural enterprises.

The lesson of Newton Gunasinghe's essay is that policies create conditions under which certain kinds of group formation take place. He brilliantly illustrated the course one might take in trying to draw the lines of connection between policy and violence, connections that the RSL and CAS documents seem to ignore. Questions concerning the connections between prior policies and violence seem not even to be askable in these models. As Hettige has shown in his contribution to this volume, youth across the country feel they are being exploited or ignored. New social and political cleavages are emergent in Sri Lankan society, yet none of the proposed pro-poor strategies considers the ways in which people, young and old, of one social group or another, differentially experience their relation to the economy. The planners discuss the development of empowerment, but they do not recognize the forms of empowerment people have already created in the course of their everyday lives to provide for their families, to deal with the local representatives of the state, and to survive in civil war.

The essays in this volume show that people are never completely powerless. They create spaces to live in despite the many constraints they may experience. In those spaces, they also live their identities, their sense of their place in the world. What is not yet clear in the proposals being fielded is how the new programs will connect to the identities and strategies so hard won over the past twenty years. What will happen when the sense of self and empowerment already lived is undermined by these proposed strategies for growth? And in the end, what sort of empowerment will common people be afforded in these schemes? What forms of empowerment will not be allowed? What kind of participation is expected of them? What forms of participation will not be allowed? Clearly no one will be empowered to contest the foregone conclusion that a growth strategy is best, nor will they be allowed to participate in ways that will impede the accumulation of capital. If anything, power is being taken away by the removal of avenues of grievance redress, the protection of landholdings on poor homesteads, and the legal right to say no to overtime labor in factories. At least this is the impression one gets from a study of reconstruction discourse sponsored by international development institutions (and pressed upon both parties to the negotiations). One can only wonder about the extent to which the strings attached to reconstruction loans will impede the negotiation of a new kind of democracy by committed Sri Lankans at all levels of society: from those who labor on the many negotiating committees to the young women and men who are trying to make their way in a world seemingly filled with ideological and structural obstacles.

The Economy and Not War/Not Peace

The strategies proposed for rebuilding Sri Lanka appear, in large part, to be "donor driven," as was noted by Dr. Paikiasothy Saravanamuttu, executive director at the Center for Policy Alternatives in Colombo, in his presentation to donors at the Tokyo Conference on Reconstruction and Development of Sri Lanka (June 9–10, 2003). He meant that the process was undemocratic and the outcomes were " 'economic centric' and technical in nature, failing to recognize the symbiotic relationship between the political and economic" (2003: 3). Citing comments by Sunil Bastian, the director of the Center for Policy Alternatives in Colombo, at a recent workshop on the RSL document, Saravanamuttu added that economic growth was inadequate as a solution to poverty. There also need to be specific mechanisms to ensure that the distribution of resources be carried out equitably. The processes of peace and development have to be inclusive and human rights have to be at the center of the processes if the people of Sri Lanka are "to move beyond a situation of NO WAR/NO PEACE to one of lasting peace" (2003: 4).

Similarly, Jayadeva Uyangoda has argued cogently that "negative peace," the absence of war, or the de-escalation of war, can be seen as "basically a conflict management, pragmatic approach that falls short of a 'positive peace,' meaning the eradication of conditions that produced, and may reproduce, the conflict" (Uyangoda 2003a: 5). So while the donors and the World Bank say peace and development go hand in hand, in reality, development cannot be treated as necessarily a guarantor of peaceful relations of production. Growth-focused development may find obstacles in war, but the absence of war is still not a road map to utopia. While the war may subside, the struggle for peace will remain. Yet according to some observers, neither of the primary adversaries at the negotiating table, nor the potential donors pressuring both sides, seem interested in more transformative objectives that would address underlying "structural causes of the conflict, reforming the state and political structures, community reconciliation and peace building, democratization . . . human rights, re-integration of communities, and many more reconstructive measures" (Uyangoda 2003a: 5). Just as important to the process of making "positive peace" in the aftermath of war is the cultivation of a more critical recognition of the link between politics and economics. Uyangoda has noted in another context that cognizance must be taken of those constituencies "who thrive in the continuation of the conflict in the context of which they have come into being" (2003b: 8). He adds that these constituencies "are more than simple spoilers. They include a wide variety of constituencies and characters—politicians and political parties, traders and entrepreneurs, military and guerilla groups active in the protracted conflict itself. Their existence is intimately linked to the economic and political gains they make in, and by means of, war and conflict. They are in this sense material agents of the conflict and its continuation" (Uyangoda 2003b: 8).

Uyangoda's critical insights about the complex materiality of the conflict nicely avoid reducing the persistence of civil war to some essentialist form of greed; his work thus resonates deeply with the aims of this volume. Our contributors indicate in a variety of ways that there are many complex linkages and articulations to consider in the making of both war and peace. As we argued in chapter 1, the war in Sri Lanka is not simply an aberration afflicting the normal social formation, something simply added to it. Rather, the war and the multiple forms of associated violence are material elements within the articulation of what the "normal" Sri Lankan social formation has become. Along these lines, Shastri and Richardson demonstrated how the conflict is imbricated in the very policies that have shaped the structure of economic opportunities and the manner in which they are distributed and perceived to be distributed. A peace pact and concomitant influx of aid may make the formations of violence invisible but not inactive. People of all classes and statuses will find themselves in new forms of competition for resources, making for a volatile conjuncture with unpredictable outcomes, as the studies by Hettige and Gunasinghe in this volume illustrate. This is especially so because, as Bremner, Gamburd, and Lynch further illustrated, this transformation has become written into popular consciousness and public discourse about identity and community.

On the other hand, while a cease-fire on the battlefront may not mean that the habitus of violence and division in all other corners of life will miraculously disappear, it does appear to have opened up spaces in which new patterns can emerge. But these can take hold only if the discourses of ethnicity and distrust, exacerbated as they may be with the direction now being taken in and around the peace negotiations, do not close them up again. It is clear that people in Sri Lanka have welcomed even the tenuous respite from war that the past year has given them. Whether it is elite vacationers who can now explore parts of their own country long closed to them, or working-class Sri Lankans who are reacquainting themselves with their counterparts in other ethnic groups and regions, during the summer of 2003, we heard enthusiasm for this new reality that often seemed to belie the more conflicted accounts in the press. At the same time, sometimes the most enthusiastic—such as a rural potter marveling at the friendliness of Tamils in areas where, for the first time in his life, he could now travel to sell his pottery—were still adamant that the Tamils should not be given too much and that the Sinhalese had to worry about "losing their country." The violence has produced a formation in which the divisions among Sinhala, Tamil, and Muslim identities have been made all the more real through nearly a generation of increasing physical separation. Structures, interests, attitudes, and motivations have been transformed and are being encountered anew by a generation who have known nothing but this formation of violence, which is now written into all aspects of their lives. Peace may give them alternative experiences, but the constant barrage against peace takes its toll, and the more so, the longer "no war, no peace" goes on.

Additionally, there needs to be concerted and practical recognition that goes beyond the statistical: real family members have died, routine and tested modes of sustenance have disappeared, and familiar localities have been transformed into wastelands, minefields, and graveyards—all in the wink of an eye. These, too, must be remembered as part of the unspeakable, uncountable inventory of destruction left in the wake of this war. People will still be feeling the pain of these violent transformations. Against the backdrop of a devastated infrastructure, those who have been physically maimed by war and torture will remain as visible symbols of the violence that is now woven into the social fabric. As much of the recent literature on violence and its aftermath has shown (see, e.g., the insightful contributions to Das, Kleinman, Lock, Ramphelle, and Reynolds 2001; Das, Kleinman, Ramphelle, and Reynolds 2000; Kleinman, Das, and Lock 1997; Sluka 2000), the ineffable experience of fear and the memories of the loss of home, family, livelihood, and sense of place defy quantification and will not be easily bought off with pledges of development aid. There is indeed a danger that such memories, fears, and emotions will be used to rouse people to new sorts of violence articulating a new space of death with its own justifications (Taussig 1984). And as noted previously, development has been shown to open up new spaces for violence and political manipulation as new resources become the object of desire up and down the hierarchy of agency.

New structures, new agencies, new forms of violence, exclusion, and identity may unfold, drawing on the fractured pieces of prior articulations. Will ethnicity once again emerge as the organizing principle around which these experiences are articulated? Peace is not a matter of promoting forgiveness or reconciliation and then making it possible to get on with economic growth. It is also a question of how the passions, emotions, symbols, and memories of this dark history can be channeled into something other than the production of more violence. In this sense, peace negotiation will be a never-ending task.

August 2003

Postscript

As we go to press, Sri Lanka's fragile peace process seems to be unraveling. One newspaper headline reads, "Power Struggle in Sri Lanka Stalls Peace Bid" (*Boston Globe*, November 11, 2003). The tension between Sri Lanka's President Chandrika Kumaratunge and her opponent, Prime Minister Ranil Wickremasinghe, close to the surface ever since the cease-fire was declared, has finally broken through. The president claims that the prime minister is giving the LTTE too much and that they will have a de facto state in the end if he is left to run the show. Her position echoes sentiments that extremist elements within the Buddhist establishment and sectors of the Sinhala public have been expressing for months, the "Sri Lanka for the Sinhalese" position that has become so entrenched in Sri Lankan society, polity, and economy.

So on November 2 and 3, 2003, while Prime Minister Wickremasinghe was out of the country, the president suspended Parliament, fired the three most powerful ministers (security, finance, and media), took over their jobs herself, and then instituted, briefly, a State of Emergency. The threat of these actions, which are the president's constitutional prerogative, has always underlain the tension between the country's two highest officials. But now the uncertainty in the peace process has been taken to a new level. As barricades reappeared in the streets, people began to wonder what security forces might be ordered to do under the president's control. Would Tamils in Colombo again be attacked or detained in increasing numbers? Would the army be used to stop protests and other efforts to support the peace process? When the prime minister returned from Washington, D.C., the State of Emergency was lifted, but the peace talks were suspended, so that the two sides can sort out who is to be in charge (Senanayake 2003). Meanwhile, Sri Lanka's stock market again has plummeted, and tourists by the thousands again are canceling their tours (Senanayake 2003). For now, this seems to be the character of Sri Lanka's ongoing social formation of No War/No Peace. Within it, the struggle for the sweet taste of power seems endless, while the costs of that struggle are seen in the repeated opening and closing of spaces in which people can forge their daily lives.

November 2, 2003

References Cited

123India.com
    2001   Sri Lanka Sacks 31 Airmen over Airport Attack. Electronic document, http://www.123india.com, accessed November 11.

ABC News Online
    2003   Sri Lanka's President Warns PM against Accepting Aid. June 10. Electronic document, http://www.abc.net.au/news/newsitems/s876655.html, accessed June 12.

Abeyesekere, Gamini
    1986   Facets of Development in Sri Lanka: Social Development. In *Facets of Development in Independent Sri Lanka: Felicitation Volume to Commemorate the 10th Successive Budget of Hon. Ronnie de Mel, Minister of Finance and Planning.* Warnasena Rasaputra, W. M. Tilakaratna, S. T. G. Fernando, and L. E. N. Fernando, eds. Pp. 291–309. Colombo: Ministry of Finance and Planning of Sri Lanka.

Abeyratne, Sirimal
    1997   Trade Strategy and Industrialization. In *Dilemmas of Development: Fifty Years of Economic Change in Sri Lanka.* W. D. Lakshman, ed. Pp. 341–385. Colombo: Sri Lanka Association of Economists.
    1999   *Economic and Political Change in Developing Countries: With Special Reference to Sri Lanka.* Amsterdam: VU University Press.

Abeysekera, Charles, and Newton Gunasinghe, eds.
    1984   *Sri Lanka: The Ethnic Conflict—Myths, Realities, and Perspectives.* New Delhi: Navrang.
    1985   *Ethnicity and Social Change in Sri Lanka.* Colombo: Social Scientists Association.
    1987   *Facets of Ethnicity in Sri Lanka.* Committee for Rational Development. Colombo: Social Scientists Association.

AFP (Agence France-Presse)
    2000a   Sri Lanka War Budget Bites Hard. Electronic document, http://asia.dailynews.yahoo.com, accessed August 13.
    2000b   Sri Lanka's "War Footing" Begins to Affect Economy. Electronic document, http://asia.dailynews.yahoo.com, accessed July 16.

Alailima, Patricia J.
    1997   Social Policy in Sri Lanka. In *Dilemmas of Development: Fifty Years of Economic Change in Sri Lanka.* W. D. Lakshman, ed. Pp. 127–170. Colombo: Sri Lanka Association of Economists.

Alles, A. C.
    1990   *The JVP, 1969–89.* Colombo: Lake House Investments.

Amerasinghe, E. F. G.
    1998   Wage Fixation in Sri Lanka. *Island,* August 10: 8.

Amnesty International
    1990   *Sri Lanka: Extrajudicial Executions, "Disappearances," and Torture, 1987 to 1990 (ASA 37/21/90).* London: Amnesty International.

Arunatilake, Nisha, Sisira Jayasuriya, and Saman Kelegama
    2000   *The Economic Cost of the War in Sri Lanka.* Research Studies, Macroeconomic Policy and Planning Series, 13. Colombo: Institute of Policy Studies.

Asian Survey
    2002   Sri Lanka 2001: Year of Reversals. *Asian Survey,* February 42(1): 177–182.
    2003   Sri Lanka 2002: Turning the Corner? *Asian Survey,* February 43(1): 215–221.

Associated Press
    2003   Sri Lanka's Rebels Reject Latest Government Attempt to End Standoff. June 11. Electronic document, http://64.225.57.18/asianews/data/3189.htm, accessed June 14.

Athas, Iqbal
    2000a   Military Procurements and Corruption. *Sunday Times.* June 25: 11.
    2000b   What the Censor Did Not Want You to Know. *Sunday Times.* July 2: 11.

Athukorala, Premachandra, and Sisira Jayasuriya
    1994   *Macroeconomic Policies, Crises, and Growth in Sri Lanka, 1969–1990.* Washington: World Bank.

Azar, Edward E.
    1987   *Codebook of the Conflict and Peace Data Bank (COPDAB): A Computer-Assisted Approach to Monitoring and Analyzing International and Domestic Conflict.* College Park, MD: Center for International Development and Conflict Management.
    1990   *The Management of Protracted Social Conflict: Theory and Cases.* Aldershot, Hampshire: Dartmouth.

Balachanddran, P. K.
    2003   LTTE Flays Lankan Govt for Internationalising Conflict. Electronic document, http://www.hindustantimes.com/news/181_278194,00050002.htm, accessed June 14.

Balakrishnan, N., and H. M. Gunasekera, compilers
    1977   Statistical Appendix. In *Sri Lanka: A Survey.* K. M. de Silva, ed. Pp. 257–278. Honolulu: University of Hawaii Press.

Bandarage, Asoka
    1988   Women and Capitalist Development in Sri Lanka, 1977–87. *Bulletin of Concerned Asian Scholars* 20(2): 57–81.

Bandaranayake, Senake, Lorna Dewaraja, Roland Silva, and K. D. G. Wimalaratne, eds.
    1990   *Sri Lanka and the Silk Road of the Sea.* Colombo: UNESCO and the Central Cultural Fund.

Bartholomeusz, Tessa J., and Chandra R. de Silva, eds.
    1998   *Buddhist Fundamentalism and Minority Identities in Sri Lanka.* Albany: SUNY Press.

Bastian, Sunil
    1990   The Political Economy of Ethnic Violence in Sri Lanka: The July 1983 Riot. In *Mirror of Violence: Communities, Riots, and Survivors in South Asia.* Veena Das, ed. Pp. 286–304. Delhi: Oxford University Press.

BBC World News Online
    2001   Sri Lanka Lifts Ban on Anti-War Movie. Electronic document, http://news.bbc.co.uk/1/hi/entertainment/film/147064.stm, accessed May 7, 2003.
    2003a   Norwegians—"Salmon-Eating Busybodies." Electronic document, http://news.bbc.co.uk/2/hi/south_asia/2950698.stm, accessed June 24.
    2003b   US Tells Tigers to Restart Talks: The United States Says It Expects the Tamil Ti-

ger Rebels and Sri Lankan Government to Resume Talks Immediately. Electronic document, http://news.bbc.co.uk/2/hi/south_asia/2986876.stm, accessed June 14.

Berdal, Mats, and David M. Malone, eds.
2000   *Greed and Grievance: Economic Agendas in Civil Wars.* A project of the International Peace Academy. Boulder: Lynne Rienner.

Bhalla, Surjit S., and Paul Glewwe
1986   Growth and Equity in Developing Countries: A Reinterpretation of the Sri Lankan Experience. *World Bank Economic Review* 1(1): 35–63.

Bhargava, Pradeep
1987   *Political Economy of Sri Lanka.* New Delhi: Navrang.

Biyanwala, Janaka
1997   A Letter to Susanthika. *Options* 10: 25, 27.

Brass, Paul R.
1997   *Theft of an Idol: Text and Context in the Representation of Collective Violence.* Princeton: Princeton University Press.

Brinton, Crane
1965   *The Anatomy of a Revolution.* New York: Vintage Books.

Brohier, R. L.
1955/56 D. S. Senanayake as Minister of Agriculture and Lands. *Ceylon Historical Journal* 5: 68–80.

Brow, James
1990   Nationalist Rhetoric and Local Practice: The Fate of the Village Community in Kukulewa. In *Sri Lanka: History and the Roots of Conflict.* Jonathan Spencer, ed. Pp. 125–144. New York: Routledge.
1996   *Demons and Development: The Struggle for Community in a Sri Lankan Village.* Tucson: University of Arizona Press.

Carby, Hazel
1997   Policing the Black Woman's Body in an Urban Context. In *Women Transforming Politics: An Alternative Reader.* Cathy J. Cohen, Kathleen B. Jones, and Joan C. Tronto, eds. Pp. 151–166. New York: New York University Press

Carnegie Commission on Preventing Deadly Conflict
1997   *Final Report—Preventing Deadly Conflict.* Washington: Carnegie Commission.

Cat's Eye
1997   Susanthika: Sexism, Racism, and the Body Politic. *Island,* November 26.

Central Bank of Ceylon
1982   *Review of the Economy.* Colombo: Department of Economic Research, Central Bank of Ceylon.
1983   *Review of the Economy.* Colombo: Department of Economic Research, Central Bank of Ceylon.

Central Bank of Sri Lanka
1995–   *Annual Reports of the Central Bank of Sri Lanka.* Rajagiriya: Central Bank of Sri
2002   Lanka Printing Press.
1998   *Economic Progress of Independent Sri Lanka.* Rajagiriya: Central Bank of Sri Lanka Printing Press.

Central Intelligence Agency
1998   World Factbook 1998. Electronic document, http://www.odci.gov/cia/publications/factbook/index.html, accessed August 16, 1999.

Chandraprema, C. A.
   1991   *Sri Lanka: The Years of Terror. The JVP Insurrection, 1987–89.* Colombo: Lake
           House Investments.
Chengappa, Raj
   2000   Return of the Tigers. *India Today* 25(21): 28–34.
Cohen, Stanley
   1972   *Folk Devils and Moral Panics: The Creation of the Mods and Rockers.* London:
           MacGibbon and Kee.
Collier, Paul
   2000a   Economic Causes of Civil Conflict and Their Implications for Policy. Electronic
           document, http://www.worldbank.org/research/conflict/papers/civilconflict.pdf,
           accessed June 15.
   2000b   Doing Well Out of War: An Economic Perspective. In *Greed and Grievance: Eco-
           nomic Agendas in Civil Wars.* A project of the International Peace Academy.
           M. Berdhal and D. Malone, eds. Pp. 91–111. Boulder: Lynne Rienner.
Columbage, S., and S. A. Karunaratne
   1986   Development Planning and Investment. In *Facets of Development in Independent
           Sri Lanka: Felicitation Volume to Commemorate the 10th Successive Budget of Hon.
           Ronnie de Mel, Minister of Finance and Planning.* Warnasena Rasaputra, W. M.
           Tilakaratna, S. T. G. Fernando, and L. E. N. Fernando, eds. Colombo: Ministry
           of Finance and Planning of Sri Lanka.
Danforth, Loring
   1995   *The Macedonian Conflict: Ethnic Nationalism in a Transnational World.* Prince-
           ton: Princeton University Press.
Daniel, E. Valentine
   1996   *Charred Lullabies: Chapters in an Anthropography of Violence.* Princeton: Prince-
           ton University Press.
Das, Veena, Arthur Kleinman, Margaret Lock, Mamphela Ramphele, and Pamela Reynolds, eds.
   2001   *Remaking a World: Violence, Social Suffering, and Recovery.* Berkeley: University
           of California Press.
Das, Veena, Arthur Kleinman, Mamphela Ramphele, and Pamela Reynolds, eds.
   2000   *Violence and Subjectivity.* Berkeley: University of California Press.
Davies, James C.
   1962   Toward a Theory of Revolution. *American Sociological Review* 27: 5–19.
   1969   The J-Curve of Rising and Declining Satisfactions as a Cause of Some Great
           Revolutions and a Contained Rebellion. In *Violence in America: Historical and
           Comparative Perspectives.* A Report to the National Commission on the Causes
           and Prevention of Violence, June 9. Hugh Davis Graham and Ted R. Gurr, eds.
           Pp. 671–709. New York: New American Library Signet Special.
de Alwis, Malathi
   1998   *Maternalist Politics in Sri Lanka: A Historical Anthropology of Its Conditions of Possi-
           bility.* Ph.D. dissertation, Department of Anthropology, University of Chicago.
de Mel, Neloufer
   1998   Agent or Victim? The Sri Lankan Woman Militant in the Interregnum. In *Sri
           Lanka: Collective Identities Revisited,* vol. 2. Michael Roberts, ed. Pp. 199–220.
           Colombo: Marga Institute.
de Silva, Chandra Richard
   1974   Weightage in University Admissions: Standardization and District Quotas in Sri
           Lanka, 1970–75. *Modern Ceylon Studies* 5: 151–178.

1984a   Sinhala-Tamil Relations and Education in Sri Lanka: The University Admissions Issue—the First Phase, 1971–77. In *From Independence to Statehood: Managing Ethnic Conflict in Five African and Asian States*. Robert B. Goldmann and A. Jeyaratnam Wilson, eds. Pp. 125–146. New York: St. Martin's Press.

1984b   Plebiscitary Democracy or Creeping Authoritarianism? The Presidential Election and Referendum of 1982. In *Sri Lanka in Change and Crisis*. James Manor, ed. Pp. 35–50. London and Sydney: Croom Helm.

de Silva, Jani
1998   Praxis, Language, and Silences: The JVP Uprising in the 1980s. In *Sri Lanka: Collective Identities Revisited*, vol. 2. Michael Roberts, ed. Pp. 163–198. Colombo: Marga Institute.

de Silva, Kingsley M.
1986   *Managing Ethnic Tensions in Multi-Ethnic Societies: Sri Lanka, 1880–1985*. Lanham, MD: University Press of America.

1993   *Sri Lanka: Problems of Governance*. New Delhi: Konark.

1998   *Reaping the Whirlwind: Ethnic Conflict, Ethnic Politics in Sri Lanka*. New Delhi: Penguin Books.

de Silva, Kingsley M., and G. H. Peiris, eds.
1995   *The University System of Sri Lanka: Vision and Reality*. Kandy: International Center for Ethnic Studies.

de Silva, Kingsley M., and Howard W. Wriggins
1988   *J. R. Jayewardene of Sri Lanka: A Political Biography—Volume One: The First Fifty Years*. Honolulu: University of Hawaii Press.

1994   *J. R. Jayewardene of Sri Lanka: A Political Biography. Volume Two: From 1956 to His Retirement (1989)*. Honolulu: University of Hawaii Press.

de Silva, Pramod
1992a   Fearing a Threat to their Supremacy . . . Some Aristocrats Out to Destroy Government Programs—President. *Daily News* (Colombo), October 20.

1992b   Remarkable Economic Growth Despite Ongoing War, Says President. *Daily News* (Colombo), November 3.

1993   We Seek Support on the Strength of Our Record—President. *Daily News* (Colombo), March 16.

de Silva, Soma
1997   Population. In *Arjuna's Atlas of Sri Lanka*. T. Somasekaram, M. P. Perera, M. B. G. de Silva, and H. Godellawatta, eds. Pp. 47–52. Dehiwala, Sri Lanka: Arjuna Consulting.

Defense Correspondent
2000   After Months of Anxiety and Heartbreak, the "Phoney War" Is Back. *Sunday Island*, July 2: 11.

Diyasena, W.
1983   The Formal School Education System of Sri Lanka. In *University Education and Graduate Employment in Sri Lanka*. Bikas Sanyal, ed. Pp. 62–111. Colombo: Marga Institute.

du Gay, Paul
1997   Introduction. In *Production of Culture/Cultures of Production*. Paul du Gay, ed. Pp. 1–10. London: Sage.

Dugger, Celia W.
2001   As Sri Lanka War Brings Ruin, Villages Live Off It. *New York Times on the Web:* www.nytimes.com, August 17.

Dunham, David, and Charles Abeysekera
   1987   The Sri Lankan "Open Economy" in an Asian Perspective. In *Essays on the Sri Lankan Economy, 1977–83.* David Dunham and Charles Abeysekera, eds. Pp. 1–24. Colombo: Social Scientists Association.
Economist
   2000   A Prize from Norway. *Economist,* February 26: 51.
Economist Intelligence Unit (EIU)
   1994–   Sri Lanka. *Quarterly Country Reports.*
   2000
Edirisinghe, Roland
   2000   Colombo Dispatch: War Effort. *New Republic,* July 31: 15–16.
Eller, Jack David
   1999   *From Culture to Ethnicity to Conflict: An Anthropological Perspective on International Ethnic Conflict.* Ann Arbor: University of Michigan Press.
Elson, Diane, and Ruth Pearson
   1981   Nimble Fingers Make Cheap Workers: An Analysis of Women's Employment in Third World Export Manufacturing. *Feminist Review* 7(spring): 87–107.
Esman, Milton J., and Ronald J. Herring, eds.
   2001   *Carrots, Sticks, and Ethnic Conflict: Rethinking Development Assistance.* Ann Arbor: University of Michigan Press.
Fairbanks, Gordon H., James W. Gair, and M. W. S. de Silva
   1968   *Colloquial Sinhalese.* 2 vols. Ithaca: South Asia Program, Cornell University.
Farmer, B. H.
   1976   *Pioneer Peasant Colonization in Ceylon: A Study in Asian Agrarian Problems.* Reprint of 1st ed. published by Oxford University Press, London. Westport, CT: Greenwood Press.
   [1957]
Fernando, A. S.
   1992   Two Hundred Garment Factories, 100,000 Jobs. *Daily News* (Colombo), February 19: 14.
Fine, Janice, with Matthew Howard
   1995   Women in the Free Trade Zones of Sri Lanka. *Dollars and Sense,* November/December: 26–27, 39–40.
Fuentes, Annette, and Barbara Ehrenreich
   1983   *Women in the Global Factory.* Boston: South End Press.
Gamage, Siri
   1999   Post-independent Political Conflicts in Sri Lanka: Elites, Ethnicity, and Class Contradictions. In *Conflict and Community in Contemporary Sri Lanka: "Pearl of the East" or the "Island of Tears"?* Siri Gamage and I. B. Watson, eds. Pp. 325–355. New Delhi: Sage.
Gamage, Siri, and I. B. Watson, eds.
   1999   *Conflict and Community in Contemporary Sri Lanka: "Pearl of the East" or the "Island of Tears"?* New Delhi: Sage.
Gamburd, Geraldine
   1972   *The Seven Grandparents: Locality and Lineality in Sinhalese Kinship and Caste.* Ph.D. dissertation, Department of Anthropology, Columbia University.
Gamburd, Michele Ruth
   1995   Sri Lanka's "Army of Housemaids": Control of Remittances and Gender Transformations. *Anthropologica* 37: 49–88.
   1999   Wearing a Dead Man's Jacket: State Symbols in Troubled Places. In *Conflict and*

Community in Contemporary Sri Lanka: "Pearl of the East" or "Island of Tears"? Siri Gamage and Bruce Watson, eds. Pp. 165–177. New Delhi: Sage.

2000   The Kitchen Spoon's Handle: Transnationalism and Sri Lanka's Migrant House-maids. Ithaca: Cornell University Press.

Goffman, Erving
1963   Stigma: Notes on the Management of Spoiled Identity. Englewood Cliffs, NJ: Prentice-Hall.

Gombrich, Richard F., and Gananath Obeyesekere
1988   Buddhism Transformed: Religious Change in Sri Lanka. Princeton: Princeton University Press.

Goode, Erich, and Nachman Ben-Yehuda
1994   Moral Panics: The Social Construction of Deviance. Oxford: Blackwell.

Goodhand, Jonathan, David Hulme, and Nick Lewer
2000   Social Capital and the Political Economy of Violence: A Case Study of Sri Lanka. Disasters 24(4): 390–406.

Goonewardena, Kanishka
1996   Cultural Politics of Global Capital: National Socialism in Sri Lanka. Paper presented at the 25th Annual Conference on South Asia, Madison, Wisconsin, October 17–20.

Gramsci, Antonio
1971   Selections from the Prison Notebooks of Antonio Gramsci. Edited and translated by Quentin Hoare and Geoffrey Nowell Smith. New York: International.

Gunaratna, Rohan
1990   Sri Lanka: A Lost Revolution? The Inside Story of the JVP. Kandy: Institute of Fundamental Studies.
1997   International and Regional Security Implications of the Sri Lankan Tamil Insurgency. Colombo: Alumni Association of the Bandaranaike Center for International Studies.

Gunasekera, Manisha
1996   Jatika Chintanaya and Identity Crisis: A Feminist Reappraisal. Paper presented at the National Convention on Women's Studies, Centre for Women's Research, Colombo. March.

Gunasinghe, Newton
1976   Social Change and the Disintegration of a Traditional System of Exchange Labor in Kandyan Sri Lanka. Sociological Bulletin 25(2): 168–184.
1986   Ethnic Conflict in Sri Lanka: Perceptions and Solutions. South Asia Bulletin 6(2): 34–37.

Gunatilleke, Godfrey
1989   Sustainable Development and Social Welfare. Paper presented at the International Center for Ethnic Studies Four Decades of Independence Workshop, Colombo, August 11–13.
2000   The Ethnic Dimension of Socio-Economic Development. Mimeographed paper. Colombo: Marga Institute.

Gunawardana, R. A. L. H.
1985   The People of the Lion: Sinhala Consciousness in History and Historiography. In Ethnicity and Social Change in Sri Lanka. Social Scientists Association, ed. Pp. 55–107. Colombo: Social Scientists Association.
1990   The People of the Lion: Sinhala Identity and Ideology in History and Histori-

ography. In *Sri Lanka: History and the Roots of Conflict.* Jonathan Spencer, ed. Pp. 64–78. New York: Routledge.

Gunawardena, R. S., and M. D. Nelson
1987   *Trade Activities in Kandy with Special Reference to Aspects of Ethnic Participation.* ICES Research Report. Kandy: International Center for Ethnic Studies.

Guneratne, P. R., S. Medagama, M. R. Samaranayake, M. D. Dayaratne, and N. D. Chandrapala
1983   Universalization of Primary Education in Sri Lanka. Report. Colombo: Ministry of Education.

Gurr, Ted R.
1970   *Why Men Rebel.* Princeton: Princeton University Press.

Gurr, Ted R., and Barbara Harff
1994   *Ethnic Conflict in World Politics.* Boulder: Westview Press.

Hall, Stuart
1996a   Gramsci's Relevance for the Study of Race and Ethnicity. In *Stuart Hall: Critical Dialogues in Cultural Studies.* David Morley and Kuan-Hsing Chen, eds. Pp. 411–449. New York: Routledge.
1996b   On Postmodernism and Articulation: An Interview with Stuart Hall. In *Stuart Hall: Critical Dialogues in Cultural Studies.* David Morley and Kuan-Hsing Chen, eds. Pp. 131–150. New York: Routledge.
1996c   Introduction: Who Needs "Identity"? In *Questions of Cultural Identity.* Stuart Hall and Paul du Gay, eds. Pp. 1–17. London: Sage.
1997   Introduction. In *Representation: Cultural Representations and Signifying Practices.* Stuart Hall, ed. Pp. 13–64. London: Sage.

Haraway, Donna
1986   Situated Knowledges: The Science Question in Feminism and the Privilege of the Partial Perspective. In *Simians, Cyborgs, and Women: The Reinvention of Nature.* Donna Haraway, ed. Pp. 183–201. New York: Routledge.

Harrison, Frances
2003   Sri Lanka Peace Protest. March 11. Electronic document, http://news.bbc.co.uk/2/hi/south_asia/2838077.stm, accessed June 12.

Harriss, John
2002   *Depoliticizing Development: The World Bank and Social Capital.* London: Anthem Press.

Heng, Geraldine, and Janadas Devan
1992   State Fatherhood: The Politics of Nationalism, Sexuality and Race in Singapore. In *Nationalisms and Sexualities.* Andrew Parker, Mary Russo, Doris Sommer, and Patricia Yaeger, eds. Pp. 343–364. New York: Routledge.

Herring, Ronald J.
2001   Making Ethnic Conflict: The Civil War in Sri Lanka. In *Carrots, Sticks and Ethnic Conflict: Rethinking Development Assistance.* Milton J. Esman and Ronald J. Herring, eds. Pp. 140–174. Ann Arbor: University of Michigan Press.

Hettiarachchi, Kumudini.
1998   How Do Sri Lankans Eat? *Sunday Times Plus,* July 12: 2.

Hettiarachchy, T.
1991   A Report on the Socio-Economic Problems of the Workforce at Katunayake Export Processing Zone. *Island,* December 29.

Hettige, Siri T., ed.
1992   *Unrest or Revolt: Some Aspects of Youth Unrest in Sri Lanka.* Colombo: Goethe-

Institute, German Cultural Institute, and American Studies Association (Sri Lanka).

1998　*Globalization, Social Change and Youth.* Colombo: German Cultural Institute.

Hettige, Siri T.

1996　Economic Liberalization and the Emerging Patterns of Social Inequality in Sri Lanka. *Sri Lanka Journal of Social Sciences* 20(1–2): 89–115.

1997　Economic Liberalization, Social Class, and Ethnicity: Emerging Trends and Conflicts. Special issue, "Conflict and Community in Contemporary Sri Lanka," *South Asia* 20: 331–358.

1998　*Readership Survey, 1997–1998.* Colombo: Ministry of Cultural Affairs.

1999a　Impact of Economic Change on Social Inequality: Some Empirical Evidence. Paper presented at the 7th Sri Lanka Studies Conference, Canberra, December 3–6.

1999b　National Youth Survey of Sri Lanka. Ms, Center for Anthropological and Sociological Studies, University of Colombo.

2000　Survey on Social Mobility. Ms. Colombo: Center for Anthropological and Sociological Studies.

Holt, John C.

1996　*The Religious Works of Kirti Sri.* Oxford: Oxford University Press.

Horowitz, Donald L.

1985　*Ethnic Groups in Conflict.* Berkeley: University of California Press.

2001　*The Deadly Ethnic Riot.* Berkeley: University of California Press.

Isenmann, Paul

1987　A Comment on Growth and Equity in Developing Countries: A Reinterpretation of Sri Lankan Experience. *World Bank Economic Review* 13: 521–531.

Island

2000a　Nearly 1000 Army Desterers [*sic*] Arrested. *Island,* July 5: 1.

2000b　Censorship. *Island,* May 7: 1.

2000c　Lanka Gets Israeli Jets. *Sunday Island,* May 14: 1.

2000d　The Historic Judgment and Censorship. *Island,* July 4: 6.

2000e　Heavy Fighting Continues in Jaffna. *Island,* May 13: 3.

2000f　Tigers Intensify Attacks on Kilaly. *Island,* May 3: 1.

Jabbar, Zacki

2000　Troops Consolidate Defences: 250 Tigers Killed. *Island,* May 15: 1.

Japan Times Online

2003　Sri Lanka Envoy Offers Leadership Role to Rebels. June 10. Electronic document, http://www.japantimes.co.jp/cgi-bin/getarticle.p15?nn20030610a4.html, accessed June 14.

Jayasinghe, Amal

2000　Tigers to Make Fresh Bid to Wrest Jaffna—the Prize Catch. *Island,* April 30: 3.

Jayasundera, P. B.

1986　Fiscal Policy in Sri Lanka since Independence. In *Facets of Development in Independent Sri Lanka: Felicitation Volume to Commemorate the 10th Successive Budget of Hon. Ronnie de Mel, Minister of Finance and Planning.* Warnasena Rasaputra, W. M. Tilakaratna, S. T. G. Fernando, and L. E. N. Fernando, eds. Pp. 43–82. Colombo: Ministry of Finance and Planning of Sri Lanka.

Jayasuriya, J. E.

1979　*Educational Policies and Progress, 1796–1948.* Colombo: Associated Educational Publishers.

Jayawardena, Kumari

1994 Some Aspects of Religious and Cultural Identity and the Construction of Sin-
[1992] hala Buddhist Womanhood. *Nivedini: A Sri Lankan Feminist Journal* 2(1): 111–
139.

Jeganathan, Pradeep

2000 On the Anticipation of Violence: Modernity and Identity in Southern Sri Lanka.
In *Anthropology, Development, and Modernities: Exploring Discourses, Counter-
tendencies and Violence.* Alberto Arce and Norman Long, eds. Pp. 112–126. New
York: Routledge.

Jeganathan, Pradeep, and Qadri Ismail, eds.

1995 *Unmaking the Nation: The Politics of Identity in Modern Sri Lanka.* Colombo:
Social Scientists Association.

Kakar, Sudhir

1996 *Colors of Violence: Cultural Identities, Religion, and Conflict.* Chicago: University
of Chicago Press.

Kanes

1998 Globalization and the Labor Market in Sri Lanka IV—Labour Skills and Legislation. *Island,* July 19: 18.

Kannangara, Ananda

2000 Rs 400 Private Sector Payraise. Electronic document, http://www.lanka.net/
lakehouse/, accessed July 29.

Kapferer, Bruce

1988 *Legends of People, Myths of State: Violence, Intolerance, and Political Culture in Sri
Lanka and Australia.* Washington: Smithsonian Institution Press.

Karunatilake, H. N. S.

1987 *The Economy of Sri Lanka.* Colombo: Center for Demographic and Socioeconomic Studies.

Karunatillake, W. S.

1992 *An Introduction to Spoken Sinhala.* Colombo: Gunasena.

Katz, Jackson

1995 Advertising and the Construction of Violent White Masculinity. In *Gender,
Race, and Class in Media.* Gail Dines and Jean M. Humez, eds. Pp. 133–141. London: Sage Publications.

Kelegama, Saman

1999 Economic Costs of Conflict in Sri Lanka. In *Creating Peace in Sri Lanka.* Robert
I. Rotberg, ed. Pp. 71–88. Washington: Brookings Institution Press.

Kemper, Steven

1991 *The Presence of the Past: Chronicles, Politics, and Culture in Sinhala Life.* Ithaca:
Cornell University Press.

Kerbo, Harold R.

1982 Movements of "Crisis" and Movements of "Affluence": A Critique of Deprivation and Resource Mobilization Theories. *Journal of Conflict Resolution* 26(4):
645–663.

Kiribanda, B. M.

1997 Population and Employment. In *Dilemmas of Development: Fifty Years of Economic Change in Sri Lanka.* W. D. Lakshman, ed. Pp. 223–249. Colombo: Sri
Lanka Association of Economists.

Kleinman, Arthur, Veena Das, and Margaret Lock, eds.

1997 *Social Suffering.* Berkeley: University of California Press.

Kumaratunga, Chandrika Bandaranaike
    2000   The Public Security Ordinance (Chapter 40). *Island,* May 6: 7.
Lacnet
    2003   Sri Lanka: Gov't Gets 4.5 Billion Dollars in Pledges, Tied to Peace. June 10. Elec-
            tronic document, http://www.theacademic.org/stories/10552555700/story.shtml,
            accessed June 14.
Lakshman, W. D.
    1997a   Introduction. In *Dilemmas of Development: Fifty Years of Economic Change in Sri
            Lanka.* W. D. Lakshman, ed. Pp. 1–27. Colombo: Sri Lanka Association of Econo-
            mists.
    1997b   Income Distribution and Poverty. In *Dilemmas of Development: Fifty Years of
            Economic Change in Sri Lanka.* W. D. Lakshman, ed. Pp. 171–222. Colombo: Sri
            Lanka Association of Economists.
Ladduwahetty, Ravi
    2000   Rs. 4.3 Billion for Government Interim Allowance. Electronic document,
            http://www.lanka.net/lakehouse/, accessed August 1.
Lal, Deepak, and Sarath Rajapatirana
    1989   *Impediments to Trade Liberalization in Sri Lanka.* Thames Essay, 51. London:
            Gower, for the Trade Policy Research Center.
Latour, Bruno
    1988   *The Pasteurization of France.* Trans. Alan Sheridan and John Lay. Cambridge:
            Harvard University Press.
Lebovics, Herman
    1992   *True France: The Wars over Cultural Identity, 1900–1945.* Ithaca: Cornell Univer-
            sity Press.
Levy, Brian
    1989   Foreign Aid in the Making of Foreign Policy in Sri Lanka, 1977–1983. *Policy Sci-
            ences* 22: 437–461.
Lewer, Nick, and Joe William
    2002   Sri Lanka: Finding a Negotiated End to Twenty-five Years of Violence. In *Search-
            ing for Peace in Central and South Asia: An Overview of Conflict Prevention and
            Peacebuilding Activities.* Monique Mekenkamp, Paul van Tongeren, and Hans
            van de Veen, eds. Pp. 483–502. Boulder: Lynne Rienner.
Liyanage, Sumanasiri
    1997   The State, State Capital and Capitalistic Development. In *Dilemmas of Develop-
            ment: Fifty Years of Economic Change in Sri Lanka.* W. D. Lakshman, ed. Pp. 423–
            455. Colombo: Sri Lanka Association of Economists.
Lynch, Caitrin
    1999   The "Good Girls" of Sri Lankan Modernity: Moral Orders of Nationalism and
            Capitalism. *Identities: Global Studies in Culture and Power* 6(1): 55–89.
    2000   The "Good Girls" of Sri Lankan Modernity: Moral Orders of Nationalism, Gen-
            der, and Globalization in Village Garment Factories. Ph.D. dissertation, Depart-
            ment of Anthropology, University of Chicago.
    2002   The Politics of White Women's Underwear in Sri Lanka's Open Economy. *Social
            Politics: International Studies in Gender, State, and Society* 9(1): 87–125.
Malkki, Liisa H.
    1995   *Purity and Exile: Violence, Memory, and National Cosmology among Hutu Refu-
            gees in Tanzania.* Chicago: University of Chicago Press.

Manor, James, ed.
1984   *Sri Lanka in Change and Crisis.* London: Croom Helm.
Marga Institute
1978   *Analytical Description of Poverty in Sri Lanka.* Document M/40. Colombo: Marga Institute.
McGilvray, Dennis B.
1998   Arabs, Moors, and Muslims: Sri Lankan Muslim Ethnicity in Regional Perspective. *Contributions to Indian Sociology* (n.s.) 32(2): 433–483.
1999   Tamils and Muslims in the Shadow of War: Schism or Continuity? In *Conflict and Community in Contemporary Sri Lanka: "Pearl of the East" or "Island of Tears"?* Siri Gamage and Bruce Watson, eds. Pp. 217–228. New Delhi: Sage.
Meadows, Donella, and Jennifer Robinson
1985   *The Electronic Oracle: Computer Models and Social Decisions.* Chichester: Wiley.
Mehta, Pratap B.
1998   Ethnicity, Nationalism and Violence in South Asia. *Pacific Affairs* 71(3): 380.
Meyer, Eric
1984   Seeking the Roots of the Tragedy. In *Sri Lanka in Change and Crisis.* James Manor, ed. Pp. 137–152. London: Croom Helm.
Mohamed, Suresh
1992a   Mrs. B's Regime of Shortages and Queues: Govt. Will Never Take People Back to That "Miserable Era"—President. *Island,* June 3: 3.
1992b   President Explains Rationale for Garment Factories on Estate. *Island,* October 24.
Moore, Mick
1985   *The State and Peasant Politics in Sri Lanka.* Cambridge: Cambridge University Press.
1990a   Economic Liberalization versus Political Pluralism in Sri Lanka. *Modern Asian Studies* 24(2): 341–383.
1990b   Economic Liberalization, Growth, and Poverty: Sri Lanka in Long-Term Perspective. Discussion Paper #274. Sussex: Institute of Development Studies.
1993   Thoroughly Modern Revolutionaries: The JVP in Sri Lanka. *Modern Asian Studies* 27: 593–642.
Morrison, Barrie M., M. P. Moore, and M. U. Ishak Lebbe, eds.
1979   *The Disintegrating Village? Social Change in Rural Sri Lanka.* Colombo: Lake House Investments.
Muller, H. P., and Siri T. Hettige, eds.
1995   *The Blurring of a Vision: The Mahaweli.* Ratmalana, Sri Lanka: Sarvodaya.
Mwanasali, Musifiky
2000   The View from Below. In *Greed and Grievance: Economic Agendas in Civil Wars.* A project of the International Peace Academy. Mats Berdal and David M. Malone, eds. Pp. 137–153. Boulder: Lynne Rienner.
Nakamura, Hishashi, Pyadasa Ratnayake, and S. M. P. Senananayake
1997   Agricultural Development: Past Trends and Policies. In *Dilemmas of Development: Fifty Years of Economic Change in Sri Lanka.* W. D. Lakshman, ed. Pp. 250–292. Colombo: Sri Lanka Association of Economists.
Nash, June, and Maria Patricia Fernandez-Kelly, eds.
1983   *Women, Men, and the International Division of Labor.* Albany: SUNY Press.
National Peace Council
1998   The Cost of the War. Paper presented at the Convention for National Peace Delegates, Colombo, January 4.

O'Sullivan, Meghan
    1997   Household Entitlements during Wartime: The Experience of Sri Lanka. *Oxford Development Studies* 25(1): 95–121.
Obeyesekere, Gananath
    1970   Religious Symbolism and Political Change in Ceylon. *Modern Ceylon Studies* 1(1): 43–63.
    1988   *A Meditation on Conscience.* Colombo: Social Scientists Association.
Observer
    1992   Investing in the People—A Durable Security against Violence. *Observer* (Colombo), February 23: 4.
Ong, Aihwa
    1987   *Spirits of Resistance and Capitalist Discipline: Factory Women in Malaysia.* Albany: SUNY Press.
    1991   The Gender and Labor Politics of Postmodernity. *Annual Review of Anthropology* 20: 279–309.
Options
    2001   Ahinsa. *Options* 25: 11.
Peebles, Patrick
    1982   *Sri Lanka: A Handbook of Historical Statistics.* Boston: G. K. Hall.
    1990   Colonization and Ethnic Conflict in the Dry Zone of Sri Lanka. *Journal of Asian Studies* 49(1): 30–55.
Peiris, G. H.
    1993a   Government Intervention in Industrial Development. In *Sri Lanka: Problems of Governance.* K. M. de Silva, ed. Pp. 231–249. New Delhi: Konark.
    1993b   Economic Growth, Poverty, and Political Unrest. In *Sri Lanka: Problems of Governance.* K. M. de Silva, ed. Pp. 250–272. New Delhi: Konark.
Perera, Sasanka
    1996   The Social and Cultural Construction of Female Sexuality and Gender Roles in Sinhala Society. Paper presented at the National Convention on Women's Studies, Centre for Women's Research, Colombo. March.
    1998   *Political Violence in Sri Lanka: Dynamics, Consequences, and Issues of Democratization.* Colombo: Centre for Women's Research.
Phillips, Richard
    2000   The Struggle of the Common Man for Self-Dignity Is Very Profound. Interview of Prasanna Vithanage. March 1. Electronic document, http://www.wsws.org/articles/2000/mar2000/pras-m01.shtml, accessed May 7, 2003.
Porteous, Samuel D.
    2000   Targeted Financial Sanctions. In *Greed and Grievance: Economic Agendas in Civil Wars.* A project of the International Peace Academy. Mats Berdal and David M. Malone, eds. Pp. 173–188. Boulder: Lynne Rienner.
Putnam, Robert, with Robert Leonardi and Raffaelli Y. Nanetti
    1993   *Making Democracy Work: Civic Traditions in Modern Italy.* Princeton: Princeton University Press.
Rabushka, Alvin T.
    1981   Adam Smith in Sri Lanka. *Policy Review* 18(54): 54–62.
Rajasingham-Senanayake, Darini
    1999   The Dangers of Devolution: The Hidden Economies of Armed Conflict. In *Creating Peace in Sri Lanka.* Robert I. Rotberg, ed. Pp. 57–69. Washington: Brookings Institution Press.

Ram, Mohan
    1989   *Sri Lanka: The Fractured Island.* New Delhi: Penguin.

Rasaputram, Warnasena, W. M. Tilakaratha, S. T. G. Fernando, and L. E. N. Fernando, eds.
    1986   *Facets of Development in Independent Sri Lanka: Felicitation Volume to Commemorate the 10th Successive Budget of Hon. Ronnie de Mel, Minister of Finance and Planning.* Colombo: Ministry of Finance and Planning of Sri Lanka.

Ratnapala, Nandasena
    1989   *Rural Poverty in Sri Lanka.* Nugegoda, Sri Lanka: Deepanee.

Ray, Himashu P.
    1996   *The Winds of Change: Buddhism and the Maritime Links of Early South Asia.* New Delhi: Oxford University Press.

Richardson, John M. Jr.
    1990a   *Sri Lanka Political Conflict Data, 1948–1988.* American University School of International Service.
    1990b   *Coding Instructions for Political Conflict Events.* Mimeographed manual for field research team.
    1991   Understanding Violent Conflict in Sri Lanka: How Theory Can Help. *Ethnic Studies Report* 9(1): 40–55.
    1999   Problems of a Small State in a Big World: How Global Economic Trends and Great Power Politics Have Impacted Sri Lanka. In *History and Politics—Millennial Perspectives: Essays in Honor of Kingsley M. de Silva.* Gerald Peiris and S. W. R. de A. Samarasinghe, eds. Pp. 55–76. Colombo: Law and Society Trust.

Richardson, John M., Jr., and Shinjinee Sen
    1997   Ethnic Conflict and Economic Development: A Policy Oriented Analysis. *Ethnic Studies Report* 15(1): 85–108.

Risseeuw, Carla
    1991   *Gender Transformation, Power, and Resistance among Women in Sri Lanka: The Fish Don't Talk about the Water.* New Delhi: Manohar.

Roberts, Michael
    2001   Ethnicity after Edward Said: Post-Orientalist Failures in Comprehending the Kandyan Period of Sri Lankan History. *Ethnic Studies Report* 14(1): 69–98.

Rogers, John D.
    1993   Colonial Perceptions of Ethnicity and Culture in Early Nineteenth-Century Sri Lanka. In *Society and Ideology: Essays in South Asian History Presented to Professor K. A. Ballhatchet.* Peter Robb, ed. Pp. 97–109. Delhi: Oxford University Press.
    1994   Post-Orientalism and the Interpretation of Premodern and Modern Political Identities: The Case of Sri Lanka. *Journal of Asian Studies* 53(1): 10–23.

Rogers, John D., Jonathan Spencer, and Jayadeva Uyangoda
    1998   Sri Lanka: Political Violence and Ethnic Conflict. *American Psychologist* 53(7): 771–777.

Rosa, Kumudhini
    1991   Strategies of Organisation and Resistance: Women Workers in Sri Lankan Free Trade Zones. *Capital and Class* 45: 27–34.

Ross, Russell R., and Andrea Matles Savada, eds.
    1990   *Sri Lanka: A Country Study.* Country Studies. Area Handbook Series, Federal Research Division of the Library of Congress. Washington: Government Printing Office for the Department of the Army.

Rotberg, Robert I.
    1999   Sri Lanka's Civil War: From Mayhem toward Diplomatic Resolution. In *Creating*

Peace in Sri Lanka: Civil War and Reconciliation. Robert I. Rotberg, ed. Pp. 1–16. Washington: Brookings Institution.

Rotberg, Robert I., ed.
1999   Creating Peace in Sri Lanka: Civil War and Reconciliation. Washington: Brookings Institution.

Royal Norwegian Government, Royal Ministry of Foreign Affairs.
2002   Parties Have Decided to Explore a Political Solution Founded on Internal Self-Determination Based on a Federal Structure within a United Sri Lanka. Statement of the Royal Norwegian Government. December 5. Electronic document, http://www.peaceinsrilanka.org/insidepages/Pressrelease/RNG/RNG5thDec.asp, accessed June 20, 2003.
2003   Press release of the Royal Norwegian embassy, Berlin. February 8. Electronic document, http://www.peaceinsrilanka.org/insidepages/Pressrelease/RNG/RNEBerlin080203.asp, accessed August 29.

Ryan, Bryce, and Sylvia Fernando
1951   The Female Factory Worker in Colombo. International Labour Review 64(5–6): 438–461.

Samarasinghe, S. W. R. de A.
1988   Sri Lanka: A Case Study from the Third World. In Health, Nutrition and Economic Crises: Approaches to Policy in the Third World. David E. Bell and Michael R. Reich, eds. Pp. 39–79. Dover, MA: Auburn House.
N.d.   Ethnic Conflict and Economic Development in Sri Lanka. Ms.

Samath, Feizal, and Kumudini Hettiarachchi
2000   A Village in the Lurch. Sunday Times Plus, May 21: 1.

Sanyal, Bikas C.
1983   University Education and Graduate Employment in Sri Lanka. Colombo: Marga Institute.

Saravanamuttu, Paikiasothy
2003   Civil Society Presentation. Paper presented at the Tokyo Conference on Reconstruction and Development of Sri Lanka, June 9–10. Electronic document, http://www.cpalanka.org/roadmap_programme.html, accessed June 14.

Sarkar, N. K., and S. J. Tambiah
1957   The Disintegrating Village. Colombo: Ceylon University Press.

Sassen, Saskia
1998   Globalization and Its Discontents: Essays on the New Mobility of People and Money. New York: Free Press.

Scudder, Thayer
1995   Constraints to the Development of Settler Incomes and Production-Oriented Participatory Organizations in Large-Scale Government Sponsored Projects: The Mahaweli Case. In The Blurring of a Vision: The Mahaweli. H. P. Muller and Siri T. Hettige, eds. Pp. 148–173. Ratmalana, Sri Lanka: Sarvodaya Book Publishing Services.

Seizer, Susan
1997   Dramatic License: Negotiating Stigma on and off the Tamil Popular Stage. Ph.D. dissertation, Department of Anthropology, University of Chicago.
2000   Roadwork: Offstage with Special Drama Actresses in Tamilnadu, South India. Cultural Anthropology 15(2): 217–259.

Senanayake, Shimal.
2003   Power Struggle in Sri Lanka Stalls Peace Bid. Boston Globe, November 11: A10.

Shah, Nasra
    1995   Emigration Dynamics from and within South Asia. *International Migration*
            33(3–4): 559–626.
Shahul, Mohamed
    2002   Country Report on the Trade Union Situation in Sri Lanka. Electronic docu-
            ment,   http://fesportal.fes.de/pls/porta130/docs/FOLDER/WORLDWIDE/
            GEWERKSCHAFTEN/BERI CHTE/SRILANKA.HTML, accessed June 14,
            2003.
Shastri, Amita
    1997   Transitions to a Free Market: Economic Liberalization in Sri Lanka. *Round Table*
            344: 485–511.
    2002   Sri Lanka 2001: Year of Reversals. *Asian Survey* (Berkeley) 42(1): 177–182.
    2003   Sri Lanka 2002: Turning the Corner? *Asian Survey* (Berkeley) 43(1): 215–221.
Skocpol, Theda
    1994   *Social Revolutions in the Modern World.* Cambridge: Cambridge University Press.
Slack, Jennifer
    1996   The Theory and Method of Articulation in Cultural Studies. In *Stuart Hall:
            Critical Dialogues in Cultural Studies.* David Morley and Kuan-Hsing Chen, eds.
            Pp. 112–127. New York: Routledge.
Slaves of "Free" Trade: Camp Sri Lanka.
    2001   Kashyapa A. S. Yapa, dir. 26 min. Joint Association of Workers Councils of Free
            Trade Zones. Seeduwa, Sri Lanka.
Sluka, Jeffrey, ed.
    2000   *Death Squad: The Anthropology of State Terror.* Philadelphia: University of Penn-
            sylvania Press.
Snodgrass, Donald R.
    1966   *Ceylon: An Export Economy in Transition.* Homewood, IL: Richard D. Irwin, for
            the Economic Growth Center of Yale University.
    1999   The Economic Development of Sri Lanka: A Tale of Missed Opportunities. In
            Creating Peace in Sri Lanka: Civil War and Reconciliation. Rorbert I. Rotberg, ed.
            Pp. 89–108. Washington: Brookings Institution.
Social Scientists Association (SSA), ed.
    1985   *Ethnicity and Social Change in Sri Lanka.* Colombo: Social Scientists Association.
Somasundram, M.
    1999   Introduction: Convivencia. In *Reimagining Sri Lanka: Northern Ireland Insights.* M.
            Somasundram, ed. Pp. ix–xxvi. Colombo: International Centre for Ethnic Studies.
Sorokin, Pitrim A.
    1937   *Social and Cultural Dynamics.* Vol. 3. New York: Bedminster Press.
Special Correspondent
    1992   200 Garment Factory Program—A Bold Bid to End Rural Poverty. *Daily News*
            (Colombo), September 30.
Spencer, Jonathan
    1990   *A Sinhala Village in a Time of Trouble.* Delhi: Oxford University Press.
Spencer, Jonathan, ed.
    1990   *Sri Lanka: History and the Roots of Conflict.* New York: Routledge.
Sri Lanka Department of Census and Statistics
    1944–   *Surveys of Labor Force Participation.* Colombo: Government Printer.
    1979,
    1996

1971   *Census of Population, District Reports.* Colombo: Government Printer.

1981a   *Report of the Census of 1981.* Colombo: Government Printer.

1981b   *Census of Population, District Report 1981.* Colombo: Government Printer.

1996   Census Statistics. Electronic document, http://www.li/national/census/sl_figures95.html#populations, accessed September 3, 1998.

2002a   Statistical Abstract 2002. Table 2.8: Population by Ethnic Group, Census Years. Electronic document, http://www.statistics.gov.lk/abstract/population/tab0208.pdf, accessed June 12, 2003.

2002b   Sri Lanka Statistical Data Sheet, Year 2002. Publications Division. Ministry of Interior. Electronic document, http://www.statistics.gov.lk/misc/ds2002.pdf, accessed June 12, 2003.

Sri Lanka, Department of Information

2001a   Govt Welcomes LTTE Cease-Fire. Electronic document, http://www.news.lk/NewsDecember201.html, accessed June 11, 2003.

2001b   Cessation of Hostilities Begin Today. December 24. Electronic document, http://www.news.lk/december2001.html, accessed June 11, 2003.

2002a   Government Extends Truce. January 22. Electronic document, http://www.news.lk/january2002.html, accessed June 12, 2003.

2002b   Agreement on a Cease-Fire between the Government of the Democratic Socialist Republic of Sri Lanka and the Liberation Tigers of Tamil Eelam. February 24. Electronic document, http://www.news.lk/Newsfebruary242.html, accessed June 12, 2003.

Sri Lankan Government

1951   *Ceylon: Report of the Kandyan Peasantry Commission.* Sessional Paper XVIII. Colombo: Government Press.

1988   *Report by the High Level Committee of Officials on Poverty Alleviation through People-Based Development. Final Report on an Action Programme.* Sessional Paper no. 12. Colombo: Government Printer.

1990   *Report of the Presidential Commission on Youth.* Sessional Paper I. Colombo: Government Printer.

2003   Bandaranaike-Chelvanayakam Pact of 1957. Electronic document, http://www.

[1957] peaceinsrilanka.org/insidepages/Agreement/Ban.asp, accessed June 20.

2003   Dudley Senanayake-Chelvanayakam Pact of 1965. Electronic document, http://

[1965] www.peaceinsrilanka.org/insidepages/Agreement/Dudley.asp, accessed June 20.

2003   Regaining Sri Lanka. Electronic document, http://regainingsrilanka.org/docum.htm, accessed June 14.

Standing, Guy

1989   Global Feminization through Flexible Labor. *World Development* 17(7): 1077–1095.

Stokke, Kristian

1995   Poverty as Politics: The Janasaviya Poverty Alleviation Programme in Sri Lanka. *Norsk Geografisk Tidsskr* 49: 123–135.

Sturgess, Diane

2000   Sri Lankan Government Bans Anti-War Film. Electronic document, http://www.wsws.org/articles/2000/aug2000/film-a07.shtml, accessed May 7, 2003.

Suchman, Lucy A.

1987   *Situated Actions: The Problem of Human-Machine Communication.* Cambridge: Cambridge University Press.

Sunday Observer
  1997   *Sunday Observer* (Colombo), Internet edition: Business News, May 25.
Sunday Times
  2000a   Susanthika Renews Sex Charge. *Sunday Times* (Colombo), October 1: 1.
  2000b   Censor Bombarded in Supreme Court. *Sunday Times* (Colombo), June 11: 3.
  2000c   Indictment to Be Amended in Athas Case. *Sunday Times* (Colombo), May 28: 2.
Tambiah, Stanley J.
  1986   *Sri Lanka: Ethnic Fratricide and the Dismantling of Democracy.* Chicago: Univer-
           sity of Chicago Press.
  1992   *Buddhism Betrayed? Religion, Politics, and Violence in Sri Lanka.* Chicago: Uni-
           versity of Chicago Press.
  1996   *Leveling Crowds: Ethnonationalist Conflicts and Collective Violence in South Asia.*
           Berkeley: University of California Press.
Tambiah, Yasmine
  1997   Women's Sexual Autonomy: Some Issues in South Asia. *Options* 9: 28–32.
TamilNet News
  2001   LTTE Declares Monthlong Cease-Fire. December 19. Electronic document,
           http://news.tamilnet.com/art.html?artid=6568&catid=13, accessed June 12,
           2003.
  2002a   LTTE Extends Unilateral Cease-Fire. January 20. Electronic document, http://
           news.tamilnet.com/art.html?artid=6636&catid=13, accessed June 11, 2003.
  2002b   Norway Announces Permanent Cease-Fire in Sri Lanka. February 22. Electronic
           document, http://news.tamilnet.com/art.html?artid=6727&catid=13, accessed
           June 12, 2003.
  2003a   Tigers Call Off Rehabilitation Talks Pending "Tangible Action on the Ground."
           April 24. Electronic document, http://news.tamilnet.com/art.html?artid=8844&catid=13,
           accessed June 11.
  2003b   LTTE Insists on Draft Framework for Interim Administration to Resume Talks,
           June 11. Electronic document, http://news.tamilnet.com/art.html?artid=9186&catid=13,
           accessed June 14.
Taussig, Michael
  1984   Culture of Terror—Space of Death: Roger Casement's Putumayo Report and the
           Explanation of Torture. *Comparative Studies in Society and History* 26(3): 467–
           497.
Tennekoon, Serena
  1986   "Macho" Sons and "Man-Made" Mothers. *Lanka Guardian,* June 15.
  1987   Symbolic Refractions of the Ethnic Crisis: The *Divaina* Debates on Sinhala
           Identity. In *Facets of Ethnicity in Sri Lanka.* Charles Abeysekera and Newton
           Gunasinghe, eds. Pp. 1–59. Colombo: Social Scientists Association.
  1988   Rituals of Development: The Accelerated Mahaveli Development Program of
           Sri Lanka. *American Ethnologist* 15(2): 294–310.
Thaheer, Minna
  1997   Friendship Houses for Hapless Workers. *Midweek Mirror,* Internet edition (Co-
           lombo), May 28, Women: 4–5.
Thompson, Kenneth
  1998   *Moral Panics.* London: Routledge.
Tilley, Charles
  1978   *From Mobilization to Revolution.* Reading, MA: Addison Wesley.

Times of India
  2000   Susantika [*sic*] Dropped from Lanka Relay Team. *Times of India,* online edition, September 9.
Tiruchelvam, Neelan
  1999   Devolution and the Elusive Quest for Peace. In *Creating Peace in Sri Lanka: Civil War and Reconciliation.* Robert I. Rotberg, ed. Pp. 189–201. Washington: Brookings Institution.
Trautmann, Thomas R.
  1997   *Aryans and British India.* Berkeley: University of California Press.
Traven, B.
  1971   *Government.* Chicago: Elephant Paperbacks.
Tsing, Anna
  2000   Inside the Economy of Appearances. Special issue, "Globalization. Millennial Quartet, Vol. 2." Arjun Appadurai, guest editor. *Public Culture: Society for Transnational Cultural Studies* 30: 115–144.
United Nations Development Program
  1991   *Human Development Report.* New York: Oxford University Press.
Uyangoda, Jayadeva
  2003a   Sri Lanka: A "Pragmatic" Peace Agenda. In *Sri Lanka's Peace Process 2002: Critical Perspectives.* Uyangoda Jayadeva and Morina Perera, eds. Pp. 3–6. Colombo: Social Scientists Association.
  2003b   Sri Lanka's Peace Process: Surprising Possibilities? In *Sri Lanka's Peace Process 2002: Critical Perspectives.* Uyangoda Jayadeva and Morina Perera, eds. Pp. 7–15. Colombo: Social Scientists Association.
Uyangoda, Jayadeva, and Janaka Biyanwila, eds.
  1997   *Matters of Violence: Reflections on Social and Political Violence in Sri Lanka.* Colombo: Social Scientists Association.
van der Veer, Peter
  1994   *Religious Nationalism: Hindus and Muslims in India.* Berkeley: University of California Press.
Vidanapathirana, Upananda
  1986   Pattern of Industrialization. Strategies and Responses. In *Facets of Development in Independent Sri Lanka: Felicitation Volume to Commemorate the 10th Successive Budget of Hon. Ronnie de Mel, Minister of Finance and Planning.* Warnasena Rasaputra, W. M. Tilakaratna, S. T. G. Fernando, and L. E. N. Fernando, eds. Pp. 165–193. Colombo: Ministry of Finance and Planning of Sri Lanka.
Voice of Women
  1983   *Women Workers in the Free Trade Zone of Sri Lanka.* Colombo: Voice of Women.
Walton, John, and David Seddon
  1994   *Free Markets and Food Riots: The Politics of Global Adjustment.* Cambridge, MA: Blackwell.
Weerarathne, Chitra
  2000   SC Orders Ban on Leader Publications to Be Lifted: "Competent Authority Has No Authority to Censor." *Island,* July 1: 1.
Weerasinghe, Rohini
  1989   Women Workers in the Katunayake Investment Promotion Zone (KIPZ) of Sri Lanka: Some Observations. In *Women in Development in South Asia.* V. Kanesalingam, ed. Pp. 306–21. New Delhi: Macmillan.

White, Howard, and Ganeshan Wignaraja
  1992   Exchange Rates, Trade Liberalisation, and Aid: The Sri Lankan Experience. *World Development* 20: 1471–1480.
Wickremasuriya, Sarathchandra
  1978   "Decoration before Dress": A Study of Sir Ponnambalam Arunachalam's Attitudes to Colonial English Education in Sri Lanka. *Ceylon Historical Journal* 25: 213–238.
Wickremeratne, Ananda
  1995   *Buddhism and Ethnicity in Sri Lanka: A Historical Analysis.* New Delhi: International Centre for Ethnic Studies.
Wijetunga, W. M. K.
  1983   Development of University Education in Sri Lanka (1942–1980). In *University Education and Graduate Employment in Sri Lanka.* Bikas Sanyal, ed. Pp. 112–148. Colombo: Marga Institute.
Williams, Raymond
  1973   *The Country and the City.* New York: Oxford University Press.
Wilson, A. Jeyaratnam
  1977   Politics and Political Development since 1948. In *Sri Lanka: A Survey.* K. M. de Silva, ed. Pp. 281–311. Honolulu: University of Hawaii Press.
Winslow, Deborah
  2002   Co-opting Co-operation in Sri Lanka. *Human Organization* 61(1): 9–20.
Women of the Zone: Garment Workers of Sri Lanka.
  1994   Kashyapa A. S. Yapa, dir. 24 min. Labor Video Project. San Francisco.
Woost, Michael D.
  1990   Rural Awakenings: Grassroots Development and the Cultivation of a National Past in Rural Sri Lanka. In *Sri Lanka: History and the Roots of Conflict.* Jonathan Spencer, ed. Pp. 164–183. New York: Routledge.
  1993   Nationalizing the Local Past in Sri Lanka: Histories of Nation and Development in a Sinhalese Village. *American Ethnologist* 20(3): 502–521.
World Bank
  1953   *The Economic Development of Ceylon: Report of a Mission Organized by the International Bank for Reconstruction and Development at the Request of the Government of Ceylon.* Baltimore: Johns Hopkins University Press for the World Bank.
  1997   *World Development Report 1996/97: The State in a Changing World.* New York: Oxford University Press for the World Bank.
  2000a   *World Development Report 1999/2000: Entering the 21st Century.* New York: Oxford University Press, for the World Bank.
  2000b   *Sri Lanka: Recapturing Missed Opportunities.* World Bank Report no. 20430–CE. Poverty Reduction and Economic Management Unit, South Asia Region. Electronic document, http://www.worldbank.org/sar, accessed June 16.
  2003a   Sri Lanka Country Assistance Strategy. Electronic document, http://lnweb18.worldbank.org/sar/sa.nsf/8b211d2239d56913852567d7005d8e54/370fe6a061ba6 25b85256d1f005787c0?OpenDocument, accessed June 12.
  2003b   World Bank Stresses Link between Peace and Development at Sri Lanka Donor Conference. June 10, news release no. 2003/408/SAR. Electronic document, http://web.worldbank.org/WBSITE/EXTERNAL/NEWS/0,,contentMDK%3A20115013~menuPK%3A34463~pagePK%3A34370~piPK%3A34424~theSitePK%3A4607,00.html#, accessed June 12.

Yahoo Asia News Online
  2003a   Sri Lankan Tigers Make Fresh Demands before Reentering Talks. May 21. Elec-
          tronic document, http://story.news.yahoo.com/news?tmpl=story&u=/afp/20030521/
          wl_sthasia_afp/srilanka_tamil_norway_030521093647, accessed June 12.
  2003b   Sri Lanka PM Moves to Break Deadlock with Tigers. June 9. Electronic docu-
          ment, http://in.news.yahoo.com/030609/137/24zgw.html, accessed June 12.
Yahoo News Singapore Online
  2003   Sri Lankan President Vows to Renegotiate Aid from Tokyo Meet. June 10.
          Electronic document, http://sg.news.yahoo.com/030610/1/3bom5.html, accessed
          June 12.
Yalman, Nur
  1967   *Under the Bo Tree: Studies in Caste, Kinship, and Marriage in the Interior of Cey-
          lon.* Berkeley: University of California Press.

Contributors

Francesca Bremner is an instructor in sociology at Montclair State University and a doctoral candidate in sociology at Columbia University. She received her B.A. from Montclair State University and an M.A. and an M.Phil from Columbia University. She was an advertising executive and a journalist in Sri Lanka. Her dissertation research was carried out over eight months while she was a research fellow at the International Center for Ethnic Studies in Colombo in 2001. Her research documents the everyday processes, material and symbolic, that led to the July 1983 riots in Sri Lanka. This is accomplished through an analysis of narratives of the violence of 1983 collected from people from one neighborhood who actually participated in the violence. She has also been involved in numerous human rights/refugee projects in the United States and Sri Lanka. She has directed three films, two of which focus on violence in Sri Lanka.

Michele Ruth Gamburd is associate professor of anthropology at Portland State University. She received her Ph.D. in anthropology from the University of Michigan in 1995. She also holds B.A. degrees from Balliol College (Oxford) and Swarthmore College. She is the author of *The Kitchen Spoon's Handle: Transnationalism and Sri Lanka's Migrant Housemaids* (2000), which was reprinted in India by Vistaar under the title *Transnationalism and Sri Lanka's Migrant Housemaids* (2002). She also has published over a dozen articles, including "Nurture for Sale: Sri Lankan Housemaids and the Work of Mothering" (in *Home and Hegemony: Domestic Service and Identity Politics in South and Southeast Asia,* edited by Sara Dickey and Kathleen M. Adams, 2000); "Class Identity and the International Division of Labor: Sri Lanka's Migrant Housemaids" (in *Anthropology of Work Review,* 1999); "Wearing a Dead Man's Jacket: State Symbols in Troubled Places" (in *Conflict and Community in Contemporary Sri Lanka,* edited by Siri Gamage and Bruce Watson, 1999); and "Violence Studies: An Introductory Curriculum" (*Political and Legal Anthropology Review,* 1999). Her work and studies have been supported by the National Science Foundation (Senior Research Award, Graduate Research Fellowship, Dissertation Research Award, and Summer Research Award), the Andrew W. Mellon Foundation, and the Keasbey Memorial Foundation (for study at Oxford).

Newton Gunasinghe (1946–88) was senior lecturer in sociology at the University of Colombo. He received an M.A. degree in sociology in 1973 from Monash University, Australia, and a Ph.D. in 1979 from the Institute for Development Studies at the University of Sussex. He left behind a rich record of publications. He was coeditor of *Facets of Ethnicity in Sri Lanka* (1987). His dissertation was published posthumously as *Changing Socio-Economic Relations in the Kandyan Countryside* (1990). *Newton Gunasinghe: Selected Essays* (1996), edited by Sasanka Perera, contained a dozen important works on topics ranging from agrarian relations and social structure to economic change and the politics of ethnicity and religion.

Siri T. Hettige is professor of sociology at the University of Colombo, Sri Lanka, where he is also director of the Centre for Sociological and Anthropological Studies. He received his B.A. and B.Phil degrees in sociology from the University of Colombo and his Ph.D. in social anthropology from Monash University (Australia) in 1980. His research interests include rural social stratification in Sri Lanka, seasonal labor migration, urban social structure, cultural aspects of Sri Lankan workers migrating to the Middle East, comparative health systems research, rural development, impact of political violence on women, the youth revolt in the south, the impact of the open economy on rural and urban youth, and globalization. He is author, editor, or coeditor of ten books, including *Wealth, Power, and Prestige: Emerging Patterns of Social Inequality in a Peasant Context* (1984), *Sri Lanka at the Crossroads: Dilemmas and Prospects after Fifty Years of Independence* (2000), and *Globalization, Social Change, and Youth* (1998), as well as dozens of articles. He was principal researcher of the 1999 National Youth Survey of Sri Lanka, funded by the UNDP, and the 1998 survey of business executives funded by the University of Colombo. He has received numerous awards and fellowships, including a 1994–95 Fulbright Senior Scholar Award to the South Asia Research Center at the University of Pennsylvania.

Caitrin Lynch is assistant professor of anthropology at Drew University. She was a Mellon Postdoctoral Fellow (Program for the Study of Women, Gender, and Sexuality and the Department of Anthropology) at Johns Hopkins University, and managing editor of the journal *Public Culture*. She received her Ph.D. in anthropology from the University of Chicago in 2000. Her dissertation, supervised by Arjun Appadurai, was entitled "The 'Good Girls' of Sri Lankan Modernity: Moral Orders of Nationalism, Gender, and Globalization in Village Garment Factories." She is the author or coauthor of numerous articles and reviews, including "The Politics of White Women's Underwear in Sri Lanka's Open Economy" (*Social Politics,* spring 2002); "Millennial Transitions" (in *Millennial Capitalism and the Culture of Neoliberalism,* edited by Jean and John L. Comaroff, 2001); "Good Girls or Juki Girls? Learning and Identity in Garment Factories" (*Anthropology of Work Review,* spring 1999); and "The 'Good Girls' of Sri Lankan Modernity: Moral Orders of Nationalism and Capitalism" (*Identities: Global Studies in Culture and Power,* 1999). She has received numerous fellowships and research grants including awards from the National Science Foundation, the Social Science Research Council, and Fulbright, as well as the Ruth Murray Essay Prize (University of Chicago).

John M. Richardson Jr. is director of the American University Center for Teaching Excellence and professor of international development in the School of International Service at American University, where he has been since 1975. In 1988 he was visiting professor of international relations, Department of History and Political Science, University of Colombo, Sri Lanka. He has held teaching and/or research appointments in the Department of Systems Engineering, Systems Research Center, and Department of Political Science, Case Western Reserve University, and the System Dynamics Group, Sloan School of Management, MIT. He received his Ph.D. in political science from the University of Minnesota in 1968. He was an early contributor to the field of global modeling, under the auspices of the Club of Rome, and played a major role in the global modeling "clearinghouse" activities organized by the International Institute for Applied Systems Analysis. Dr. Richardson is the author, coauthor, or editor of five books. Earlier works include *Partners in Development* (1969), *Groping in the Dark: The First Decade of Global Modeling* (1982), *Making It Happen: A Positive Guide to the Future* (1982), and *Ending Hunger: An Idea Whose Time Has Come* (1985). He contributed to *Breakthrough: New Global Thinking* (1988), published jointly in the United States and the USSR. His most recent book is *Democratization in South Asia: The First Fifty Years* (1998; coedited with S. W. R. de A. Samarasinghe). He was an editorial board member for *History and Politics: Millennial Perspectives—Essays in Honor of Kingsley de Silva* (1999), to which he also contributed. He has also published numerous professional papers and research reports.

Amita Shastri is professor of political science at San Francisco State University. She received her doctoral degree from Nehru University, New Delhi. She has been a University Grants Commission Research Fellow, India (1977–81) and a Pew Faculty Fellow in International Affairs at the JFK School of Government, Harvard University (1990–91). She has also been a research fellow/visiting scholar at the California Institute of Technology; University of California, Los Angeles; University of California, Berkeley; and the International Center for Ethnic Studies at Colombo. Her research interests focus on the processes of democracy and democratization, political economy of development, and ethnic conflict. She has edited the volume *Post-Colonial States of South Asia: Democracy, Identity, Development, and Security* (2001) with A. J. Wilson, and contributed chapters to books and articles to a number of international scholarly journals, including *Journal of Asian Studies, Electoral Studies, Round Table, Asian Survey,* and *Contemporary South Asia.*

Deborah Winslow is associate professor of anthropology at the University of New Hampshire. She received her Ph.D. in anthropology from Stanford University. She also has been a Fulbright lecturer in India and a resident scholar at the School of American Research. She edits the Monographs in Economic Anthropology series for the Society for Economic Anthropology and AltaMira Press.

The primary focus of her research is rural Sri Lanka, where she has followed the fortunes of a community of Sinhalese potters since 1973, both before and after the opening up of the Sri Lankan economy. She also has done research among potters in India. She is coeditor of *Economic Analysis beyond the Local System* (1997). Her published articles include "Potters' Progress: Hybridity and Accumulative Change in Sri Lanka" (*Journal of Asian Studies*, 2003), "Co-opting Cooperation in Sri Lanka" (*Human Organization*, 2002), and "Pottery, Progress, and Structural Adjustments in a Sri Lankan Village" (*Economic Development and Cultural Change*, 1996). Her research support has included grants from the National Science Foundation and the National Endowment for the Humanities.

Michael D. Woost is associate professor and chair of the Department of Anthropology at Hartwick College. He received his Ph.D. in anthropology from the University of Texas at Austin in 1990. He has been visiting lecturer in the Department of Sociology at the University of Peradeniya in Sri Lanka and has received grants from the Fulbright-Hays Program, the National Science Foundation, the American Institute for Sri Lanka Studies, and the Social Science Research Council. He has been engaged in research in Sri Lanka since 1983, with a primary focus on the role of development programs and development discourse as an extension of "state" power. His published articles include "The Common Sense of Development and the Struggle for Participatory Development in Sri Lanka" (in *Development beyond the Twenty-first Century*, edited by J. Cohen and N. Dannhaeuser, 2002), "From Shifting Cultivation to Shifting Development in Rural Sri Lanka" (*Journal of the Anthropology of Work*, 1999), and "Developing a Nation of Villages: Rural Community as State Formation in Sri Lanka" (*Critique of Anthropology*, 1994).

Index

Page numbers in italics refer to illustrations.

in military, 18, 156–157, 160, 189n10
morality of Juki girls, 22–23, 171–177, 183–187
morality of white women, 171–172, 175–176
motivation for military service, 22–23, 160
nationalism effects on, 187
in open economy, 168
poverty and absent parents, 166–167n13
women and tradition, 179, 190n17
Globalization
effects of, on civil war, 74, 87–90, 90–91
effects of, on nationalism, 187
effects of, on structure of economy, 54–60,
81, 84, *84*, 90–91
effects of, on values, 190n20
with "human face," 73
producing anxiety about national purity, 180
Goffman, Erving, theories about stigma,
183–184
Goodhand, Jonathan
analysis of social capital and civil war, 8,
10, 13
description of life during civil war, 13
Government expenditure in relation to GDP,
82–83
Government Consumer Finance Surveys, 56
Greater Colombo Economic Commission
(GCEC), 50, 69n32, 108
Greed, as explanation for civil war, 12, 14–17,
154–156
Gross Domestic Product (GDP)
1980–2000, *79*
in 2000, 42n16
as cause of civil war, 15
government expenditures in relation to,
82–83
in relation to 1978–2000 sectoral composition
of economy, 84
in relation to debt, 80–81
in relation to defense spending, 8, 9, 77, 80,
92n21
in relation to domestic savings, 78
in relation to government revenues, 80
in relation to industrial investment, 78
per capita in 2000, 92n16
Gross National Product (GNP)
relation to foreign debt, 69n35
relation to sectoral composition of
economy, *84*
rise under UNP, 55
variability, 56
Gunasinghe, Newton, 3, 13, 19–20, 22, 24n5, 96,
97, 98, 133, 168, 187, 200, 203
Gurr, Ted Robert, relative deprivation theory
by, 44

Hall, Stuart, articulation theory by, 17–18
Haraway, Donna
"god-trick" explanations, 17
theory of situated knowledge, 21–22, 23,
27n23
theory of technology of vision, 3, 23
Hartal (strike) of 1953, 33–34
Harvard University Institute of International
Development, 58–59
Health care
effects on urban poor, 58, 110
health services under UNP, 58, 61–62, 101
migration of doctors, 71n65
military hospitals, 167n16
public health indicators, 61
reduction in funding for, 58, 61, 101
Hettige, Siri, 3, 13, 97, 98, 199, 201, 202–203
Hinduism, 140
Hoeffler, Anke, 15
Housing construction
cuts in support for, 52
foreign aid financed, 48
Gam Udawa (Village Awakening Program),
49–50
loan from Ceylon General Railway
for, 161
Hulme, David
analysis of social capital and civil war, 8,
10, 13
description of life during civil war, 13

Identity
construction of, 95, 137–143, 145–146,
150, 184
ethnographical representation of, 133–134,
137–138
in explanations of violence, 44
types of, 25–26n10
Import substitution
contrasted with open economy, 48, 108, 113
as macro-economic policy, 35, 36–37
public sector role in, 100, 102–103
Income distribution
changes under open economy, 56–57,
70nn47,49,52, 74
increasing inequalities in, 56–57, 66, 87–88,
110–111
inequalities in, 88, 91–92n13, 107
Income per capita, 87
India
role in civil war, 46
stigmatized women in, 183–184
trade loan from, 77
trade with, 106, 109

changing identities of, in peace process, 203
competition with, in public sector employment, 122
in eastern districts, 198
how affected by civil war, 21, 89
leadership among, 197
location of, in Sri Lanka, 6, 196
morality of, 172
role of, in peace talks, 193, 196
as social group, 4, 166n12
Tamil relations with, 196

high Sri Lanka indicators, 152
Sri Lanka compared to South Asia, 33
Pieris, G. L., 75
Plantation sector
    capital accumulation in, 105
    citizenship of workers, 128n3
    employment in, 116, 118, 120
    nationalization of, 100
    privatization of, 76
    reform of, 54
Police
    accused of corruption, 147, 154
    involvement in 1983 riots, 2, 145
    relations with urban residents, 141
Political-organizational mobilization theory of
    violent conflict, 44
Poor
    effects of cuts in education on, 62, 66
    effects of cuts in health care on, 61, 66
    effects of open economy on, 55–59, 66–67,
        76, 91–92n13
    employment in garment factories, 174
    military enlistment by, 157, 166–167n13
    not benefited by Mahaweli project, 48
    ultra-poor, 57
    urban poor, 103, 108, 109–111, 139–140
    urban poor and Sinhala chauvinism, 113
    urban poor and state, 113, 148
Population
    1946 ethnic composition of, 39n2
    growth, 152, 153
    male/female ratios of, 69n43
Portuguese colonialism, 24–25n6
Post-ethnicity argument, as explanation of civil
    war, 8
Prabhakaran, Velupillai, 151, 165n2
Premadasa, Ranasinghe (President of Sri Lanka,
    1989–1993). See also United National Party
    1993 assassination of, 38
    economic policies of, 37–38, 61, 74, 77–78, 80–
        81, 88, 90, 188n2
    election of, 37–38
    Garment Factories Program of, 168–177,
        188n3
    housing programs of, 49–50, 200
    JVP uprising under, 188n4
Presidential Commission on Youth
    findings on JVP, 170, 190n17
    findings on unemployment, 59–60
Private sector
    discrimination and employment in, 60, *124*
    English language and employment in, 64, 123
    ethnicity and employment in, 111–112, 127
    in housing, 49

in open economy, 54, 85, 102, 123–127
rural recruiting by, 126
savings in, 78
in social services, 61–62, 111
in state-controlled economy, 100–102, 121
urban bias of, 120
urban district recruiting, 126
youth aspirations for employment in, 112,
    124, 126
wages in, 77
Privatization
    under PA government, 76, 88, 90
    of public sector enterprises, 76
Public sector
    district and employment in, 126
    employment in, 117, 129n14
    ethnicity and employment in, 105
    hiring practices in, 126
    language bias in, 129nn7,8
    patronage in, 101, 104
    privatization of, under PA government, 76
    Tamil employment in, 106
    upward mobility within, 127
Pura Handa Kaluwara (*Death on a Full Moon
    Night;* Sinhala film)
    censorship of, 186–187
    effects of, on 200 Garment Factories Pro-
        gram, 186

Rajasingham-Senanayake, Darini, on informal
    economy and civil war, 3, 10–11, 89
Ratnapala, Nandasena, ethnographic research
    on poor, 57–58
Refugees, in civil war, 9, 86
Relative deprivation
    as cause of civil war, 44, 87–88
    experienced by Tamils, 105–106
    in open economy, 19
    perception of, 60–61, 66
    relation to ethnicity, 67n9, 105–106, 108, 110,
        112–114
    use of, by politicians, 66
Remittance income. See also Employment
    from globalization, 90
    from Sri Lanka government, 10, 26–27n17
    from work abroad, 51, 76, 78, 88, 90
Richardson, John M., Jr., 3, 190n20, 202
Riots and violence. See also Riots of July 1983
    anti-Muslim, 99
    anti-Tamil, 47, 99
    because of economic policy, 99
    class in, 97
    normalization of, 163
    terrorism in, 149–150

Riots of July 1983
  catalysts for, 1–2, 43, 65–67, 74, 87–91, 95–98,
    98n1, 99–100, 113, 134, 137, 143–150
  comparatively, 42
  costs of, 2, 86
  identity constructed in, 140
  media coverage of, 146
  participation in, 137–150
  police involvement in, 2, 145
  Tamil diaspora because of, 89, 148
  violence patterns, 144, 145
Roadblocks. See Checkpoints and roadblocks
Rural vs. urban
  Buddhist values, 184–185
  English language skills, 123
  gender ideologies, 169, 182
  morality divide, 175–177, 179
  PQLI disparities, 117
  romantic notion of village, 190n17
  youth employment, 123–124

Sales tax (GST), 76
Samarasinghe, S. W. R. de A.
  poverty research by, 57
  research on employment discrimination, 60
Savings
  domestic and foreign 1980–2000, 79
  increase in domestic in open economy, 78
  by poor, 57, 158
Scale-making projects (theory of). See also
    Tsing, Anna
  in civil war, 20–21
  about gem trade in Sri Lanka, 20–21
  living within, 133
  meaning in, 4
Seizer, Susan, 183
Sen, Shinjinee, 68n16
Senanayake, Don Stephen (D. S.; Prime Minis-
    ter, 1948–1952), as minister of lands and agri-
    culture, 32
Senanayake, Dudley (Prime Minister, 1952–
    1953), resignation of, 34
Shastri, Amita, 3, 8, 9, 22, 188n2, 200, 202
Sinhalese
  economic differentiation, 60
  Low country/Kandyan distinction, 4–5
  in northern dry zone, 32
Skocpol, Theda
  on social revolutions, 67n10
  on state competence and violence, 44
Slack, Jennifer, on theory of context, 3
Social capital
  in civil war, 8, 12–14
  defined, 12–13

  Robert Putnam on, 12
  World Bank interest in, 27n19
Social formation, defined, 24n4
Sorokin, Pitrim, 67n5
Space
  religious construction of, 140
  urban class composition of, 139, 140
Spencer, Jonathan, 68n13
Sri Lanka Freedom Party (SLFP). See also
    United Front
  coalition with PA, 190n20
  economic policies under, 32, 75
  patronage under, 100, 104–105
  pro-Sinhala policies of, 32
Sri Lanka Monitoring commission, 193
Sri Lanka Rupee (SL Rs.)
  2000–2001 exchange rates, 167n15
  depreciation of, 52, 69n39, 80
Sri Lanka Transport Board, allocations to, 69n40
Sri Lankan Youth Surveys, 97
State. See also Public sector
  1980–2000 fiscal operations of, 82–83
  competence of, as explanation of violence, 44
  control of economy, 48, 50–51, 53, 73, 80, 88,
    100–104, 113–114
  economic agendas of, 168–171
  local experience of, 139, 141–142, 143, 170
  relation to urban lower class, 142
  response to "underwear critique," 183
  social production of, 137
  spatial limits of power of, 89–90
  state personnel, 105
  state policies and opportunities for youth,
    115–130
  theories of, 27n20
  village distrust of, 152, 154, 165
Structural adjustment policies, 69n33, 152.
  See also Open economy
Swabasha (native language) education. See also
    English
  in colonial private sector employment, 120
  effect on colonial public sector employ-
    ment, 116
  in post-colonial employment, 122, 123, 128

Tambiah, Stanley J., 57
Tambiah, Yasmine, 182
Tamils. See also Liberation Tigers of Tamil
    Eelam; Tamil United Liberation Front
  advantage during colonialism, 118–122
  casualties, estimates of, 166n11
  as category, 4, 26n12, 166n12, 179
  in Colombo neighborhood, 138–139, 143–148
  comparative PQLI, 117–118